# BUILDINGS &

# LANDSCAPES

JOURNAL OF THE VERNACULAR ARCHITECTURE FORUM
VOLUME 25 | NUMBER 2 | FALL 2018

# BUILDINGS &

# LANDSCAPES

JOURNAL OF THE VERNACULAR ARCHITECTURE FORUM
VOLUME 25 | NUMBER 2 | FALL 2018

JEFFREY E. KLEE

# *Viewpoint:* Fieldwork, Mind, and Building

Opposition has been central to the mythology of vernacular architecture studies in North America since the 1970s—most emphatically, opposition to scholarly practices that emphasize elite buildings and academically trained architects.[1] The rhetoric of revolution appears in much late twentieth-century work on ordinary buildings, in which resistance came to define the contours of its scholarship as effectively as any set of shared assumptions about the built environment.[2] This generation of scholars critiqued perspectives that seemed too narrow in outlook, too focused on the powerful, and above all, too elitist. According to Henry Glassie, "the goal of history must not be the chronicle of the *outré,* the obvious, and the violent; it must be a record of what happened."[3] Such work did not always proceed "from the bottom up" but the spirits of E. P. Thompson and Jesse Lemisch preside over many of the most influential texts in vernacular architecture studies of the last forty years.[4]

Essential to this rhetoric of opposition has been a reluctance to define the parameters of vernacular architecture (a reluctance not shared by more resolutely antiquarian scholars in the United Kingdom).[5] Anything that questioned the notion that only the most accomplished architectural monuments merited serious study was theoretically fair game, although in practice, much of the scholarship on vernacular architecture in the closing decades of the twentieth century focused on housing, often preindustrial or rural. Faced with the problem of bringing order to such a broad spectrum of buildings, thoughtful scholars argued that the study of vernacular

architecture coheres not around a class of structures but rather an approach to the built environment. What mattered was not what one studied, but how.[6] Studies of the vernacular were characterized by their humanism, their attention to the social and cultural history of communities, and their grounding in architectural fieldwork.

This is as true as ever, but two things have changed recently to reveal how significantly the terrain of vernacular architecture studies is shifting in its maturity. First, the critical and contextual approach that emerged in the 1970s and 1980s is increasingly applied to objects that were once beyond the pale for the folklorists, historians, preservationists, and geographers who pioneered the modern study of vernacular architecture. The expanding field of vernacular architecture scholarship now includes important studies of architect-designed suburban churches, hospitals, and insane asylums, as well as reconsiderations of iconic singular buildings such as Thomas Jefferson's Monticello.[7] The second, related shift is a decline of the centrality of field-based research to the study of architecture among scholars of ordinary buildings.[8] To some degree, this is a consequence of the field's increasing achievement of its longstanding ambition to cover the entirety of the built environment. Taking articles published in the journal *Buildings & Landscapes* as an index for the range of scholarship, twentieth-century topics now outnumber papers considering all other periods combined.[9] If fieldwork was necessary for the study of Maryland tobacco barns or Massachusetts timber framing, it is a less obviously essential technique for engaging with condominiums or ranch houses.[10]

At the same time, the object of critique has changed. If vernacular architecture studies could once be understood as the critical complement to traditional architectural history, this role is no longer available, or necessary.[11] The articles published in the *Journal of the Society of Architectural Historians* over the past two decades well illustrate the reach of this shift. Though many essays continue to address the work of architects and elite patrons, they are situated more securely in their social context. It is partly for this reason that leading scholars of vernacular architecture have occasionally called for the retirement of the term "vernacular" altogether. As early as 1991, Bernard Herman and Thomas Carter suggested renaming the emergent field "The New Architectural History," but their proposal was not widely embraced.[12]

Serious scholars of the full range of buildings recognize the importance of cultural context; those who do not court irrelevance. The drift in North American scholarship toward a materialist, socially engaged approach to architecture has been pervasive and is not restricted to the study of ordinary buildings. But critical methodological divisions remain in the larger field of architectural scholarship and criticism and it is worth taking a new look at where those fault lines lie. The most important differences are no longer between cathedral experts and bicycle shed enthusiasts, nor between rural and urban specialists, nor between historians of the modern and preindustrial periods. Architectural scholars are, instead, divided by faith: whether we believe that architecture is an autonomous, idealist practice that is governed by its own internal and transcendent principles or whether we think that architecture is a human endeavor that is embedded in the social world, a participant in a much larger field of cultural exchange. While both perspectives can inform the broader culture of design and building, the latter, materialist approach characterizes the most insightful recent scholarship and promises to explain more fully the widest range of artifacts. It has continued to guide the most influential work in the expanded field of architectural history.

## Idealism

Throughout the second half of the twentieth century, the prevailing literature on architectural history and theory endorsed a view that design is a practice driven by careful reflection: on the nature of modernity, or capitalism, or building and dwelling itself. In this conceptualization, actual buildings serve chiefly as illustrations of premises expressed more clearly elsewhere. The work of the scholar is to locate the relevant discourse and then to show how an artifact embodies that discourse. Despite the narrowness of this approach and its dependence upon articulate, literate designers as subjects, many architects, critics, and historians have accepted this idealist view of the production of buildings. Often this idealism has emphasized the relatively simple relationship between a designer's expressed body of theory and the form of his or her buildings, but its more ambitious adherents have sought more widely for sources of value. In his ambitious *Space, Time, and Architecture*, Sigfried Giedion aimed to show how international modern architecture was the inevitable product of an industrialized economy and a scientific, progressive culture. A student of the German art historian Heinrich Wölfflin, Giedion argued that Ludwig Mies van der Rohe, Walter Gropius, Le Corbusier, and other leaders of twentieth-century design were perceptive, heroic interpreters of a "universal architecture" for a "universal civilization."[13] Giedion was joined in this effort by Reyner Banham, Peter Blake, and other chroniclers of the modern movement, who sought to identify a Hegelian Zeitgeist, or spirit of the age, to show how the principles of the factory system, industrial technology, and the scientific method had inspired perceptive architects to produce the principal monuments of the modern era.[14] Giedion's belief in the generative power of a universal spirit is derived from the notion developed by Alois Riegl, a contemporary of Wölfflin, of the *Kunstwollen*, literally, the "art will" of a period. Riegl argued that the *Kunstwollen* drove aesthetic development toward perfection and was materialized by an ingenious intermediary in the form of the artist or architect. Riegl's *Kunstwollen* embraced Hegel's progressivism, in which art, following history and social life, proceeds to higher planes of perfection.[15]

If the attempt to identify a Zeitgeist seemed especially pressing for scholars of modernism, historians of earlier periods also found notions of a disembodied generative force driving artistic change useful. William H. Pierson invoked the *Kunstwollen* to explain what he saw as the progress of design from the ill-formed early colonial to the elegant federal style:

> Throughout western history, the evolution of style in architecture . . . has been the same. In its formative stage, each style at first merely hints at its ultimate character. Then . . . it evolves a mature architectural idiom, unique, coherent and expressive. From this high point, it then spreads outward and downward through the entire fabric of the civilization which brought it in to being.[16]

For Pierson, as for many of his contemporaries, the key figure in this process of translating spirit into form is the architect: "It is to him that all the generative forces flow, and it is through his practical skills and poetic imagination that these same forces are commingled and freshened."[17] Henry Chandlee Forman did not cite Riegl but adopted his premises in his history of early Maryland architecture. His *Maryland Architecture: A Short History from 1634 through the Civil War* illustrated neatly his faith in a disembodied "goal" of early architecture that can hardly have been perceived in any single individual.[18] Forman thought of changes in design as stages toward an ideal with an ethos, and a will, of its own that was expressed by but independent of human builders.

As the shared assumptions of these histories of early American architecture and high modernism illustrate, an approach that casts buildings principally as materialized, transcendent ideas has been deployed across a wide range of cultures and periods. In his groundbreaking *Gothic Architecture and Scholasticism*, Erwin Panofsky, with more subtlety than Pierson or Giedion, enlisted the structure of medieval argument to explain the new visual order brought to cathedral design in the era after Abbot Suger.[19] Similarly, and more influentially, Rudolph Wittkower used the humanist love of mathematical proportion and faith in divine order to root Renaissance architecture in rigorous thought rather than epicurean pleasure or a simple-minded antiquarian admiration for the classical past. The very title of his *Architectural Principles in the Age of Humanism* announced his ambition to repudiate Geoffrey Scott's *Architecture of Humanism: A Study in the History of Taste*. Scott sought to systematize the study of the Renaissance to show its leading lights as men of discernment and learning but to Wittkower, he had only succeeded in establishing the period as retrograde, devoted to beauty and luxury, not intellect.[20] In seeking to recuperate Alberti and Palladio as designers of intelligence, rather than creators of "pure form," his analysis emphasized abstraction, proportion, and geometry, with simple line drawings showing hypothetical organizing systems for select church façades. He located meaning first of all in math, only tangentially in theology, and very little in the social and political life of cinquecento Italy. In his effort to de-emphasize the importance of ornament in the scholarly literature on Palladio and his contemporaries and replace it with an analysis of proportion, principle, and system, Wittkower made the Renaissance intellectually respectable, safe even for modernists to admire.[21] Like his contemporaries Giedion and Panofsky, he strove to make the study of architecture a rigorous philosophical activity, elevating it from the realms of the dilettante and the antiquarian and from the unthinking formalism he saw exemplified in Scott. Wittkower's focus on the abstraction of geometry and proportion removed architecture further from the social world than either Wölfflin or Riegl, legitimating new avenues of inquiry that dematerialized the study of architecture and licensed interpretations that severed buildings from their social, political, and historical context.

In the same difficult decade in which Wittkower was preparing *Architectural Principles,*

Carroll Meeks explored the possibility of a different kind of architectural scholarship that was more attuned to the importance of context and might make, additionally, a contribution to cultural history. He saw the potential of a history that placed buildings at the heart of a broader humanistic project. "What an opportunity it gives for integrating political and social movements, literary and musical achievements, in one coordinated course, centered on material evidence—the buildings themselves!"[22] By shifting the focus of research from architectural theories to architectural performances in their broader context, he pointed the way toward more rigorous and wide-ranging analyses, grounded in artifacts.

Despite Meeks's enthusiasm for an object-centered architectural history, the free-wheeling interpretive implications of *Architectural Principles in the Age of Humanism* have exerted a more powerful force on scholarship. In his "Mathematics of the Ideal Villa," Colin Rowe, a student of Wittkower, used it to develop an inventive comparison of Andrea Palladio's Villa Malcontenta with Le Corbusier's Villa Stein, an exercise that depends on the degree to which Wittkower's argument is ahistorical.[23] Even otherwise sober-minded scholars fell under its spell. Marcus Whiffen traced equilateral triangles on the elevations of buildings in Williamsburg to claim that a rigid geometric sensibility governed the design of colonial Chesapeake architecture and contributed to its longstanding appeal.[24] Such diagrams did little to advance anyone's understanding of the George Wythe House or Bruton Parish Church but the notion that pure geometry played a significant role in Chesapeake design has been stubbornly persistent.[25] As Alina Payne has observed, savvy design professionals embraced Wittkower's arguments, too, especially his representation of the architect as a theoretician above all.[26] His was that rare work of scholarship that has been regarded respectfully by both historians and serious-minded professionals.

In parallel with the scholarly effort to set the history of architectural design on theoretical foundations, some twentieth-century architects sought to bolster their reputations through public collaborations with famous brains. In the postwar period, these were most often scientists. Le Corbusier and Frank Lloyd Wright both courted the approval of Albert Einstein for some of their more ambitious projects.[27] In the same period, architects and planners worked to portray themselves as similar to medical professionals, working to cure all manner of urban ailments.[28] At a 1956 conference on urban design, Richard Neutra rallied the assembly with an urgent but hopeful exhortation:

> It is being discovered that many diseases—not only nervous diseases—have to do with environmental planning. . . . We are all facing a common danger, a common threat to survival, and if we planners, architects, landscape architects, can rouse the public to awareness of this danger, we may in one or one and a half generations become as honored and powerful as the American Medical Association.[29]

Norwegian architect Christian Norberg-Schulz pursued a scientific synthesis of architectural generation—what he called an "integrated theory of architecture." In his *Intentions in Architecture,* his goal was to establish the practice of architecture as something akin to a social science, to claim a respectability for the profession that he thought it had not yet attained.[30]

Beginning the in the late 1960s, as dissatisfaction grew with the degree to which the revolutionary promises of modern architecture had failed to materialize, the tenor of this theoretical discourse changed, although the essential notion that architecture was principally an intellectual activity, only secondarily a practice, remained fully intact. Increasingly, designers and critics turned to thinkers who provided models with which to critique the orderly, scientific, and positivist presumptions of their predecessors.[31] In its oppositional rhetoric and its dissatisfaction with the revolutionary claims of high modernism, this critical discourse paralleled the contemporary development of vernacular architecture studies. In a few cases, such as the work of Philadelphia architects Robert Venturi and Denise Scott Brown, it explored similar material terrain, though to entirely different purposes. Venturi and Scott Brown provocatively turned their attention to the American suburbs and the Las Vegas strip to reconsider the importance of ornament and symbolism in a critique of the sterile, geometric abstraction of what they termed "orthodox Modern architecture."[32] Anticipating criticism that commercial signage and colonial kitsch could hardly be taken seriously as sources for contemporary design, they framed their work in a complex theoretical armature grounded in semiotics.[33] Unlike other writers of this period who took up ordinary buildings and landscapes as a field of careful study, such as Henry Glassie and Fred Kniffen, they maintained a careful ironic rhetorical distance from their subjects, affirming that the strip and the cul-de-sac were only "almost alright," redeemable as models through the studious intervention of the theoretically sophisticated critic.

In a similar way, designers Peter Eisenman and Bernard Tschumi engaged in a public, sometimes competitive correspondence with the philosopher and literary theorist Jacques Derrida, working to burnish their poststructuralist bona fides.[34] All of these practitioners insisted their designs were the product of careful theorizing, as have their chroniclers. At a recent celebration of Tschumi's work at the Pompidou Center, the exhibition opened with a display of texts that the architect had read and admired, to make a claim for the primacy of theorizing in his buildings. In the mythology of Tschumi and his peers, books come first, not buildings, or even drawings.[35] And in 2017, the Chicago Architectural Biennial featured a display celebrating the career of Chicago architects Stanley Tigerman and Margaret McCurry by exhibiting selections from their library but minimizing the presentation of buildings themselves, relegating them to a handful of small photographs.[36]

Although the principles taken to be the drivers of design were different from those proposed by Norberg-Schulz or Wittkower, and although they sought to distance themselves from their modernist predecessors, the premise that theorizing produces buildings through the intervention of the architect remained. Eisenman and Tschumi distinguished themselves by the degree to which they insisted on the primacy of theory to the ex-

clusion of other considerations. When pressed on the necessary concern that architects must have for pragmatic factors for their designs to be occupied, or even built, Eisenman demurred: "You have to transcend use; you have to say, yes, there are certain givens, but they will no longer generate the system of values."[37] In part, this assertion distanced him from a certain strain of modernist thought, emphasized by Norberg-Schulz, that held that careful attention to the prosaic concerns of a client was sufficient to generate good design. But it was also a way to assert, however implausibly, the centrality of theory to the generation of architectural form, to the exclusion of social, practical, or aesthetic factors. As Tschumi put it, "architecture that does not have a concept is not architecture." He qualifies and negates Pevsner's old formulation, holding that "a bicycle shed with a concept is architecture, a cathedral without one is not."[38] Always implicit in such arguments, and often explicit, is a belief that theoretical premises not only parallel, and dignify, built form but that careful theorizing is the primary cause of architecture and therefore, is sufficient to explain it. The building itself, in fact, may be of only secondary interest, simply an illustration of a principle that might be expressed equally well through text or drawing or model.

Wittkower, Rowe, and their many successors, including Tschumi, embraced the view that good architecture is caused by good theory; bad architecture is the product of bad theory, or no theory at all. This view is seductive. It is romantic. It is inspirational for those who must do the difficult and often tedious work of designing buildings. But the view that architecture is above all a principled activity and that theoretical propositions do not just influence but drive practice is grounded in premises that are themselves bad theory. Faith in a ghostly force that guides design according to its own prerogatives, and the conviction that theoretical premises are the chief causes of architectural form, are both echoes of René Descartes's notion of the relationship between mind and body, in which a disembodied and immaterial substance nonetheless, by mysterious means, exerts a causal force on the material body.[39] Idealist historians such as Wittkower share the French philosopher's faith in a division between the embodied material world and a disembodied spirit that brings it into being, a faith characterized as Cartesian dualism. This is not to say that Wittkower and Descartes are engaged in the same philosophical project. But Wittkower's views on architecture are dualist in conception in that he argued that architectural theorizing takes place outside of, and prior to, the production of buildings. In this view, architecture, like the Cartesian mind, has an existence that is independent of actual building. Recall Tschumi: "a bicycle shed with a concept is architecture." Compare Descartes: "I think, therefore I am." For the idealist, architecture is separate from building in the same way that being does not reside in the body.

For contemporary philosophers, as well as neurologists, the critical weakness of Cartesian dualism is that there is no verifiable way to demonstrate how a disembodied mind produces action in the body.[40] The mind-body problem as formulated by Descartes is simply irreconcilable in his terms without resorting to magic. Its resolution demands either divine intervention or an embodied understanding of consciousness. And yet in the work of Wittkower, Rowe, and their many sympathizers, Cartesian dualism remains the predominant metaphor for explaining the production of architecture. Architectural minds, whether in the form of individual genius or a collective *Kunstwollen*, are taken to produce embodied buildings, whose value is established by the quality of the mind that brought them into being.

Dualism is an illustration of what sociologist Pierre Bourdieu terms idealism, the notion that conscious human thought always precedes and produces social practice, a faith that pervades academic disciplines. This tendency to see thinking, or, more precisely, writing, as the essential activity demanding scholarly interpretation is a disposition that Bourdieu describes as a "scholastic bias," a characteristic of academic discourses across many fields, from the humanities to the social sciences and the hard sciences. His development of the notion of "habitus," the collection of practices, assumptions, and predispositions that govern individuals' actions in the social world but are only rarely articulated, was intended as an explicit critique of this bias.[41] Central to the mythology of the thinking architect is the belief in a creator as a special, privileged agent who sits outside the ordinary world of social and economic exchange, a faith captured in the popular notion of the starving artist or the consumptive poet in his garret. Bourdieu regards this belief as fundamental to the fields of art and literature but it applies equally to architectural criticism and history: "Cultural production distinguishes itself from the production of the most common objects in that it must produce not only the object in its materiality, but also the value of this object, that is, the recognition of artistic legitimacy. This is inseparable from the production of the artist or the writer as artist or writer, in other words, as a creator of value."[42] For many scholars, the creation of architectural value occurs at the moment the architect expresses him- or herself in writing, not at the moment of construction.

One of the qualities of an idealist understanding of practice is that it privileges mental over physical work, supposing that a conscious mind everywhere and always governs action. It is, therefore, a fiction that flatters both academics and professionals. And it is an ancient fiction, one that courses through Greek thought as well as early modern conceptions of gentility.[43] Yet for all its ontological weakness and its class-centrism, it permeates social and intellectual life. It afflicts the sciences, as in the relative status of mathematics over engineering, for example, or theoretical over experimental physics; in architecture, it manifests itself in the notion that a few highly theorized structures, like the Villa Rotunda or the Vanna Venturi House, deserve special attention, while those that are untethered to explicit philosophical premises may be ignored, unworthy of praise or even consideration. This is not to suggest that architectural theory should be dismissed out of hand as irrelevant. Art historian Keith Moxey argues that when theoretical considerations are germane, as they are with the work of Venturi and Scott Brown, they should be treated as evidence alongside the created work, not as a simple explanation for it, the *clavis interpretandi*: "Rather than invoke the traditional metaphors of surface and depth, according to which theory is said to lie at a deeper, more foundational level than practice, I would argue that both types of cultural activity lie in the same intellectual plane."[44]

Beyond its theoretical weakness, idealist notions of architecture fail to account for too many things: buildings without identifiable architects, to begin with; and for any building, the complex interaction between client, builder, and community interests; or the critical role of financing in determining what gets built, and how. The idealist fails to acknowledge that buildings are embedded in multiple contexts. They cannot be principally understood as manifestations of an immaterial, architectural mind.

Nonetheless, this perspective has pervaded modern architectural practice and criticism for decades. And because this work cannot begin without some evidence of intent, an architect who writes copiously is an ideal subject—his or her buildings can be parsed for the degree to which they embody a set of stated intentions. But following this trail of interpretive bread crumbs significantly circumscribes interpretive possibilities. Although some buildings may indeed embody particular notions about design and architecture, this does not remove them from their prosaic contexts in the social world.[45] Frank Gehry's Disney Concert Hall is an exceptional structure and makes a significant contribution to contemporary debates about form, but it is also, inescapably, a building in Los Angeles (Figure 1). It sits across the street from an apartment complex; it is the home of a symphony orchestra; its construction was underwritten by a major media corporation; and at the risk of belaboring the obvious, it had to obey the city's building codes, fire regulations, and the laws of physics. Finally, its designer is a canny professional, running a service business that is dependent upon the vagaries of the world economy and local real estate markets.[46] Photographs often isolate it from that context, enabling the fantasy that it is a pure instance of architectural thought, rather than part of a fluid urban and human context.

## Materialism

Idealist notions of architecture are entirely deficient in dealing with the artifacts that comprise the overwhelming majority of the built environment (Figure 2). For buildings that lack a known designer, such interpretations often argue that they are the offspring of a collective mind, or, for structures thought to be especially humble, a product of the earth itself. William Pierson, unable to decide which explanation he preferred, deployed both, describing the Parson Capen house as simple and austere, "the very embodiment of the Puritan mind," whose "unrefined surfaces harmonize quietly with the stark gray-brown countryside, making the house a natural extension of the earth upon which it stands."[47]

Those who must do the hard work of interpreting such buildings on their own terms have developed a more useful and perceptive set of interpretive tools by beginning with the material facts of buildings and working outward to the wider cultural world of which they are a part.[48] Where the idealist architectural historian begins with a theoretical framework and seeks buildings to illustrate it, the materialist scholar begins with buildings and works outward toward social life. This allows the Capen house to be recognized for what it is: a large, respectable residence, stylishly outfitted with a handsome stair and boldly chamfered summer beams, built in the 1680s for a young minister of the gospel in a small town on the North Shore north of Boston.

In its careful attention to material facts, materialist scholarship is empirical at its core. Among humanists, empiricism has a marginal reputation. It is seen by many as a useful but not entirely serious endeavor, focused on data collection rather than interpretation; for many students of material culture, it sits a little too close for comfort to connoisseurship.[49] Like classification or description, it seems theoretically simple-minded, a not entirely respectable epistemology that stinks a little of the dilettante. But connected to larger social patterns, the materialist

historian can magnify the smallest data points to open interpretive avenues that are foreclosed to the dualist. The empirical analysis of material life, properly situated in its context, allows for much wider-ranging investigations of architecture than those offered by idealism.

Consider, for example, the interpretations of Monticello, in which Thomas Jefferson is most commonly portrayed as an ingenious designer, bringing the obsessiveness and intellectual rigor of his political writings to the creation of his mountaintop house in Albemarle County, Vir-

Figure 2. Parson Capen house, Topsfield, Massachusetts, built 1683, restored 1913 by George Francis Dow. Photograph by Jeffrey E. Klee, 2008.

ginia. For Marcus Whiffen and Frederick Koeper, it is "one of the most fascinating self-portraits in the history of architecture. From its site to its gadgetry—wind-dial, geared double doors, dumb waiter—it is all Jefferson."[50] Finding Jefferson's genius manifest in some key aspect of his house has been irresistible quarry for many scholars, who have observed a singular mind at work in his dumbwaiters, the suppression of the service wings out of view from the main house, his attention to proportion, and his seeming ability to translate conceptions of freedom into material form.[51] For others, beginning with Fiske Kimball, his brilliance has been evident in the scrupulously researched classical sources of his design in pattern books and European buildings.[52] In this hagiographical literature, authors address only those aspects of the building that reveal his brilliant, discerning architectural mind at work most clearly. Kimball focused on his knowledgeable use of classical sources; Christian Norberg-Schulz thought he saw a unique sensitivity to the *genius loci* of the North American continent; Buford Pickens, following the lead of Wittkower, thought the key to the building was his attention to ideal proportions and perfect geometric shapes. Such speculative readings of the house begin with a principle presumed to be significant and then conclude their analysis when they locate its manifestation in the built fabric.

Recently, materialist scholars have found more prosaic and more plausible explanations for many of Monticello's apparently distinctive qualities by observing that it was the home of a Virginia planter whose social life, like those of his peers, was dependent upon the enslaved labor of an enormous workforce. Edward Chappell notes the care with which the everyday work of Jefferson's domestic staff in and around the house was kept out of sight, concealing the degree to which he was dependent upon the work of slaves.[53] The subterranean service passages, dumbwaiters, and hidden staircases all contribute to an illusion of solitude and independence that Dell Upton describes as supporting "an interpretive myth of domestic life" that diminishes or even denies the prosaic underpinnings of that life.[54] Upton accepts the premise that the house is a careful self-portrait but reads that portrait more critically, noting its elisions to observe how that portrait is constructed, and why: "Just as the slaves' work spaces are hidden by the terrace, the family quarters are concealed behind balustrades. The only storey that we see is the patriarch's. Visually Jefferson's house claims that the home of many people, white and black, is the home of one man."[55] Upton's and Chappell's explorations of Monticello do not deny that Jefferson used dumbwaiters to support domestic service, nor that the house's ornament was derived from European models. They simply look outward to observe how such devices were in the service of a larger social program. They recognize the architecture of Monticello as part of a cultural and economic system that was dependent upon enslaved labor even as it required, for rhetorical and political purposes, that dependence to be concealed.

Materialists understand, in other words, that buildings are embedded in social contexts in much the same way that minds are embodied in flesh. All buildings are discursive and represent a theoretical perspective, whether or not they engage with the preoccupations of design theorists. Monticello makes a claim for the role of architecture in social life, a claim that situates and contextualizes its deployment of classical architecture. In the arrangement and finish of spaces for preparing meals and doing laundry, Jefferson's house reveals much about his attitudes toward the nature and status of his enslaved domestic staff. Recent excavations at Mulberry Row, the avenue of work buildings and slave dwellings at Monticello, illustrate how Jefferson manipulated slave structures over time to move them out of sight and below ground, even if this meant the great expense of relocating them closer to the mansion (Figure 3). In its disposition of ornament, the house asserts a view about the respectability of its occupants and visitors. In its degree of stylishness, finally, it illustrates the cultural capital of its owner.[56] For attentive researchers, such questions are observed in and raised by buildings themselves, including those put up by owners who are less well documented than the third president of the United States.

All buildings are equally "about" something or other. To the limited extent that a structure can be said to have narrative content, a bicycle shed is about community life and the civic provision of transportation infrastructure. Lincoln Cathedral may be said to be about many things, including secular and religious authority, community devotion, public art, and medieval theology. In its siting, its design and choice of materials, a shopping center takes a position on the social role of consumption. Only a little imagination is required to recognize that even the most commonplace structure exists for a reason and that this reason for being can be described, analyzed, and carefully historicized. Through their plans, form, and finish, all buildings embody social values. Sometimes those values are those of political theorists and architecture critics, as they need places to live and work like the rest of us. Bishops have things to say about the design and construction of churches; industrialists write about factories. Architects and builders are paid to listen to them and to account for their notions about what buildings should look like and how they should function but they do not have the last word in these negotiations.

**Fieldwork**
An architectural history that attends to context and social meaning is better able to explain a wide range of buildings and the multiple forces that bring them into being, give them significance, and situate them in the social world. Such scholarship is a singular form of what is more generally described as the history of material life, which provides, in Cary Carson's terms, "an account of people's growing dependence on inanimate objects to communicate their relationships with one another and mediate their daily progress through the social worlds they inhabited."[57] Material histories of architecture center on buildings, whether or not they incorporate detailed field-based research. Fieldwork may not be necessary or even useful to account for buildings already well documented or those captured thoroughly in professional drawings and photographs, such as housing towers, or those that are no longer standing. There are many avenues of architectural research that cannot be pursued in the field. An understanding of legislative and administrative structures, such as the practice of redlining, or setback requirements, requires time in the municipal archives. We must look to

Figure 3. Monticello, begun 1768, as enlarged and improved 1796–1809. View of subterranean service wing with mansion house visible in the background. Photograph by Jeffrey E. Klee, 2008.

deed, tax, and census records for the history of ownership and occupation. Similarly, the social and professional context of a structure's owner, builder, and designer are not embodied in any durable way in buildings. There are limits to what the fieldworker can learn in isolation.

But if fieldwork is not always central to a materialist method, it often provides insights that may not be available elsewhere. Many of the contexts in which buildings are embedded do not leave traces in the written record. Material traces are recorded and interpreted through careful fieldwork and only discernable through close examination. The most informative work of this kind involves both careful looking and careful recording, in drawings, photographs, and written notes. It records the layout of a structure in a measured plan, accompanied by significant details. It develops hypotheses about the use and significance of individual spaces. It moves beyond the singular, the curious, and the aesthetically appealing to the commonplace and the ordinary to identify patterns and account for commonalities as well as difference.[58] Architectural fieldwork is attentive, above all, to history. Buildings have a life cycle, they change over time,

and sorting out what was done when and why is one of the most important jobs of the fieldworker. Studies that fail to account for historical context remove buildings from any meaningful relationship to history, diminishing them through isolation. Ahistorical scholarship on commonplace buildings reinforces notions of the vernacular as timeless, unchanging, and thoughtless, thereby segregating them from the purview of humanistic scholarship.[59] All buildings are embedded in a context and only possess significance to the extent that that context is clearly understood.

As Dell Upton has pointed out, the roots of this method are antiquarian.[60] In the early twentieth century, field-based research was done to help architects design houses for dentists and bankers, with the same professional motivations that took Robert Adam to Split in the 1750s. Today, the purely antiquarian building investigator is a figure of ridicule or pity, more the dilettante than the scholar, seeking to be a world expert in the screw, or the scarf joint. A certain apprehension attends fieldwork, therefore, in the twenty-first century. None of us want to be mistaken for a member of the Society of Dilettanti. But if some antiquarians have been fieldworkers, not all fieldworkers are antiquarians. Occasional arguments about how much detail is appropriate for a field drawing reflect this anxiety.[61] Such debates obscure the fact that fieldwork is part of a much larger domain of analytical activity that includes, but is not the same as, the recording of plans. In that it slows the researcher down so that analysis can take place, drawing is a very effective way to encounter and analyze a building in the field, but it is not the only means to that end. The purpose of fieldwork is analysis, not illustration.[62] Fieldwork is not drawing any more than writing is typing.

Fieldwork, finally, is a special category of a materialist analysis of architecture in its embodiment. It is embodied in the metaphorical sense of attending to architectural bodies rather than the ineffable architectural mind. Philosopher of science Davis Baird observes how scientific devices, models, and instruments embody kinds of knowledge that are not often written down or articulated through language.[63] What he describes as a materialist epistemology can only be recovered and understood through the careful examination of these artifacts, as this "thing knowledge" has not always left a trace in the written record. In the same way, buildings record their own architectural epistemology, capturing an understanding of domestic life, for example, or construction practices, social systems, or religious belief that is not reliably preserved in texts. As antiquarians as well as scholars of material culture have long maintained, artifacts are evidence.[64] But fieldwork is also embodied in the literal sense that it involves an agent moving through a building with his or her body in order to make sense of it. The fieldworker, like all occupants, passes through doors, sweats in attics, and bumps his or her head against collar ties. It is no accident that there is a rich genre of story among fieldworkers involving bodily mishaps: falling through floors and ceilings, being confronted by animals, swarmed by fleas, and threatened by unsympathetic occupants.

It is axiomatic, now, that discourse conditions our knowledge of things in the world and that genuine understanding is elusive. Historians have become adept at analyzing texts to identify the ways in which they limit that understanding. The analytical fieldworker seeks to understand how the material world participates in this conditioning—how buildings, as much as language, structure our interpretive lives.[65] When we speak of what a building means, or how a house organizes domestic life, we recognize the participation of objects in the production of social life.

As a particular kind of materialist scholarship, fieldwork, as a method, serves as a criticism of idealist notions of architecture. Its performance is a rebuke to perspectives that subordinate the material practice of building to the immaterial, disembodied practice of thinking as it enacts an embodied way of understanding buildings. To measure and photograph a building is to insist that the fabric of building is key to understanding architecture. Fieldwork recognizes that knowledge is embodied in building, not only in texts, and still less in a phantasmic Cartesian otherworld, accessible only to genius. It is a critique of an essentializing perspective on architecture that imagines absolute, immutable, transcendent values for design. The recording of buildings as a means to get at thought is the inverse of the view that architecture is a series of theoretical propositions that are materialized in a small number of exceptional buildings. That such work is often dismissed as antiquarian, anti-modern, or reactionary by those arguing for a Cartesian view of building should come as no surprise. But fieldwork is a more humane, more complete, and more intellectually robust means of engagement with buildings, and we should take courage from that understanding.

Whether field-based or not, materialist scholarship has a distinctive moral and intellectual center. It insists, first of all, that the study of architecture should be inclusive, covering the full range of environments that humans inhabit; and second, that buildings must be studied as the product of many forces, including social, technological, intellectual, financial, and legal. Idealist or art-historical methods that focus only on the origins of form are both ethically and intellectually impoverished. Even the most provincial, antiquarian forms of fieldwork participate in this critique of idealist architectural history. Whether as a component of a materialist understanding of architecture, undertaken as part of a Section 106 survey, or pursued for its own sake, fieldwork rejects notions of architecture as a privileged, insular activity. Nonetheless, the fieldworker is a freakish figure for many, and a threatening one to a certain view of architecture. But many ideas need threatening. In looking carefully at buildings, we make a public claim for an embodied understanding of architecture that contributes to a durable, humanistic scholarship on the material world. Fieldwork insists that the world is not divided into high architecture and vernacular building, cathedrals and bicycle sheds. It has been said many times before but it bears repeating that there is nothing but language to separate the vernacular from fine architecture. There is no architectural mind. There are only buildings, and our attempts to make sense of them.

AUTHOR BIOGRAPHY

**Jeffrey E. Klee** is the Shirley and Richard Roberts Architectural Historian for the Colonial Williamsburg Foundation.

NOTES

1. An early articulation of how little notice the principal journal of architectural history in the United States took of ordinary buildings is found in John Maass, "Where Architectural Historians Fear to Tread," *Journal of the Society of Architectural Historians* 28, no. 1 (March 1969): 3–8. Among other concerns, Maass objected to a persistent focus on urban elites, calling for greater attention to "the anonymous architecture of early and rural societies."

2. See, e.g., the introduction to Dell Upton and John Michael Vlach, eds., *Common Places: Readings in American Vernacular Architecture* (Athens: University of Georgia Press, 1986), where Upton and Vlach observe the already commonplace practice of defining the vernacular by what it is not rather than what it is.

3. Henry Glassie, *Folk Housing in Middle Virginia: A Structural Analysis of Historic Artifacts* (Knoxville: University of Tennessee Press, 1975), 10.

4. Jesse Lemisch, "The American Revolution Seen from the Bottom Up," in *Towards a New Past: Dissenting Essays in American History,* ed. Barton J. Bern-

stein (New York: Pantheon Books, 1968), 3–45; Jesse Lemisch, "Jack Tar in the Streets: Merchant Seamen in the Politics of Revolutionary America," *William and Mary Quarterly* 25, no. 3 (July 1968): 371–407; Edward Palmer Thompson, *The Making of the English Working Class* (New York: Pantheon Books, 1964).

5. Cary Carson, "Whither VAG?" *Vernacular Architecture* 15 (1984): 3–5. More recently, Daniel Maudlin has exhorted British scholars to expand the traditional boundaries of what constitutes the vernacular in the U.K., but he acknowledges that, for most, such boundaries remain carefully drawn around regional traditions of the pre-Georgian era. Daniel Maudlin, "Crossing Boundaries: Revisiting the Thresholds of Vernacular Architecture," *Vernacular Architecture* 41 (2010): 10–14.

6. Dell Upton, "The Power of Things: Recent Studies in American Vernacular Architecture," *American Quarterly* 35, no. 3 (1983): 262–79; Camille Wells, "Old Claims and New Demands: Vernacular Architecture Studies Today," in *Perspectives in Vernacular Architecture II,* ed. Camille Wells (Columbia: University of Missouri Press, 1986), 1–10; Thomas Carter and Bernard L. Herman, "Introduction: Toward a New Architectural History," in *Perspectives in Vernacular Architecture III,* ed. Thomas Carter and Bernard L. Herman (Columbia: University of Missouri Press, 1991), 1–6.

7. The Architecture, Landscape, and American Culture series, published by the University of Minnesota Press and edited by Abigail Van Slyck and Katherine Solomonson, illustrates this shift well. See, e.g., Annmarie Adams, *Medicine by Design: The Architect and the Modern Hospital, 1893–1943* (Minneapolis: University of Minnesota Press, 2007); Gretchen Buggeln, *The Suburban Church: Modernism and Community in Postwar America* (Minneapolis: University of Minnesota Press, 2015); Abigail A. Van Slyck, *A Manufactured Wilderness: Summer Camps and the Shaping of American Youth, 1890–1960* (Minneapolis: University of Minnesota Press, 2010); Carla Yanni, *The Architecture of Madness: Insane Asylums in the United States* (Minneapolis: University of Minnesota Press, 2007).

8. In his remarks at the 2004 meeting of the Vernacular Architecture Forum, Dell Upton cautioned his audience against making a fetish of fieldwork, noting that a single-minded empiricism could foreclose more thoughtful analysis. In the decade since,

however, field methods have been less in evidence at the annual meetings of the VAF. Dell Upton, "The VAF at 25: What Now?," *Perspectives in Vernacular Architecture* 13, no. 2 (2006): 7–13.

9. Anna Vemer Andrzejewski, " 'Perspectives in Vernacular Architecture,' the VAF, and the Study of Ordinary Buildings and Landscapes in North America," *Perspectives in Vernacular Architecture* 13, no. 2 (January 2006): 55–63.

10. Orlando V. Ridout, "Work in Progress: The Chesapeake Farm Buildings Survey," ed. Camille Wells, *Perspectives in Vernacular Architecture*, 1 (1982): 137–49; Abbott Lowell Cummings, *The Framed Houses of Massachusetts Bay* (Cambridge, Mass.: Belknap Press of Harvard University Press, 1979); Henry Glassie, *Vernacular Architecture* (Bloomington: Indiana University Press, 2000); James A. Jacobs, *Detached America: Building Houses in Postwar Suburbia* (Charlottesville: University of Virginia Press, 2015); Matthew Gordon Lasner, *High Life: Condo Living in the Suburban Century* (New Haven, Conn.: Yale University Press, 2012).

11. Upton, "The Power of Things," 263.

12. Carter and Herman, "Introduction: Toward a New Architectural History."

13. Sigfried Giedion, *Space, Time and Architecture: The Growth of a New Tradition*, 5th ed. (Cambridge, Mass.: Harvard University Press, 1967).

14. Peter Blake, *The Master Builders* (New York: Knopf, 1960); Reyner Banham, *Theory and Design in the First Machine Age* (New York: Praeger, 1960).

15. Allister Neher, "Riegl, Hegel, Kunstwollen, and the Weltgeist," *RACAR: Revue d'art Canadienne / Canadian Art Review* 29, no. 1/2 (2004): 5–13.

16. William H. Pierson, *American Buildings and Their Architects, Volume 1: The Colonial and Neoclassical Styles* (New York: Oxford University Press, 1986), 12.

17. Pierson, *American Buildings and Their Architects, Volume 1*, 12.

18. Henry Chandlee Forman, *Maryland Architecture: A Short History from 1634 through the Civil War*, ed. Morris Leon Radoff (Cambridge, Md.: Tidewater Publishers, 1968).

19. Erwin Panofsky, *Gothic Architecture and Scholasticism* (New York: Meridian Books, 1957).

20. Rudolf Wittkower, *Architectural Principles in the Age of Humanism* (London: Alec Tiranti, 1952); Geoffrey Scott, *The Architecture of Humanism: A Study in the History of Taste*, 2nd ed. (London: Constable and Company, 1924).

21. Alina A. Payne, "Rudolf Wittkower and Architectural Principles in the Age of Modernism," *Journal of the Society of Architectural Historians* 53, no. 3 (September 1994): 322–42.

22. Carroll L. V. Meeks, "The New History of Architecture," *Journal of the American Society of Architectural Historians* 2, no. 1 (January 1942): 7.

23. Colin Rowe, *The Mathematics of the Ideal Villa, and Other Essays* (Cambridge, Mass.: MIT Press, 1976), 1–28.

24. Marcus Whiffen, *The Eighteenth-Century Houses of Williamsburg* (Williamsburg, Va.: The Colonial Williamsburg Foundation, 1969), 83–88; Marcus Whiffen, *The Public Buildings of Williamsburg, Colonial Capital of Virginia: An Architectural History* (Williamsburg, Va.: Colonial Williamsburg, 1958), 80–82.

25. See, e.g., William M. S. Rasmussen, "Sabine Hall, A Classical Villa in Virginia," *Journal of the Society of Architectural Historians* 39, no. 4 (December 1980): 289.

26. Payne, "Rudolf Wittkower and Architectural Principles in the Age of Modernism," 324–325.

27. Milton Cameron, "Albert Einstein, Frank Lloyd Wright, Le Corbusier, and the Future of the American City," Institute for Advanced Study, https://www.ias.edu/ideas/2014/cameron-einstein.

28. José Luis Sert, *Can Our Cities Survive? An ABC of Urban Problems, Their Analysis, Their Solutions* (Cambridge, Mass.: Harvard University Press, 1942); "Slum Surgery in St. Louis," *Architectural Forum* 94 (April 1951): 128–36; "The Philadelphia Cure: Clearing Slums with Penicillin, Not Surgery," *Architectural Forum* 96 (April 1952): 112–19.

29. Neutra's remarks were made at a meeting sponsored by the Harvard University Graduate School of Design and transcribed in "Urban Design," *Progressive Architecture* 37 (August 1956): 97–111.

30. Christian Norberg-Schulz, *Intentions in Architecture* (Cambridge, Mass.: MIT Press, 1965).

31. For an account of how 1968 is treated as a watershed among contemporary historians of architectural theory, see Sylvia Lavin, "Theory into History; Or, the Will to Anthology," *Journal of the Society of Architectural Historians* 58, no. 3 (September 1999): 494–99; and Louis Martin, "Against Architecture," *Log* no. 16 (Spring/Summer 2009): 153–67.

32. Robert Venturi, Denise Scott Brown, and Steven Izenour, *Learning from Las Vegas: The Forgotten Symbolism of Architectural Form* (Cambridge, Mass: MIT Press, 1977).

33. Dell Upton, "Signs Taken for Wonders," *Visible Language* 37, no. 3 (September 2003): 332–51.

34. Bernard Tschumi, "Disjunctions," *Perspecta* 23 (1987): 108–19; Jacques Derrida and Peter Eisenman, *Chora L Works*, ed. Jeffrey Kipnis and Thomas Leeser (New York: Monacelli Press, 1997).

35. Meredith L. Clausen, "Review of *Bernard Tschumi, Architecture: Concept & Notation* Exhibition, Centre Pompidou, Paris," *Journal of the Society of Architectural Historians* 74, no. 2 (June 2015): 264–65.

36. Emma Macdonald, "MG&Co. Creates 'Rooms for Books' and Spaces for Dialogue about Architecture on Paper" (Chicagoarchitecturebiennial.org: September 19, 2017), http://chicagoarchitecturebiennial.org/blog/the-architecture-of-print/.

37. Derrida and Eisenman, *Chora L Works*, 9.

38. Bernard Tschumi and Peter Eisenman, "I Do Not Mind People Being Innocent, but I Hate When They're Naive," *Log* no. 28 (Summer 2013): 99–108. The quip that "A bicycle shed is a building; Lincoln Cathedral is a piece of architecture" appears in Nikolaus Pevsner, *An Outline of European Architecture*, 7th ed., Pelican Books (Harmondsworth, U.K.: Penguin Books, 1963), 15.

39. René Descartes, *Meditations on First Philosophy: With Selections from the Objections and Replies*, ed. Bernard Williams, trans. John Cottingham (Cambridge and New York: Cambridge University Press, 1986). Descartes's articulation of what has been subsequently referred to as the "mind-body problem," or dualism, occurs in the second meditation.

40. George Lakoff and Mark Johnson, *Philosophy in the Flesh: The Embodied Mind and Its Challenge to Western Thought* (New York: Basic Books, 1999).

41. Pierre Bourdieu, "Habitus," in *Habitus: A Sense of Place*, ed. Jean Hillier and Emma Rooksby, 2nd ed. (Aldershot, U.K.: Ashgate Publishing Company, 2005), 48.

42. Pierre Bourdieu, "Field of Power, Literary Field and Habitus," in *The Field of Cultural Production: Essays on Art and Literature*, ed. Randal Johnson (Cambridge: Policy Press, 1993), 164.

43. The inferiority of the material world to the world of Forms and the Soul is alluded to in Plato's allegory of the cave in *The Republic*. See Plato, *The Republic*, trans. G. M. A. Grube (Indianapolis: Hackett Publishing Company, 1974); it is taken up at greater length and in more detail in the *Phaedo*, in Plato, *Five Dialogues*, trans. G. M. A. Grube (Indianapolis: Hackett Publishing Company, 1981).

44. Keith P. F. Moxey, *The Practice of Theory: Poststructuralism, Cultural Politics, and Art History* (Ithaca, N.Y.: Cornell University Press, 1994), xi.

45. Sarah Williams Goldhagen, "Something to Talk About: Modernism, Discourse, Style," *Journal of the Society of Architectural Historians* 64, no. 2 (June 2005): 144–67.

46. Dell Upton, "Gehryism: American Architectural History and the Cultural Authority of Art" (Reconceptualizing the History of the Built Environment in North America, Charles Warren Center for Studies in American History, Cambridge, Mass., April 29, 2005).

47. Pierson, *American Buildings and Their Architects, Volume 1*, 51.

48. Some of the most articulate and influential discussions of the ways in which artifacts can be interpreted through carefully situating them in their material and historical context have been written by historical archaeologists. Two classics of material culture method are James Deetz, *In Small Things Forgotten: The Archaeology of Early American Life*, 1st ed. (Garden City, N.Y.: Anchor Press/Doubleday, 1977) and Ian Hodder, *Reading the Past: Current Approaches to Interpretation in Archaeology*, 2nd ed. (Cambridge: Cambridge University Press, 1991).

49. See, e.g., Upton, "The VAF at 25."

50. Marcus Whiffen and Frederick Koeper, *American Architecture 1607–1976* (Cambridge, Mass: MIT Press, 1981), 105.

51. Whiffen and Koeper, *American Architecture 1607–1976*, 102–9; Buford Pickens, "Mr. Jefferson as Revolutionary Architect," *Journal of the Society of Architectural Historians* 34, no. 4 (December 1975): 257–79; and Christian Norberg-Schulz, *New World Architecture* (New York: Princeton Architectural Press, 1988), 12–17.

52. Fiske Kimball, *Thomas Jefferson, Architect: Original Designs in the Collection of Thomas Jefferson Coolidge, Junior* (Cambridge, Mass.: Riverside Press, 1916); Walter Muir Whitehill and Frederic D. Nichols, *Palladio in America* (New York: Rizzoli International

Publications, 1982), 111–16; Richard Guy Wilson, "Thomas Jefferson's 'Bibliomanie' and Architecture," in *American Architects and Their Books to 1848,* ed. Kenneth Hafertepe and James F. O'Gorman (Amherst: University of Massachusetts Press, 2001), 59–72.

53. Edward A. Chappell, "Architecture of Urban Domestic Slavery in the Chesapeake and Jamaica: Comparative Evidence," in *Slavery in the City: Architecture and Landscapes of Urban Slavery in North America,* ed. Clifton Ellis and Rebecca Ginsburg (Charlottesville: University of Virginia Press, 2017), 29–30. For further analysis of Monticello, including a discussion of its privy and its hardware, see Edward A. Chappell, "Housing Slavery," in *The Chesapeake House: Architectural Investigation by Colonial Williamsburg,* ed. Cary Carson and Carl Lounsbury (Chapel Hill: University of North Carolina Press, 2013), 156–78; and Edward A. Chappell, "Hardware," in *The Chesapeake House,* 259–83.

54. Dell Upton, *Architecture in the United States* (Oxford and New York: Oxford University Press, 1998), 29.

55. Upton, *Architecture in the United States,* 30.

56. For the notion of cultural capital and its applicability to question of style and taste in the arts, generally, see Pierre Bourdieu, "A Sociological Theory of Art Perception," in *The Field of Cultural Production: Essays on Art and Literature,* ed. Randal Johnson (Cambridge: Policy Press, 1993), 215–37; and Pierre Bourdieu, *Distinction: A Social Critique of the Judgement of Taste* (Cambridge, Mass: Harvard University Press, 1984).

57. Cary Carson, *Face Value* (Charlottesville: University of Virginia Press, 2017), 198. Carson has argued for the utility of material artifacts to the study of history for decades. See, e.g., Cary Carson, "Doing History with Material Culture," in *Material Culture and the Study of American Life,* ed. Ian Quimby (New York: Norton, 1978); and "Material Culture History: The Scholarship Nobody Knows," in *American Material Culture: The Shape of the Field,* ed. Ann Smart Martin and J. Ritchie Garrison (Winterthur, Del.: Henry Francis du Pont Winterthur Museum, 1997), 401–28.

58. There is a rich literature on the interpretive value of architectural fieldwork, from demonstrations of its utility through careful scholarship to how-to guides for students. See, e.g., Cummings, *The Framed Houses of Massachusetts Bay*; Gabrielle M. Lanier and Bernard L. Herman, *Everyday Architecture of the Mid-Atlantic: Looking at Buildings and Landscapes* (Baltimore, Md.: Johns Hopkins University Press, 1997); Thomas Carter and Elizabeth Collins Cromley, *Invitation to Vernacular Architecture: A Guide to the Study of Ordinary Buildings and Landscapes* (Knoxville: University of Tennessee Press, 2005); Carson and Lounsbury, eds., *The Chesapeake House.*

59. A postwar fashion for architectural monographs on folk buildings that failed to take the history and context of their creation into account while presenting them in beautiful photographs is exemplified by Sibyl Moholy-Nagy, *Native Genius in Anonymous Architecture* (New York: Horizon Press, 1957); and Bernard Rudofsky, *Architecture without Architects: A Short Introduction to Non-Pedigreed Architecture* (New York: Museum of Modern Art, 1965).

60. Upton, "The VAF at 25."

61. Periodic special sessions on fieldwork at the annual meetings of the Vernacular Architecture Forum illustrate how contentious the subject of drawing can sometimes be. A demanding set of standards has been produced by the Historic American Buildings Survey: "HABS Guidelines: Recording Historic Structures and Sites with HABS Measured Drawings," United States Department of the Interior, December, 2008. Other considerations of field drawings are found in Carter and Cromley, *Invitation to Vernacular Architecture* and Lanier and Herman, *Everyday Architecture of the Mid-Atlantic.*

62. For a detailed, perceptive account of the value of analytical fieldwork, see Edward Chappell's chapter, "Fieldwork," in Carson and Lounsbury, *The Chesapeake House,* 29–47.

63. Davis Baird, "Thing Knowledge—Function and Truth," *Techné* 6, no. 2 (Winter 2002): 13–27; Davis Baird, *Thing Knowledge: A Philosophy of Scientific Instruments* (Berkeley: University of California Press, 2004).

64. Carson, *Face Value,* especially chapter 6, "Toward a History of Material Life," 191–202.

65. For the discursive role of the material world, see the introduction to Bernard L. Herman, *The Stolen House* (Charlottesville: University of Virginia Press, 1992), 3–14.

LOUIS P. NELSON

# *Object Lesson:* Monuments and Memory in Charlottesville

"There had been plenty of rumors all the evening through that a mob was gathering." As the dark of night fell, hundreds, "many having masks over their faces," marched through the streets of Charlottesville. Packed in close formation, the torch-lit masked throng marched up Second Street and then turned right on High, proceeding two more blocks to their destination: the north yard of the Albemarle County Courthouse. There they grew in numbers, eventually collecting "hundreds . . . at every corner in all directions," all fueled by "a spirit of riot." Although eerily familiar, this was not the summer of 2017, but exactly one century before.[1]

In the spring of 1917, Hampton Crosby and Richard Jones, both black, had been caught stealing a ham by white policeman Meredith Thomas. After a struggle, Thomas was shot and killed by his own gun. Just days later, Crosby and Jones found themselves detained in the old city jail, which still stands less than a block north of the courthouse. "Shouting and cat-calling" by the mob outside the jail persisted for hours. Authorities were alarmed when they learned that "a large delegation from the student body at the University was expected to join them in the grand march to seize the men and carry out a spectacular lynching at a tree selected near the place of the killing [of Thomas]." The sheriff needed reinforcements and called in an additional hundred men, half coming by train from Staunton. Just after midnight the fire department was called "but the hose was not used against the crowd. It was reported that the men declined to shift their volunteered service from fire-fighting to mob

chasing, and would not use the apparatus."[2] The night was tense, but no one pulled the trigger. Into the early hours of the morning the crowd slowly dispersed, having "furnished no leader who could risk those glistening revolvers and shining bayonets seen dimly in the dusky night." Soon after their trial in Richmond that June, Crosby and Jones were electrocuted.[3]

In both 1917 and 2017, white supremacy in Charlottesville was a public performance. White men asserted their presumed authority and public squares became stages of mass intimidation while streets became sites of domestic terrorism. Men carried torches and rope in 1917, shields and semiautomatic weapons in 2017; in both they donned masks, hoods, and capes. In 1917, they directed hours of catcalling to the jail cell windows; in 2017 they chanted "white lives matter" and "Jews will not replace us!" In the more recent events, these objects and figures live large in our imagination through photography and video clips. But in our screen-dependent, image-saturated age, visual memory seems to have dimmed our sensitivity to the power of place and the longer tradition of associating specific places with people or events. Marches, mobs, and other collective displays of intimidation inscribe racism into the very fabric of our cities. Invisible to the nonresident, the legacy of ritualized racism in the mind of the resident is not easily erased from the palimpsest of place. And these public assertions of racial hierarchies—episodic yet highly visible—reinforce the silent but unyielding geographies of race. In many inland Southern cities like Charlottesville, "historically disenfranchised African American communities have been relegated to the margins and in many places to low-lying topographic areas in their respective cities while their white counterparts have commandeered higher elevations."[4] Racism in Charlottesville is inscribed in the streets, buildings, squares, and in public monuments.

In the course of just a decade straddling the Cosby-Jones lynching attempt, from the mid-1910s to the mid-1920s, Charlottesville's elites erected a series of four monuments along a high ridge-road that connected the University of Virginia to the heart of downtown. Commissioned and funded by stockbroker and philanthropist Paul Goodloe McIntyre, these four monuments collectively transformed the city: Meriwether Lewis and William Clark (1919); Thomas Jonathan "Stonewall" Jackson (1921); George Rogers Clark (1921); and Robert Edward Lee (1924) (Figure 1).[5] While the installations were nominally monuments to heroic men, they are more importantly charged objects with a particular history that shaped how they functioned socially and politically and what they meant to period viewers. When read through the lens of their specific historic and spatial contexts, these four statues read no longer as monuments to "the Lost Cause" or

to Charlottesville's golden age. They are victory monuments, unflinching testaments to the collapse of Reconstruction and the re-establishment of white supremacy. And as public art they inscribed that victory into the fabric of the city.[6]

**The Stonewall Jackson Monument, 1921**
*(502 feet above sea level; 24 feet tall)*
On that late night in April of 1917, the torch-lit mob centered their attention on an alley between residences that gave direct access to the county jail from the county courthouse (Figure 2, numbers 5 and 6, and letter A). The mob filled High Street and the open spaces around the Thomas Jefferson–designed courthouse. As reported in the local paper, the *Daily Progress,* they also spilled down McKee Street, which divided Courthouse Square from McKee's Row, a block of rental tenements occupied largely by African Americans. Contemporary whites described the tenements as "ramshackle" and "an eyesore" (Figure 2, number 7; Figure 3).[7] In the same years that the hooded mob gathered outside the jail to threaten Crosby and Jones with lynching, Charlottesville's white community was making plans to tear down McKee's Row and replace it with a school for white children.[8] Just over four years

Figure 1. Map of Charlottesville, circa 1920, showing the location of the four monuments and two of the majority African American neighborhoods, 10th and Page and Vinegar Hill. Map by Andrew Marshall.

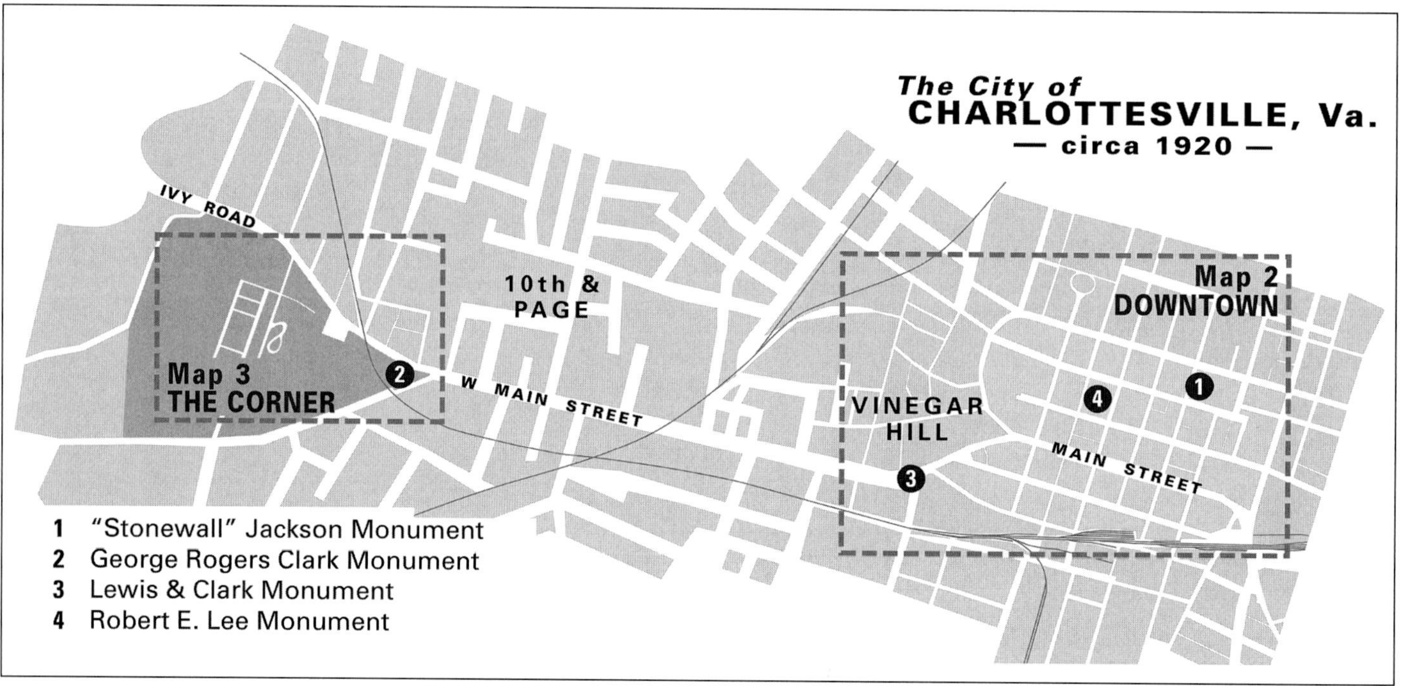

later, Senator Pat Harrison of Mississippi offered a hagiographic celebration of Stonewall Jackson at the unveiling of the new equestrian statue erected in his honor, on the spot previously occupied by McKee's Row. The "eyesore" had been replaced not with a white school but with a white memorial (Figure 2, number 2; Figure 4). The equestrian statue features Jackson leaning forward atop a horse approaching a canter. The figures are supported by a bold pink granite pedestal dominated by spectacular allegorical figures of Faith and Valor. The two strong, strikingly Aryan youth carry a shield adorned with the stars and bars. Placed at what had formerly been street level, Faith and Valor replaced the "rowdy" residents of McKee's Row. The unveiling was the capstone of three days of celebration that included a grand gala reunion of Confederate veterans and a five thousand-person march through the city. It concluded with white school children formed as a living representation of the Confederate banner in Midway Plaza, which crowned the north slope of the city's largest African American neighborhood, Vinegar Hill (Figure 2, letter B).[9]

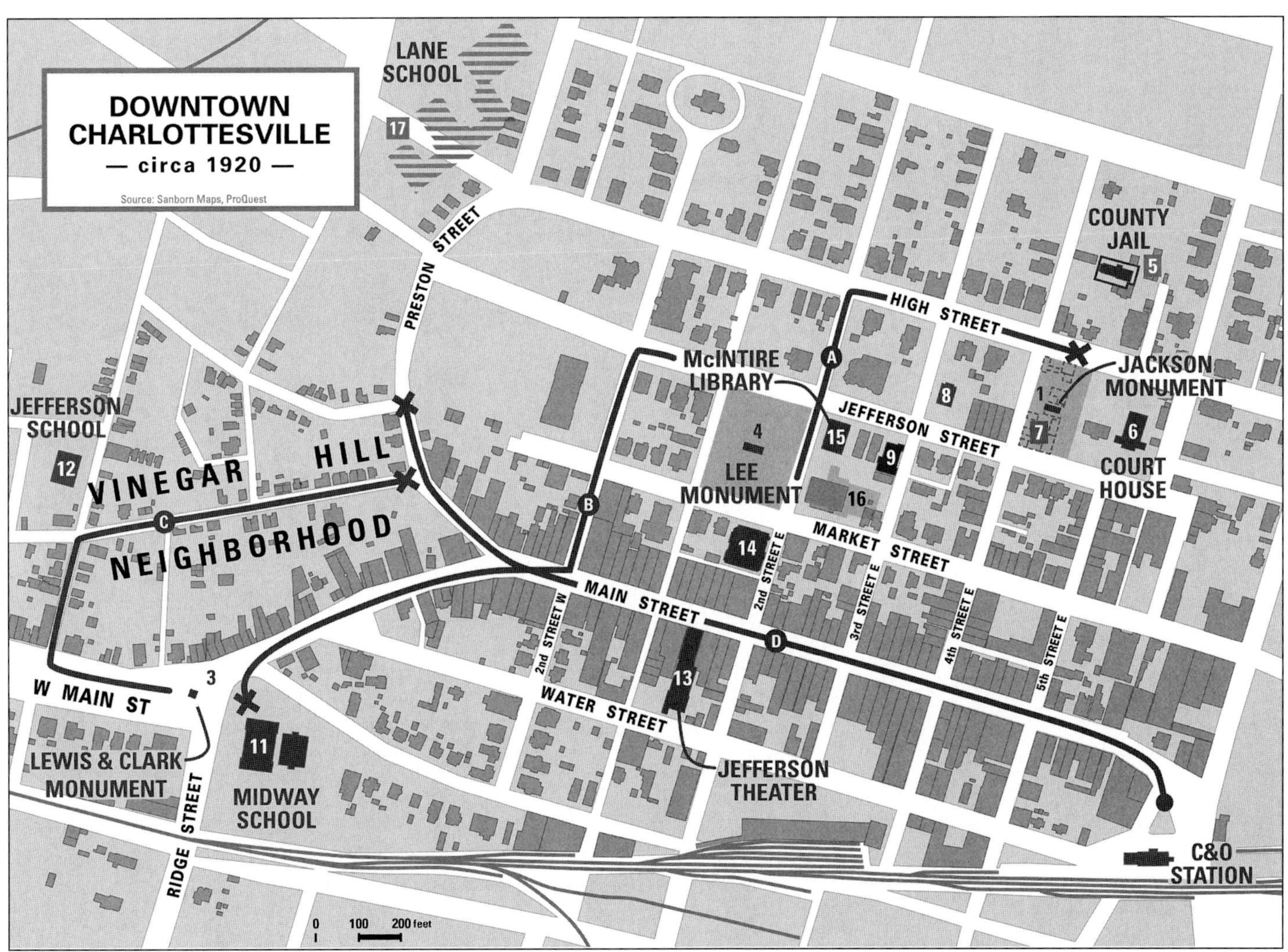


Figure 2. Detailed map of downtown Charlottesville, circa 1920, showing the location of various monuments and buildings discussed in the article and routes mapped out for marches and parades. 1: Stonewall Jackson Monument; 3: Lewis and Clark and Sacagawea Monument; 4: Robert E. Lee Monument; 5: Albemarle County Jail; 6: Albemarle County Courthouse; 7: McKee's Row; 8: Beth Israel Synagogue; 9: Holy Comforter Catholic Church; 11: Midway School; 12: Jefferson Graded School; 13: Jefferson Theater; 14: First Presbyterian Church; 15: McIntire Library; 16: Post Office, 1939 outline; 17: Lane High School; A: 1917 lynch mob; B: 1921 Confederate Veterans Parade; C: 1915 Halloween parade of KKK-clad children thorough Vinegar Hill; D: 1924 Grand Parade of the KKK. Map by Andrew Marshall.

Figure 3. McKee's Row. Rufus W. Holsinger, Holsinger Studio Collection, Albert and Shirley Small Collection, University of Virginia.

In the 1910s and 1920s, Courthouse Square—the location of McKee's Row and the courthouse with its attendant jail and the site of the lynch mob and eventually the Jackson monument—was the center of Charlottesville's political, legal, and civil authority.[10] It was here that the laws of the city, the state, and the nation shaped the lives of local citizens. It was here that in the half century following the passage of the Fourteenth Amendment black Charlottesvillians saw the legal and political recognition of their citizenship slowly recede. This square was also within two blocks of buildings housing Charlottesville's Catholic and Jewish congregations. As early as 1900, the Virginia Conference of Colored Men met at the Odd Fellow's Hall to discuss methods of resisting African American political disenfranchisement. Within ten years, black political and legal authority had been so diminished as to erase their very presence from the landscape of citizenship. In his dedication speech for the Jackson monument, Senator Harrison noted that in the Civil War a nation was torn apart by "fratricidal strife."

There was no recognition of black presence; Harrison assumed his audience to be white. As Kirk Savage has pointed out, this common postwar language draws from Sophocles's narrative of two brothers fighting on opposite sides in the war against Thebes. In such classic accounts, the brothers are worthy of honor but the slaves who also died on the battlefield were given no space in the story. And this framework for post–Civil War "reconciliation" was convenient for those working to exclude African Americans from the nation's new social contract.[11] Such familial language is part and parcel of a reconstituted Southern identity that Dell Upton has described as "unambiguously white."[12] But what did "white" mean in the 1910s and 1920s? As recent scholarship on the Ku Klux Klan (KKK) reinforces, elite Protestants constructed "white" in this period in opposition to black, but white in their view did not include all non-blacks. In this era of massive immigration, "white" also excluded immigrants, Jews, and Catholics, categories of individuals who were not considered part of the American historical and political project.[13] Like the Jackson monument itself, Harrison's speech was an act of both intimidation and erasure. So was the demolition of McKee's Row, which had stood within two blocks of the city's Catholic Church and Jewish Synagogue (Figure 2, numbers 8, 9). And so was the threat of lynching. And so was the creation of a living Confederate banner, composed of white boys and girls, immediately above the city's largest and most densely populated African American neighborhood. Taken together, these urban rituals, public speeches, and the physical remaking of the city were the product of collective action by the city's population of white Southern-born Protestants.

Asserting political authority in Charlottesville felt increasingly important to this collective of the white majority during the late 1910s. The message was clear to African Americans in the city who organized a local chapter of the NAACP in the summer of 1918, one year after the attempted lynching of Crosby and Jones.[14] The summer and early autumn of 1919 brought a series of national race riots that were quickly folded into the much broader paranoia and trauma then unfolding across the nation, including the social unrest associated with the Wall Street bombing and deep anxieties over both anarchists and communists that fueled the Palmer Raids, to name just a few. The race riots began in Charleston, South Carolina, in May, and erupted also in Washington, D.C.; Norfolk, Virginia; Knoxville, Tennessee; and Omaha, Nebraska, eventually taking place in thirty-eight cities across the country. The worst was seen in Chicago, where riots lasted for thirteen days in August. Racial tension must have been palpable in Charlottesville as riots erupted in both nearby Washington and Norfolk. And then, in August of 1920, Congress passed the Nineteenth Amendment, giving women the right to vote. Soon thereafter, the chairman of Virginia's Democratic Party sent out an appeal notifying all white women in Virginia that "the negro women are making desperate efforts to register." This was in his mind a serious problem since "the negro women are more intelligent than the negro men, therefore much

Figure 4. Charles Keck (sculptor), Thomas Jonathan "Stonewall" Jackson Monument, 1921, Charlottesville, Virginia. Photograph by Dell Upton, 2002.

more successful in meeting the requirements of the registration law." His appeal was to "look to Democratic white women of the state, whether they favor equal suffrage or not, to maintain the prestige, the integrity, the traditions, and the honor of Virginia."[15] The threat of black agency overshadowed even the arrival of women's suffrage. And finally, in February of 1921, the *Daily Progress* published a portion of a speech by an African American activist from the St. Louis Urban League. The article announced:

The New Negro of Charlottesville wants:

1. Teachers' salaries based on service not on color
2. A four year high school
3. Representation on City Council
4. 'Jim Crow' street cars abolished
5. Representation on School Board
6. Better street facilities in Negro districts

We are tax payers and law abiding citizens. We know our strength and will accept nothing short of justice![16]

With the relative freedom of an outsider, George W. Buckner gave voice to Charlottesville's structural racism: income inequities, education injustice, black political disenfranchisement, and unequal neighborhood investment. Charlottesville's white majority responded by describing the propositions as "impossible."[17]

By 1921, racial tensions in Charlottesville boiled over. That summer, the KKK organized a public address inside the courthouse just feet from where the Jackson monument would be unveiled in October (Figure 2, number 6). The public address was supported by bulletins posted around town that warned that "law and order must prevail." They announced: "All undesirables must leave town. The eye of the unknown has been and is constantly observing. . . . We See All, We Hear All, We Know All." The bulletin ended with an invitation. Any "100 percent" white native born American man who "held to the tenets of the Christian religion, Free Schools, Free Speech, Free Press, Law Enforcement, Liberty, *and White Supremacy*" (italics added) was welcome to join.[18] The KKK spoke openly in the space of the courthouse about the enforcement of white supremacy as essential to the preservation of the ideals of the Confederacy. Charlottesville's non-white audience certainly got the message. When the echoes of their voices faded and the bulletins all melted in the rain, the monumental statue of Stonewall Jackson and its Aryan youth—erected just months after the KKK spoke inside the courthouse—would serve to remind black and white Charlottesvillians of the unspoken requirements for full citizenship: a highly circumscribed conception of "whiteness."[19]

### The George Rogers Clark Statue, 1921
*(505 feet above sea level; 24 feet tall)*

Just two weeks after the unveiling of the Stonewall Jackson monument in Courthouse Square, Charlottesvillians gathered once again to reveal an even larger monument: an equestrian statue of Virginian son and Revolutionary War figure George Rogers Clark (Figure 5). In the composition, Clark faces a group of three Native Americans. A kneeling woman, wrapped in a blanket, holds up a cradleboard as if to plead for an unseen child. The central figure is a chief standing erect, also wrapped in a blanket, with long braided hair that spills across his shoulders. A second male figure, with two feathers in his hair, crouches at his feet. His blanket is open to the rear, exposing a knife that portends the possibility of resistance. With his right hand Clark gestures an invitation to join three members of his expedition grouped behind him. These men are clearly part of his regiment, but the ambiguous facial features suggest that at least one might be Native American, now acculturated and submitting to white cultural norms. The figural group sits atop a granite pedestal, much plainer than that supporting Jackson, which simply names Clark "Conqueror of the Northwest." The gesture of invitation made by Clark's extended hand is undermined by the powder keg behind him and the heroic pronouncement of Clark as conqueror. The invitation had no real options: join or perish. University of Virginia (UVA) president Edwin Alderman heralded the unveiling with a speech that extolled "the son of this soil, a hero, a pioneer, and a conqueror."[20]

The monument stands in a small triangle of grass adjacent to West Main Street and separating the eateries of the Corner from the University hospital (Figure 6, numbers 2 and 10). This location seems curious in the contemporary city, but it made sense in the early 1920s. This site, among the easternmost parcels owned by the University of Virginia, tied this monument to the three statues downtown via the critical artery of Main Street. As mentioned by one commentator, the statue "will make an imposing scene at the entrance to the University."[21] And many of those arrivals would be African Americans. Throughout the twentieth century and right up to the present, the high ground of Main Street, which connects the University to the city, is flanked by low-lying historically African American neighborhoods like the 10th and Page neighborhood, occupied by those who worked (and still work) as janitorial staff in residences in the city and in the halls and classrooms of the University (Figure 1). At their lowest point, these neighborhoods are more than thirty-three feet below Main Street and the Clark monument.

With its three groups—Clark on a horse, acculturated Native Americans, and the defiant resistance of the chief—the monument is an essay on the hierarchies of race, scientific studies of genetic superiority, and the period discourse on civility and savagery. As understood by one commentator, "The conqueror of the Northwest is evidently explaining the futility of a resistance."[22] When pitted against the clear superiority of white Americans, the racial inferiority of Native Americans was expected to be self-evident; their best hope was to abandon their savagery and take the long road of submission to white civility. This interpretation of the monument is made clearer when read in its urban context. While the Clark statue revealed to all those who passed by the futility of resisting white authority, the building complex immediately beyond—the hospital of the University of Virginia—housed the classrooms of Dr. Paul Barringer, professor of physiology, who spent his life researching white racial superiority through the study of eugenics.[23] Barringer was president of the faculty when UVA built its very first hospital in 1901. Approaching the University from the city, the new hospital was the first University building one would see after passing the Clark monument.

Barringer professed the intrinsic racial inferiority of African Americans. In his 1900 publication *The American Negro: His Past and Future,* Barringer states his case:

The American negro is the resultant of a combination of forces, each one of which can be isolated and analyzed. I will show from the study of his racial history (phylogeny) that his late tendency to return to barbarism is as natural as the return of the

Figure 5. Robert Ingersoll Aitken (sculptor), George Rogers Clark Monument, 1921, Charlottesville, Virginia. Photograph by author, January, 2018.

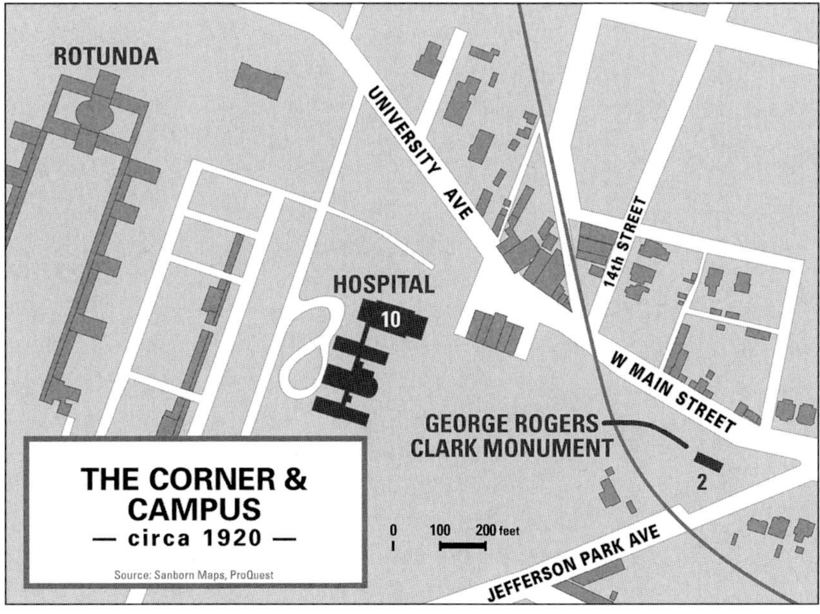


Figure 6. Detailed map of the Corner and the University hospital, circa 1920. 2: George Rogers Clark Monument; 10: University of Virginia Hospital. Map by Andrew Marshall.

sow that is washed to her wallowing in the mire. I
will show that the ages of degradation under which
he was formed and the fifty centuries of historically recorded savagery with which he came to us
cannot be permanently influenced by one or two
centuries of enforced correction.[24]

The African American community did not re-
ceive Barringer's arguments quietly. An editor of
the *Colored American,* an African American peri-
odical published in Washington, D.C., offered a
response to a Barringer lecture:

In composing the correspondence I am now sit-
ting in full view of "Monticello" where rests the
remains of the immortal Thomas Jefferson, and
I am sure if it were possible for Jefferson to arise
from his grave and find that the grand old University of Virginia, of which he is the founder, has
such a man as the chairman of the faculty, who
would make such base utterances as the Doctor is
quoted to have made against an inoffensive people,
his next request would be "Let me go back immediately to Mother Earth."[25]

Not all educated Americans adhered to views
such as Barringer's and certainly the community of educated African Americans leveled objections. Nonetheless, in Charlottesville, the tide
of popular adherence to such views was turning
with the tide of scientific racism.

Seen through this lens, "the futility of resistance" takes on a whole new meaning. Barringer and many others at the University adhered
to a biologically determinist view of humanity
that enlisted science to assert a hierarchy of the
races. Eugenicists argued that selective sterilization could and should improve the human race.
This included the selective sterilization of some
whites and the widespread sterilization of "inferior" races, including blacks but also Jews and
other non-whites. In this way, the death of resis-
tant Native Americans (or African Americans
for that matter) followed a recommended and
natural course of genetic winnowing and racial
improvement.

Barringer's teachings were closely aligned
with the convictions of the Virginia Grand
Dragon of the KKK when he spoke at a 1922
meeting of the Charlottesville chapter: "The des-
tinies of America shall remain with the white
race; they shall never be entrusted to the black,
the brown, or the yellow, or to the unclean hands
of hybrids or mongrels."[26] The newspaper article
describing this speech concluded by noting that
the Charlottesville chapter was not among the
largest in the state but that it boasted "many of
our able and influential citizens." And strong
support for the KKK's views appears also to have
permeated the student body. That same year,
the student yearbook published white-hooded
equestrian riders as the cover page to the Clubs
and Organizations section of the University yearbook, *Corks and Curls* (Figure 7). And just two
years later, these genetic assessments became
legislation with the passage of both the Racial
Integrity Act and the Virginia Sterilization Act.
Virginia's Racial Integrity Act built this definition into the legal code of the state, most clearly
through its famous "one drop rule": a Virginian
had to be 100 percent white to be identified as a
white American. The Virginia Sterilization Act
was challenged but upheld by the Supreme Court
and became a model law for other states. (The
Virginia General Assembly apologized for the
act's blatant racism in 2001.) Soon after the passage of the Racial Integrity Act, Dr. Ivey Lewis,
the Miller Professor of Biology at UVA, delivered
a public lecture on the importance of the new
law, arguing, "The mixing of whites with blacks
was the chief cause of the fall of civilizations of
Rome, Greece, Egypt, and India." Cross-racial
breeding, he continued, produced in whites a
"laxness of morals and a crumbling of culture."[27]
Then just months later, the University's Anglo-
Saxon Club announced a lecture in Madison Hall
by Earnest Sevier Cox, the legislator who worked
most fervently to see the Virginia General Assembly pass the Racial Integrity Act. This was
the party line: white elite men (by which they
meant Protestant white men born in the South)
who had enjoyed the great benefits of a UVA education had a moral, even patriotic, responsibility
to defend the purity of their race. All those passing by the entrance to the University, newly or-
namented with the monument to the Conqueror

of the Northwest, would be reminded of the in-evitable authority of whites. Contemporary medi-cal science conveniently reinforced the politics of Courthouse Square.[28]

### The Lewis and Clark (and Sacagawea) Monument, 1919
*(486 feet above sea level; 18 feet tall)*

The earliest of this series of monuments to be installed in Charlottesville's cityscape com-memorated Meriwether Lewis and William Clark, younger brother of George Rogers Clark (Figure 8). The third figure in the grouping, Sacagawea, crouching below and behind the two white men, was (and is) commonly left out of the statue's naming. Commemorating the expedi-tion commissioned by Thomas Jefferson, numer-ous contemporaries understood this work to be in conversation with that of Clark's brother since they marked each end of the street connecting the University and the city. But if George Rog-ers Clark bore the imperial charge to conquer the Northwest, his younger brother carried the charge of discovery and documentation. The pedestal of the monument bore the burden of in-terpretation. It tells viewers that these two men were "farseeing pathfinders" (when in fact that was Sacagawea's role) who "revealed an unknown empire." The expedition was made famous in part for all the artifacts returned to Virginia and exhibited in the entry hall of Monticello. This monument to the Enlightenment project of discovery stood in the midst of Midway Plaza, the park at the intersection of Main and Ridge Streets. It carried the name of the school that stood on the hill just above it: the Midway School (Figure 2, number 11). It was this same park that would two years later host the above-mentioned living Confederate banner. In February of 1890, the city's school board, "being of opinion that a high school for this community is a necessity for the completion of a thorough system of public education," embarked on the project of adding to the existing Midway School the necessary accom-modations for a high school department.[29] The Midway School was, of course, all white.

Just downhill from Midway Plaza stood Charlottesville's African American school: the

Figure 7. Clubs and Organizations cover page, *Corks and Curls*, 1922. University of Virginia library.

Jefferson Graded School (Figure 2, number 12). Although founded in the years just after the Civil War, the building that stood on the site was com-pleted in 1894. It did not include a high school. The only option for high school education for Charlottesville's black community was to board their children at schools in Richmond or Lynch-burg, a prohibitive expense for most. This injus-tice and inequity was noted even among the white readership of the Richmond newspapers when in 1895 the Charlottesville correspondent to the *Richmond Planet* urged local leaders to "unite and ask for" a high school for black students.[30] And the absence was not for lack of demand; black teach-ers reported classrooms of fifty children each.[31] Overfull classrooms meant that there was clear need for more teachers and more space and that there was an obvious pipeline that would support a high school. Charlottesville's black community leaders deeply objected to the notion—informed by the emerging field of eugenics—that Afri-can American children had only manual and no intellectual capacity. In 1914, for example, the city's black pastors all simultaneously protested from their pulpits "against colored boys being educated to work with their hands."[32] This objec-tion was not against manual labor *per se* but the

Figure 8. Charles Keck (sculptor), Meriwether Lewis and William Clark [and Sacagawea] Monument, 1919, Charlottesville, Virginia. Photograph by the author, January 2018.

residents dressed their children for Halloween as "a gay battalion of the Ku Klux Klan," which thundered down "from the heights of Midway." During this overt display of white intimidation, "many a dusky denizen of 'the bottom' was seen to shrink instinctively back into the shadows of Preston Avenue, as they swept along" (Figure 2, letter C).[33] Running from Midway Plaza to the heart of Vinegar Hill, the children descended almost fifty-six feet, a steep descent. That this public performance by white children began at the white school and ran through the neighborhood of Vinegar Hill cannot have been coincidence. As African Americans began a campaign for education justice, the city's whites enlisted their own children to perform ritualized racism through Charlottesville's racialized urban topography. Halloween was an opportunity to remind the African American residents of Vinegar Hill not to challenge the established racialized hierarchy of education. Just two years later, the white community installed the new monument to the explorers, a public monument that carried the implicit message that inquiry and discovery was a white mandate and that the work of racial others was, like Sacagawea's tracking, limited to the natural and the manual.

But such efforts at intimidation did not have the desired effect. After the World War I armistice, Reverend Clarence Long, the pastor of the African American First Baptist Church on West Main Street, took up the vigorous campaign for a black high school. His church was just a few blocks from the Jefferson School. As described by one of the first teachers at the Jefferson High School (finally opened in 1926), Long "stirred up the white people so much that they thought it better to concede to the African American community's demand for a high school than to allow him to stir up the African American community any further."[34] The resistance of the white community was so great, she reported, that Long eventually left Charlottesville. Speaking to the situation in 1921, the St. Louis Urban League called out the need for a four-year high school for black students. African American collective action eventually resulted in a successful petition to the school board for the construction of a high

supposition that all boys should be tracked toward manual labor and denied the rigorous intellectual training of a classical liberal arts education. Such tracking, of course, structurally disadvantaged a whole generation of African Americans when they applied to colleges and universities. In response, the white school superintendent closed the Jefferson school's woodshop.

The collective action for education justice by Charlottesville's African American leadership unsettled the city's Protestant white elite. Just over a year later a group of white Charlottesville school on the site of the Jefferson Graded School. But when it was opened in 1926, it offered only a two-year course of study and not a full four-year course as was the case at the Midway School. The superintendent had concluded that "it will be a long, long time before there will be pupils enough to justify a four year course for a colored high school in this city."[35] He was incorrect. The program expanded to include all four years by the 1929–30 school year.

**The Robert E. Lee Monument, 1924**
*(486 feet above sea level; 26 feet tall)*
The monument to Robert E. Lee was the last of the four to be installed (Figure 2, number 4; Figure 9). As with the Jackson monument, the week of its unveiling was filled with festivals and galas organized especially to celebrate the last surviving Confederate veterans. One of the events was the ritual opening of the Grand Camp of the Confederate Veterans of Virginia, which took place in the downtown Jefferson Theater, the center of white Charlottesville's social life (Figure 2, number 13). The ladies of the Con-

federacy were welcomed in the theater that evening. The most public spectacle, aside from the unveiling, was the grand parade of the Ku Klux Klan. "Thousands lined the sidewalks of Main Street from the C&O Station to the foot of Vinegar Hill," the newspaper reported (Figure 2, letter D). The nighttime "march of the white robed figures was impressive and directed attention to the presence of the organization in the community."[36] The conclusion of the parade at Vinegar Hill was surely no accident and certainly focused attention in Charlottesville's African American community. The week culminated in a grand Confederate Ball to be held in UVA's Memorial Gymnasium (Figure 10). Admission was limited to members of Confederate organizations, especially the Daughters and Sons of Confederate Veterans. The announcement of the ball also noted that the Sons of Confederate Veterans were now accepting applications from grandsons.[37] The KKK appears to have had a special relationship with Memorial Gym; just a decade earlier, the Klan offered a generous gift of $10,000 to UVA for the construction of that

Figure 9. Henry Shrady and Leo Lentelli (sculptors), Robert E. Lee Monument, 1924, Charlottesville, Virginia. Photograph by Bill Emory, Summer 2016.

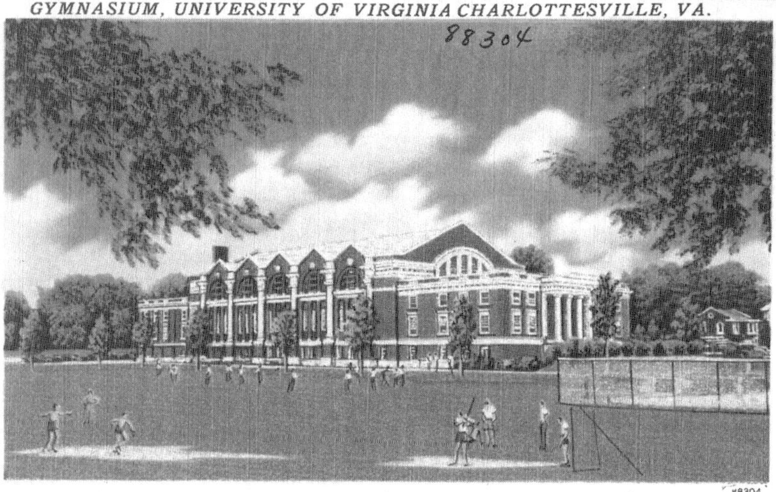


Figure 10. "Gymnasium, University of Virginia, Charlottesville, Va." Postcard, 1930–45. Tichnor Brothers Postcard Collection, Boston Public Library.

same facility. All of this for the celebration of Robert E. Lee.

If George Washington was the father of our country, then Robert E. Lee was the patriarch of the Confederacy. So said Edwin Alderman, UVA's president, on the occasion of the unveiling of the Lee monument: "The South's great Chieftain had done even more than his great prototype, Washington," Alderman continued, stating that Lee "was the embodiment of the best that there is in all the sincere and romantic history of the whole state. Its triumphs, its defeats, its joys, its sufferings, its rebirth, its pride, and its patience center in him."[38] By the opening decades of the twentieth century, the liturgies of the cult of Lee were already deeply entrenched in the self-fashioning of white Southerners. Just months after the unveiling of the Lee statue, the pastor of the First Presbyterian Church, which then faced onto the park that was then called Lee Square, "described social life in the South before and during the war . . . with all that made it ideal and charming" (Figure 2, number 14).[39] When Richmond unveiled its own Lee statue, one African American resident in that city noted its message: "The Southern white folks is on top."[40]

If the society and culture of the (presumably white) Old South were reimagined as charming, then black culture was recast as its antithesis. The Jefferson Theater, just two blocks away from the Lee monument, rescreened *Birth of a Nation* (first released in 1915) just months after the unveiling.[41] The *Daily Progress* touted the film as "the greatest picture of the age."[42] The newspaper noted that the film's rescreening "is drawing as large crowds as it did originally." The Jefferson Theater offered multiple screenings a day as "thousands want to see it a second time."[43] The picture was notorious for its portrayal of African Americans as unintelligent and oversexed. The NAACP attempted to have the film banned. Just days later the *Daily Progress* ran a series of teaser ads announcing the arrival of a minstrel show for charity in the Jefferson Theater. Made up largely of white men in blackface, the minstrel show openly mocked African Americans. Using common visual language of the day, the ads exhibited highly caricatured and stereotyped images of black men (Figures 11, 12, 13).[44] The Grand Camp of the Confederates, the screening of *Birth of a Nation,* and the openly racist minstrel shows were all part of the rebirth of the Old South in the imaginations of white Southerners. During the same months of these and other social spectacles, the KKK set off "heavy explosions from three bombs," and then burned a cross in the yard of an African American church just outside of town. The event was attended by fifty Klansmen, "only about six of them masked."[45] The notable choice of many Klansmen to attend unmasked reveals their sense that the battle for public opinion had been won. (This same confidence resurfaced in 2017 when the KKK paraded unmasked but in full regalia and then unmasked neo-Nazis stormed the streets of downtown.) It was no accident that these early twentieth-century events all took place in the Jefferson Theater. The erection of the Lee monument was the culminating act in the remaking of a city as the new Old South, with all the attendant political, racial, educational, and cultural implications.

The unveiling of the Robert E. Lee statue in 1924 was the completion of the first campaign for the remaking of the city and the beginning of the second. Paul McIntire's gift of the monument to Lee was the second of two installations on Lee Park. Begun in 1919 to house the city's public library, the McIntire Building, located

Figure 11. Detail, *Daily Progress*, Charlottesville, Virginia, January 25, 1924, page 6.

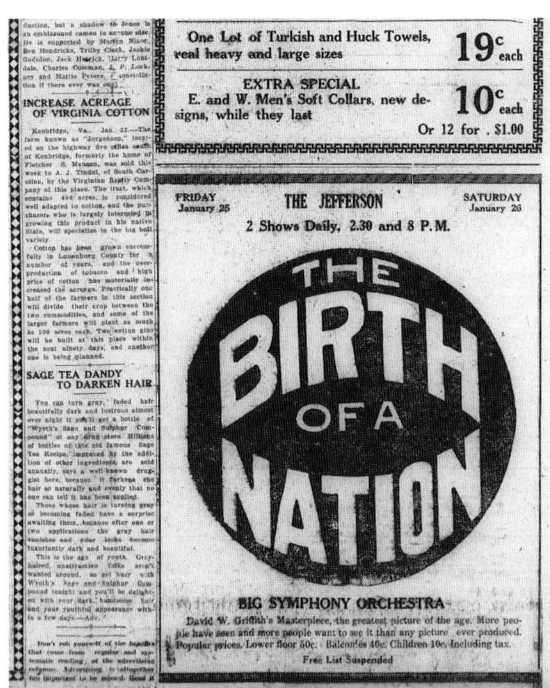


Figure 12. Detail, *Daily Progress*, Charlottesville, Virginia, January 24, 1924, page 7.

on the northeast corner of the park, served as an appropriately romanticized backdrop for the Lee monument and triggered an aesthetic transformation of the city's public architecture (Figure 2, number 15; Figure 14). Now housing the Albemarle Charlottesville Historical Society, the building was built of red brick with a crowning classical cornice and balustrade all fronted by a graceful curve of white columns. This is a stylistic tradition architectural historians identify as the colonial revival.[46] The building was distinctive enough to warrant publication in a variety of architectural magazines and regular visits by students of architecture.[47] With clear visual quotations from Monticello, the University, and local plantations like Bremo, these visual cues provided an ideal architectural setting for the rebirth of "old Virginia" as a historical past filled with all that was ideal and charming (Figures 15 and 16).

In gratitude to Paul McIntire for his generous gift of the new, spectacular library to the city, the Board of Managers wrote in 1921 asking for permission to name the library in his honor

Figure 13. Detail, *Daily Progress*, Charlottesville, Virginia, February 1, 1924, page 6.

Figure 14. McIntire Library (now the Albemarle Charlottesville Historical Society), Charlottesville, Virginia, 1921. Photograph by by author, May 2018.

Figure 15. "Monticello, Home of Thomas Jefferson, Charlottesville, Va.," Postcard, 1930–45. Tichnor Brothers Postcard Collection, Boston Public Library.

Figure 16. Bremo Plantation, Fluvanna County, Virginia. Photograph by author, 2015.

and to convey their commitment to stewarding his "high purpose in providing this beautiful building with its rich contents for the use of the people."[48] But the library was not really for all of the people of Charlottesville. Although it is never explicitly stated in any of the early records, the McIntire Library was intended for Charlottesville's white citizens. This fact was made explicit in June of 1934, when the publicly-funded library opened its first branch library, the "colored branch" in the Jefferson School (Figure 17). Even though the library in the Jefferson School quickly grew to over 850 registered borrowers per month, it had no effect on the monthly tallies of borrowers using the McIntire Library, which remains unchanged through the end of 1934. Even though the McIntire Library was a white only space (excepting of course the black janitor Albert Southall) the Board of Managers waffled on whether they should even open a "Colored Branch," describing the move to make books publicly available to Charlottesville's black citizens as "inadvisable."[49] And when they did finally make the move to open the branch library, they opened it with almost exclusively works of fiction, noting that "little or no non-fiction was available."[50] As implicitly asserted by the Lewis and Clark monument, inquiry and discovery was reserved for the white intellect. And, finally, the $240 annual salary for the Jefferson School librarian was half that of the night librarian at the McIntire Library and less than one-quarter the salary of the head librarian.[51] The McIntire Library launched an important aesthetic renaissance in Charlottesville's architecture, reviving the architectural tradition of the city's pre–Civil War landscape. But it was also an important building that—standing in the shadow of the Robert E. Lee Memorial—further institutionalized unequal access to public resources and the structural inequality of the city's public sphere. The colonial revival style of McIntire Library inaugurated the architecture of white supremacy.

Since at least the 1980s, historians have understood the connection between the increasing popularity of the colonial revival style and the rise of immigration, especially in the cities of the northeast. The first curator of the American Wing of the Metropolitan Museum of Art in New York City, for example, wanted to offer "a visual personification of home life in this country," because he feared that "the influx of foreign ideas utterly at variance with those held by the men who gave us the Republic, threaten, and unless checked, may shake the foundations," of American life.[52] But the colonial revival was also a romantic program intended to affirm white supremacy, which in Charlottesville included supremacy over blacks as well as Jews, Catholics, and immigrants.[53]

With the completion of the McIntire Building the "rebirth" imagined by Alderman would begin to take shape in architecture across the city. While the first wave of colonial revival architecture in Charlottesville was domestic, by the 1930s the style extended to the city's institutional core. The post office, now the downtown public library, was opened in 1936 boasting a brick body and a monumental portico of white columns (Figure 2, number 16; Figure 18). Two years later, the courthouse was extensively remodeled to its current colonial revival appearance (Figure 19). In a 1930s postcard of downtown Charlottesville, the photographer uses the bright red brick and stark white trim of the new colonial revival Albemarle county office buildings and courthouse as a suitable backdrop for the Jackson monument (Figure 20). In this one image, the monument and the architecture work in concert to reinforce the city's institutional and structural commitment to a political hierarchy of race. And finally, in 1939, the superintendent of schools opened Lane High School, a colonial revival structure once again, looming high above the Vinegar Hill neighborhood (Figure 2, number 17; Figure 21). The colonial revival remaking of Charlottesville was emblematic of a public program of political disenfranchisement, the crowning achievement of a campaign that had been underway for decades. Lane High School now serves as the Albemarle County Office Building.

African Americans in early twentieth-century Charlottesville traversed a city that reminded them of their second-class status at every turn.[54] Some had once lived in tenements on McKee's Row, but by the 1920s these had been demol-

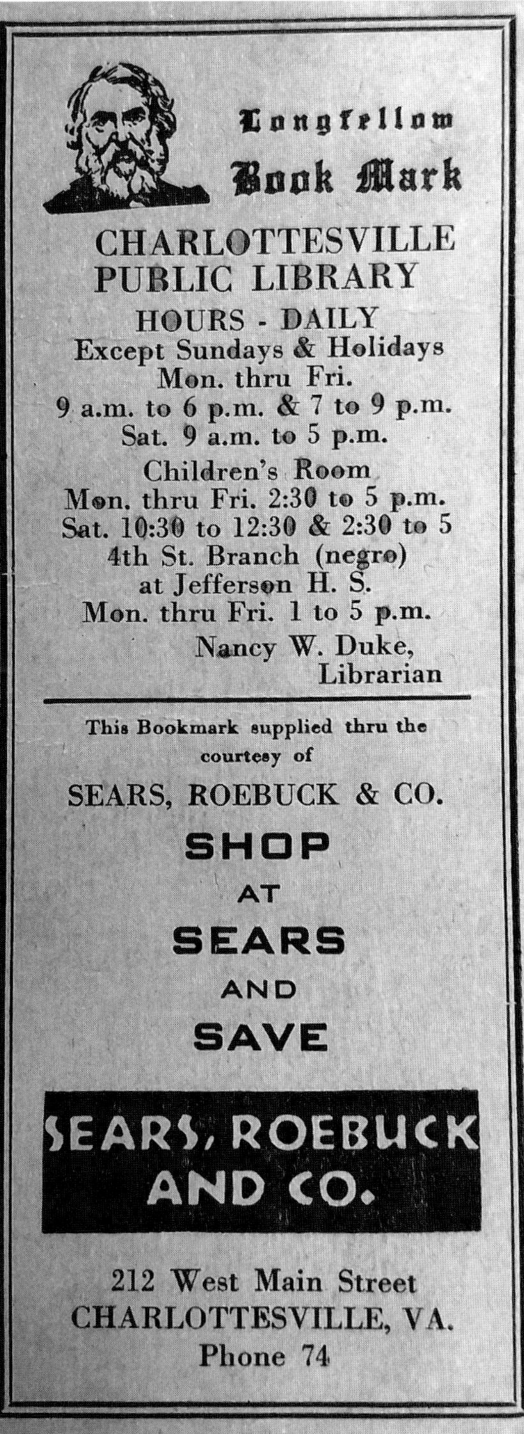


Figure 17. Charlottesville Public Library bookmark, 1940s, Charlottesville Public Library Collections, Charlottesville, Va. Note that the 4th Street Branch is marked (negro).

ished and replaced by a monument to Stonewall Jackson fronted by strong Aryan youth. Those who worked as janitors or other hourly-wage positions at the University passed by the George Rogers Clark statue and the new University hospital,

Figure 18. "Post Office, Charlottesville, Virginia." Postcard, 1930–45. Tichnor Brothers Postcard Collection, Boston Public Library.

Figure 19. "Court House and Statue of Confederate Soldier, Charlottesville, Va." Postcard, 1930–45. Tichnor Brothers Postcard Collection, Boston Public Library.

Figure 20. "Stonewall Jackson Monument Showing Albemarle County Office Buildings and Court House." Postcard, 1930–45. Tichnor Brothers Postcard Collection, Boston Public Library.

both of which communicated a strong message of the inherent superiority and inevitable authority of whites. When they walked back to their home in Vinegar Hill they passed under the eager gaze of courageous discovery by Lewis and Clark and were reminded that such inquiry was in the realm of the white intellect. This was why there was a white high school but not a black one. And if they continued down Main Street and proceeded up Second Street they would enter the sacred precinct of Lee Square, the public library, the post office, and the court house that all reminded them that Charlottesville was a city blessed with a glorious past, but one with no room for black citizens.

And these objects newly installed in the cityscape were directly correlated with a series of urban performances by whites that reinforced a clear racial hierarchy. Many of these performances appear to have had an intentional audience: the African Americans who lived in Vinegar Hill. The parade celebrating the unveiling of the Jackson monument ended in a living Confederate banner in Midway Plaza, immediately above their neighborhood. The 1924 KKK parade celebrating the unveiling of the Lee statue began at the C&O Station and ended "at the foot of Vinegar Hill." White school children spent Halloween running through that same neighborhood dressed in the white robes of the KKK. And, finally, the city school board built a colonial revival high school on a high hill looming over Vinegar Hill, a neighborhood that by 1939 was flanked by two monumental white high schools.

This is not to say that Charlottesville's African American community did not resist these impositions. They organized a chapter of the NAACP. They registered to vote. They argued for equal access to education. But to no avail. By the late 1920s, Charlottesville's white establishment had cemented their victory through the erection of a series of monuments and buildings that became surrogates for the white hoods and torches of the lynch mob. For African Americans, these were all part and parcel of the same cityscape, one of diminishment, degradation, and disenfranchisement. These four monuments are the material legacy of a comprehensive and very successful campaign of racial intimidation; while the white

Figure 21. "Lane High School, Charlottesville, Va." Postcard, 1930–45. Tichnor Brothers Postcard Collection, Boston Public Library.

population in Charlottesville/Albemarle grew by an astonishing 45 percent between 1900 and 1930, the African American population shrank by 20 percent.[55]

Through the summer of 2017, Charlottesville once again witnessed the public display of white supremacy in its streets and squares. In response to the proposed removal of the monument to the patriarch of the Confederacy, two white nationalists—both UVA alumni—began planning a massive "invasion" of the city, with now infamous results. The conflict centered on the renamed Lee Park, dominated by the Lee statue. David Duke was interviewed with the unshrouded Lee rising behind him. Private militias marched down Market Street, passing right in front of the former post office. An armed protester fired his gun in the square just yards from where a Presbyterian minister had once praised the charm of the Old South. The start of the 1924 KKK march was not far from the spots where DeAndre Harris was beaten and Heather Heyer was killed one century later. But as is very clear to all involved, these events were not really about the removal of a statue. In both events—in 1917 and in 2017—the intention was to enlist public space to explicitly assert white racial authority. In Charlottesville, the more obvious target was African Americans, but the KKK made clear their disdain for Jews and many others not like themselves. And while Charlottesville has now become synonymous with August 12, this is not a Southern story but a national condition. The deep legacies of exclusion and marginalization for some and preference and access for others are inscribed in the forms and names of buildings, bridges, sports teams, highways, parks, and statues across the Land of the Free. These historical legacies are not inert. Building on a long tradition, militias poured into the city last August equipped with shields and weapons because the removal of a monument signaled the potential destabilizing of the systems and structures that the statue had long represented: white supremacy.

## AUTHOR BIOGRAPHY

**Louis P. Nelson** is professor of architectural history and Vice Provost for Academic Outreach at the University of Virginia.

## NOTES

The author is grateful to the following readers who offered feedback on early drafts of this article: Lisa Goff, Andrus Ashoo, Bill Wilder, Ian Stevenson, Marta Gutman, Claudrena Harold, and Dell Upton. Some portions of this article were previously published in the introductory essay in Louis P. Nelson and Claudrena Harold, eds. *Charlottesville 2017: The Legacy of Race and Inequity* (UVA Press, 2018).

1. This essay depends heavily on the excellent historical research published as "1917–1924: A Timeline; The McIntire Statues and Charlottesville's African American Community," an appendix to the report of the Mayor's Blue Ribbon Commission on Race, Memorials, and Public Spaces. A deeper dive into the contexts outlined in this essay appears also in the rich online project *The Illusion of Progress: Charlottesville's Roots in White Supremacy*, available on the website of UVA's Carter G. Woodson Center: http://woodson.as.virginia.edu/woodson-projects.

2. *Daily Progress*, April 17, 1917.

3. *Daily Progress*, June 20, 1917.

4. Jeff Ueland and Barney Warf, "Racialized Topographies: Altitude and Race in Southern Cities," *Geographical Review* 96, no. 1 (January 2006): 50–78. The analysis of urban lowlands is also the subject of current research by Steven Moga at Smith College.

5. For more on the history of the patrons or artists see Aaron V. Wunsch, "From Private Privilege to Public Place: A Brief History of Parks and Park Planning in Charlottesville," *The Magazine of Albemarle County History* 56 (1998): 80–90.

6. For a broader view of these kinds of monuments across the South, see Kirk Savage, ed., *The Civil War in Art and Memory* (New Haven, Conn.: Yale University Press, 2016).

7. This section draws from research already published by Daniel Bluestone, "A Virginia Courthouse Square," *Buildings, Landscapes, and Memory: Case Studies in Historic Preservation* (New York: Norton, 2011), 220–26 and *Daily Progress*, March 19, 1914.

8. *Daily Progress*, March 19, 1914.

9. *Daily Progress*, October 19, 1921.

10. For more on the particular authority of courthouses in early Virginia see Carl Lounsbury, *The Courthouses of Early Virginia* (Charlottesville: University of Virginia Press, 2005).

11. Kirk Savage, *The Civil War in Art and Memory*, 2.

12. Dell Upton, *What Can and Can't Be Said* (New Haven, Conn.: Yale University Press, 2015), 33.

13. Linda Gordon, *The Second Coming of the KKK: The Ku Klux Klan of the 1920s and the American Political Tradition* (New York: Liveright, 2017).

14. Founded in 1909, the NAACP was at this point a fairly young organization. Blue Ribbon Commission Report, 16.

15. *Daily Progress*, October 1, 1920.

16. *Daily Progress*, February 16, 1921.

17. *Daily Progress*, February 19, 1921.

18. *Daily Progress*, July 19, 1921.

19. For more on the activity of the KKK in Charlottesville in the 1920s and 1930s, see "Chapter 1: Charlottesville's Confederate Past," from *The Illusion of Progress*, http://illusion.woodson.as.virginia.edu/index.html.

20. *Daily Progress*, November 3, 1921.

21. *Alumni News* 10 (1921): 326.

22. *Alumni News* 10 (1921): 326.

23. Gregory Dorr, "Segregation's Science: The American Eugenics Movement and Virginia, 1900–1980," PhD diss., University of Virginia, 2000.

24. Paul Barringer, *The American Negro: His Past and Future* (Raleigh, N.C.: Edwards and Broughton, 1900), 1.

25. *The Colored American*, March 3, 1900.

26. *Daily Progress,* August 23, 1922.

27. *Daily Progress,* April 6, 1924.

28. For more on the Progressive Era in Charlottesville, see "Chapter 3: The Progressive Era and the Enforcement of Racial Difference," from *The Illusion of Progress,* http://illusion.woodson.as.virginia.edu/index.html.

29. The most thorough discussion of racialized education in early Charlottesville is Scot French, "African American Civic Activism & the Making of Jefferson High School," in Andrea Douglas, ed., *Pride Overcomes Prejudice: A History of Charlottesville's African American School* (Charlottesville, Va.: Jefferson School African American Heritage Center, 2013), 41.

30. French, "African American Civic Activism," 31, 44.

31. French, "African American Civic Activism," 59.

32. French, "African American Civic Activism," 48.

33. *Daily Progress,* November 1, 1916.

34. French, "African American Civic Activism," 52.

35. French, "African American Civic Activism," 60.

36. *Daily Progress,* May 19, 1924.

37. *Daily Progress,* May 15, 1924.

38. *Daily Progress,* May 21, 1924.

39. A few decades later the church moved to a new site on Park Street. The original site is now a parking lot. *Daily Progress,* January 21, 1924.

40. Cited in Kirk Savage, *Standing Soldiers, Kneeling Slaves: Race, War, and Monument in Nineteenth-Century America* (Princeton, N.J.: Princeton University Press, 1997), 151

41. Nancy Bishop Dessommes, "Hollywood in Hoods: The Portrayal of the Ku Klux Klan in Popular Film," *Journal of Popular Culture* 32, no. 4 (March 1999): 13–22.

42. *Daily Progress,* January 25, 1924.

43. *Daily Progress,* January 25, 1924.

44. *Daily Progress,* February 1, 1924.

45. *Daily Progress,* June 21, 1924.

46. On the colonial revival, see Richard Wilson, "What Is the Colonial Revival?" in Richard Guy Wilson, Shaun Eyring, and Kenny Marotta, eds. *Recreating the American Past: Essays on the Colonial Revival* (Charlottesville: University of Virginia Press, 2006). For a deeply contextual reading of the colonial revival, see Lydia Mattice Brandt, *First in the Homes of His Countrymen: George Washington's Mount Vernon in the American Imagination* (Charlottesville: University of Virginia Press, 2016).

47. "Minutes of the Board of Managers, Charlottesville Public Library," July 9, 1923, Jefferson-Madison Regional Library, Charlottesville Virginia.

48. "Minutes of the Board of Managers, Charlottesville Public Library," May 23, 1921, Jefferson-Madison Regional Library, Charlottesville Virginia.

49. "Minutes of the Board of Managers, Charlottesville Public Library," April 13, 1934, Jefferson-Madison Regional Library, Charlottesville Virginia.

50. "Minutes of the Board of Managers, Charlottesville Public Library," January 12, 1934, Jefferson-Madison Regional Library, Charlottesville Virginia.

51. "Minutes of the Board of Managers, Charlottesville Public Library," September 14, 1934, Jefferson-Madison Regional Library, Charlottesville Virginia.

52. Quoted in William B. Rhoads, "The Colonial Revival and the Americanization of Immigrants" from Alan Axelrod, ed., *The Colonial Revival in America* (New York: Norton, 1985), 348–49.

53. For an argument about the racialized nature of the colonial revival see Catherine W. Bishir, "Landmarks of Power: Building a Southern Past, 1885–1915," in *Southern Built: American Architecture, Regional Practice* (Charlottesville: University of Virginia Press, 2013).

54. On the realities of racism and walking in more recent times, see Garnette Cadogan, "Walking While Black: Garnette Cadogan on the Realities of Being Black in America," *Literary Hub,* July 8, 2016 [republished in Jesmyn Ward, ed., *The Fire This Time: A New Generation Speaks about Race* (New York: Scribner, 2016).

55. US Census Bureau Archives online: www.census.gov/prod/www/decennial.html.

KARLA CAVARRA BRITTON

# *Object Lesson:* A Mission among the Navajo

## *The Vicar, an Architect, and Unforeseen Ghosts*

In 1917 Rudolf Otto wrote in *The Idea of the Holy* of the ephemeral idea of the ghostly. He claimed that the ghostly as well as tangible forms of architecture are both equally powerful means of expressing the numinous. Yet Otto asserted that ghosts have no place in our modern scheme of reality, despite the fact that the idea of the ghost arouses an irrepressible interest for the human mind. What is perceptibly true, Otto stated, is that our fear of ghosts is related in a far stronger sense to our fear of the "daemonic" experience itself, rather than to the sacred.[1] Otto's interest in yet disavowal of the reality of ghosts is an ironic backdrop for the investigation this essay makes of the Chapel of the Good Shepherd in Fort Defiance, Arizona, built by the renowned Southwestern architect John Gaw Meem (1894–1983) on the Navajo reservation just north of Window Rock, the Navajo Nation's capital (Figure 1). The Good Shepherd Mission provides a telling case study of the ways conflicting expectations and cultural assumptions surrounding sacred spaces can create unanticipated points of conflict which, as will become evident, are in this instance most clearly personified by the specter of ghosts— whether of a cultural or spiritual origin. And as a Christian "mission," Good Shepherd also participates in the long and nearly universal trajectory of conflict that arises when spiritual and cultural traditions attempt to integrate or even to replace one another.

Fort Defiance, located in the heart of the traditional Navajo lands, was founded in what is now northeastern Arizona in 1851 as part of the U.S. military's campaign to subdue the Navajo.[2] It be-

came notorious as the base from which Kit Carson organized the roundup of the Navajo people in 1864, leading to the forcible deportation of the Navajo by means of the genocidal three-hundred-mile "Long Walk" to Fort Sumner in eastern New Mexico. Those who survived the march were relocated in the infamous Bosque Redondo— essentially an internment camp. Along the walk and in the camp, thousands of Navajo died of disease, exhaustion, and malnutrition.

By 1868, the disastrous consequences of the relocation were inescapably evident, and the army signed a treaty that allowed the remaining Navajo to return to a greatly reduced portion of their native lands in the Four Corners area, marked by the four sacred mountains in New Mexico, Arizona, and Colorado. Following the return of the Diné (people) to what is now the Navajo Nation, the government's policy shifted from subjugation to forced cultural assimilation. Among the institutions founded in this era was the Hospital of the Good Shepherd, a medical mission of the Episcopal Church begun in 1894, located just over a hill from the original military outpost of Fort Defiance.

The mission gradually assembled a 103-acre compound of buildings constructed of native sandstone—built by local craftsmen, yet with what a "surveyor" from the national church described in 1940 as "architectural distinction"— including a hospital, eye clinic, housing for nursing and other staff, and eventually a boarding school for children, many of them orphans (Figure 2).[3] And as a mission of the church, the campus naturally included a small chapel, much

Figure 1. Good Shepherd Mission chapel, designed by John Gaw Meem, 1954, Fort Defiance, Arizona. Photograph by Karla Cavarra Britton, 2017.

like an English village church, in memory of Miss Cornelia Jay, a member of the Westchester (New York) branch of the Woman's Auxiliary of the Episcopal Church, which had a significant financial role in the mission's founding and early support.

Over the years, the size and scope of the mission expanded, and by the early 1950s the chapel was deemed insufficient for the needs of the community. According to a historical pamphlet from the period by J. Rockwood Jenkins, retired archdeacon of Arizona, the mission by then included some sixty resident children, from preschool through age sixteen, and as many as a thousand baptized members (Figure 3).[4] In 1954, a certain Father Davis Given became superintendent of the mission. Given was a recent graduate of Yale College and The General Theological Seminary in New York. He had come to Navajoland during the summers as a seminarian intern and returned in 1949 to begin his ordained ministry at Good Shepherd as the associate to then superintendent Reverend David Clark. Given remained at Good Shepherd until 1963, and those who remember him recall that he was well liked

Figure 2. Photograph of Good Shepherd Mission campus, Fort Defiance, Arizona, showing the original chapel to the left, ca. 1900. Good Shepherd Mission archives, courtesy of the Episcopal Church in Navajoland.

and respected by his Navajo parishioners and had a flourishing ministry among them. In his first year as superintendent at Good Shepherd Mission, 126 baptisms were recorded.[5]

Significantly, Given was not only the son of a wealthy industrialist (William B. Given Jr. of the American Brake Shoe Company), but also the step-grandson of Arthur Vining Davis, of the Aluminum Company of America (Alcoa). Davis had no children, and as a favorite grandson Given had the support of his grandfather for his ministry among the Navajo. The architect John Gaw Meem had already become involved with the mis-

# The Cross and The Navajo

ALICE

ETHEL CAROLINE

HEMSLEY

DICKIE

**Children of the Good Shepherd Home**

Figure 3. "The Cross and the Navajo," a publicity pamphlet for the Good Shepherd Mission children's home, ca.1950. Good Shepherd Mission archives, courtesy of the Episcopal Church in Navajoland.

sion through a request in 1949 from the Right Reverend Arthur Kinsolving, Bishop of Arizona, that he assist in the completion of the Thorne Building, a large meeting and dormitory facility.[6] Meem's firm of Meem, Zehner, Holien and Associates had also begun work on a comprehensive plan for the campus, and when Given arrived, the new associate priest asked Davis to help fund the building of a new vicarage (residence) for himself. Meem's resulting design was for a spacious 4,500 square-foot residence that included a guest suite, maid's room, library, and office in addition to the usual living quarters. As might have been expected, the house proved controversial because of its relative extravagance compared to the modest living quarters of other staff and the mission's Navajo neighbors (Figure 4).[7]

Correspondence between Given, Davis, and Meem indicates that only after plans for the house were well underway did attention shift to the building of a new chapel.[8] At Given's request, Davis is reputed to have said that not only would he fund the chapel, but he would build "a cathedral for the Navajo" (Figure 5).[9] And therein lies the beginning of a cultural mismatch between Anglo and Native concepts of the sacred that would unfold in both the building and habitation of the chapel: whereas for the Episcopalians, a cathedral-like church was an inspiring cornerstone for the mission, to the instinctively modest Navajo (whose traditional sacred spaces are simple single-family *hogans*), such a grand building spoke of an alien concept of the architectural formalization of the holy.

Nevertheless, with an ample gift from Davis of $250,000 for the chapel project in hand, Meem began developing plans. As an architect who had become famous for championing the pueblo revival style in residences, public buildings, and churches throughout the region, Meem made a striking departure from much of his previous work in his proposal for the mission chapel. Meem was himself an active Episcopalian, the son of an Episcopal missionary in Brazil, and had participated in the development of a regional church architecture not only in his own practice, but as a member of the committee on church architecture of the Diocese of the Rio Grande (New Mexico and southwest Texas), as well as the national Church Architecture Guild.[10] As a spiritually minded person, he was convinced that "contemporary man" badly needed "to be lifted from his concentration on the material world and to give life a purpose and meaning in the light of Ultimate Reality."[11]

Meem's proposal for the Good Shepherd Mission chapel is in many respects a reinterpretation of the Spanish pueblo mission churches in whose restoration he had been keenly interested, especially the church of San Esteban del Rey at the Acoma Pueblo.[12] Architectural historian Bainbridge Bunting notes in reference to the Good Shepherd chapel that "the massing of this building has strong overtones of the Southwest as seen in the greater elevation of the transepts and crossing which permit transverse clerestory lighting."[13] Its design also reflects what Meem regarded as the principal characteristics of the pueblo mission churches: simplicity of form, avoidance of bilateral symmetry, and a softening of "all outlines and surface by the hand of nature."[14] The building is also related by association with other early twentieth-century stone mission churches on reservations such as William Stanton's St. Joseph Apache Mission in Mescalero, New Mexico (1920), or Mary, Mother of Mankind Church in St. Michaels, Arizona (1930), not far from Fort Defiance.

Yet Meem introduced new modernist elements into his mission church that make it stand apart from these other ecclesiastical works, complicating the question of antecedents. Bunting, for example, suggests that the tower evokes "Swedish Modern." And in early sketches of the building Meem toyed with an unusual cruciform plan with sloping roofs crowned with a hogan-like cupola above the crossing (Figure 6). The sloping roofs may have reflected a trend in 1950s and 1960s modernist house design, or they may have made reference to the *torres* (towers) of Mesoamerican pyramids (like Antoine Predock and Pedro Marquez's much later auditorium for the National Hispanic Cultural Center in Albuquerque).[15] While such a scheme was quickly abandoned in favor of the more recognizable form of the church as it was built, the design process nevertheless clearly reflects Meem's working principle of "remembering and adapting," as he put it in a 1971 defense of his method.[16] He there expressed his intense awareness that New Mexican architecture is unique, given that nowhere else in the United States "can there be found a style of architecture which can trace its descent in an unbroken line from aboriginal American sources." As an architect, he had earlier described himself as having "an emotion approaching reverence" for this tradition, and "the

Figure 4. Vicarage, Good Shepherd Mission, John Gaw Meem, 1952. Photograph by Karla Cavarra Britton, 2017.

Figure 5. Superintendent Davis Given (far right) and philanthropist Arthur Vining Davis (third from left) at the dedication of the Good Shepherd Mission chapel, 1955. Good Shepherd Mission archives, courtesy of the Episcopal Church in Navajoland.

deepest sense of responsibility for perpetuating this truly American architecture."[17]

In any case, in lieu of the traditional adobe, Meem elected at Good Shepherd to use local light-salmon-pink sandstone, "to be laid up by Indians as at McCarty," a reference to Santa Maria de

Figure 6. Study for Good Shepherd Mission chapel, Meem, Zehner, Holien and Associates, ca. 1953. John Gaw Meem Drawings and Plans, Stack 2, Drawer 17, Special Collections and Center for Southwest Research, University of New Mexico Libraries.

Acoma at McCartys, New Mexico (1932), another of Meem's reservation churches.[18] He also took advantage of the commission to adapt the traditional pueblo revival style in other ways to design a church that has noticeably modern features. The church, for instance, is dominated by a bell tower surmounted by an aluminum cross, and at ground level the tower is also the main entrance (Figure 7). Significantly, this entrance faces east (as does the entrance to a hogan), which as the source of the dawn is a sacred direction in Navajo spirituality, toward which the morning blessing is offered. Further emphasizing this orientation, the church has a large ceremonial eastern portal, from which (at least in current use) traditional corn pollen blessings are sometimes offered at the dawn of the new day. Originally the portal was to have murals of the life of Christ, executed by Navajo artists in typical "Indian colors," which would be "easily understood and loved by the Indians."[19] (This idea became a sticking point with Given, who preferred the more European style of a famous religious artist from Washington, D.C., named Jan H. de Rosen.)[20] One of the most distinctive features of the church is the use of aluminum grills on the exterior of the tower belfry and over the otherwise clear rectangular windows (a device that Meem had previously used on his art deco–inspired 1936 Fine Arts Center on the campus of Colorado College in Colorado Springs). Indeed, Meem's ability to use such new materials

in traditional settings was one of his strengths as an architect, and the grills are evocative of the native symbols used in sand paintings, such as the corn plant and bolts of lightning, and obviously invoke the identity of the chapel's donor through the use of aluminum (Figure 8). Moreover, Meem saw in the transition from traditional adobe to materials such as stone and aluminum a parallel to the transition from ancient wooden temples to the use of stone in the Parthenon.[21]

From the main door of the church, one enters into a low-ceilinged narthex, within which the baptismal font is located. Significantly, the baptistery is at the north end of the church (the direction associated with death in Navajo cosmology). As such, its location evokes the movement from death into life through the Christian sacrament of baptism, and passing by the baptistery into the nave, one is greeted by an expansive white-stuccoed space approximately ninety feet long and thirty feet wide, with a high ceiling supported by traditional *viga* beams (Figure 9). The altar is freestanding (a liturgically advanced idea in the early 1950s) and surrounded by a multisided communion rail that evokes the traditional shape and size of a hogan. The altar is surrounded on the floor by intricate Navajo rugs, and liturgically is always approached in a clockwise movement, just as entry is made into a hogan. The furnishings are made by Southwestern artists and include silver candlesticks by Navajo silversmith Kenneth Begay and a nine-foot cross that hangs over the altar, which was designed by Meem and made by Santa Fe artist Carl Larsson, featuring silver and turquoise ceramic emblems of the Agnus Dei and four evangelists.

The church was consecrated and the vicarage dedicated on the same day, July 10, 1955, in the presence of no less than three bishops.[22] Given reported:

> It was a splendid day, in a crowded chapel, with the three Bishops also joining in confirming a class of thirty from the congregation of the Mission, its outstations and preaching stations. From our first use of the new chapel to date, all have been deeply impressed with its beauty, the fine feeling of proportion and texture of beautiful local materials,

and the wonderful way in which it seems to fit into this country and be fitted to this people.[23]

Once consecrated, the church functioned as a typical Anglican parish church, replete with the necessary vestments, processional crosses, and the Book of Common Prayer. Indeed, photographs reproduced as postcards from that era show these liturgical forms on full display, including a photograph of the elaborate dedicatory procession leading out of the church and into the open air (Figure 10).

Yet it is precisely there, where the postcard depicts the procession moving into the church-yard, that ghosts unforeseen by the vicar and architect begin to assert themselves forcefully into the picture, and where the supposed separation of religious identities begins to break down. The church is sited on a gently sloping hillside, adjacent to what is left of the previous chapel's apse, which now functions as an outdoor shrine. Behind them both lies a cemetery, affectionately referred to in some historical ecclesial documents with the traditional Anglo term "God's acre" (Figure 11).[24] Those buried in the cemetery include both Anglo and Navajo members of the Good Shepherd community, in particular a number of the children who lived at the mission, many of whom died in the great influenza epidemic of 1918–19. In most North American contexts, the presence of such a cemetery in proximity to a church would be unremarkable. As a 1953 report by the national office of the Episcopal Church on the state of the mission blithely observed, "A burial ground lies at the rear of the chapel and symbolizes the deep spiritual significance of the mission's religious ministry to the Navajos" (Figure 12).[25]

The Navajo do not, however, have a casual relationship to death, and in their worldview the ghosts of the dead are actively present and so they regard death and everything connected to it as "repulsive."[26] This attitude comes in part from the lack of a concept of an afterlife in Navajo religion equivalent to the Christian idea: the dead instead are believed to return to the place beneath the earth from where the Diné originally came, which is regarded as being located

Figure 7. Bell tower detail, Good Shepherd Mission chapel. Photograph by Karla Cavarra Britton, 2017.

Figure 8. Windows with aluminum grills depicting traditional Navajo symbols, Good Shepherd Mission chapel. Photograph by Karla Cavarra Britton, 2017.

in the north (the direction of evil). The bodies of the deceased are handled with great caution: if for example someone dies in a hogan, or family dwelling, a hole is made in the north wall in order to carry the body out, and the hogan is then destroyed.[27] In contemporary practice, to avoid the stigma of dying at home, the terminally ill are often brought to a hospital to die, where the medical staff rather than family can deal with the practical necessities.[28] Traditionally the body was touched only by a few strictly designated persons, who assumed responsibility for the entire burial and associated rituals, which were done very discretely and even secretly. A dead

person's belongings might be destroyed as part of the burial (even including livestock or a favorite horse), so that they could be of use to the deceased rather than offensively acquired by the living, thereby angering the spirit of the departed.[29] If such precautions are not taken, the dead are believed to be capable of returning to earth as ghosts to plague the living, and their presence—especially at nighttime—can be an omen of disaster.[30] In short, as Gladys Reichard (whose *Navaho Religion* is one of the most comprehensive interpretations of Navajo spirituality) somewhat derisively put it, the Diné have "an unreasoning terror of the dead."[31]

Ironically, then, the "cathedral of the Navajo" is conspicuously surrounded by a burial ground that strikes at the heart of a cultural divide between its Christian ethos on the one hand and the sensibilities of the native Navajo religious understanding on the other. Even the orientation of the graves speaks of this divide, since the graves are on a west-east axis as is customary in Christian burial grounds (with the head toward the west), whereas Navajo practice would place the body in a north-south orientation (with the head toward the north). The distinction between traditions is encapsulated in the fear of the return of spectral spirits from the place of the dead. For the Navajo, ghosts have a very prominent place, even to this day, in their cultural imagination. A *chindi,* for example, is thought to be the ghostly presence left behind when a person dies (what the Franciscan ethnographer Berard Haile described as an "ethereal, shadowy, palpable something").[32] It is made up of the residue that the individual was unable to bring into the spiritual harmony, or *hózhó,* which is the goal of Navajo life. A chindi leaves a person's body with the last breath, and then lingers near the person's burial site or possessions. So although the word "chindi" is typically translated into English as "ghost," the translation implies a more tangible idea than the Navajo meaning, which might better be described as "the contamination of the dead."[33] For someone else to come in contact with such a presence is regarded as a likely source of sickness and even death, and so chindi are much feared. The visitation of graves, therefore, as is customary in Anglo culture, has historically been relatively

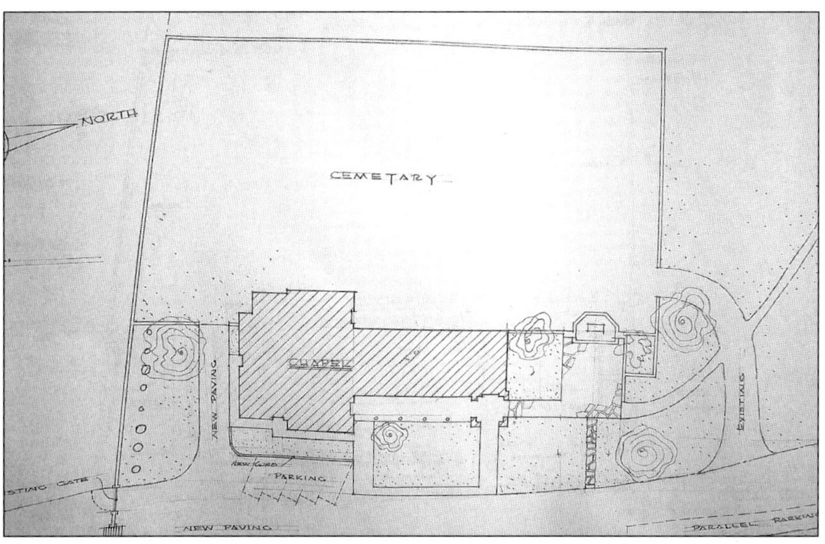

Figure 11. Site plan of the Good Shepherd Mission chapel, showing the cemetary (sic) behind the church and the remains of the apse of the old church to the north. Meem, Zehner, Holien and Associates, 1953. John Gaw Meem Drawings and Plans, Stack 2, Drawer 17, Special Collections and Center for Southwest Research, University of New Mexico Libraries.

Figure 12. Cemetery behind the church, Good Shepherd Mission chapel. Photograph by Karla Cavarra Britton, 2017.

unknown among the Navajo so as to avoid the risk of contamination.

Seen in this context, the Navajo attitude toward death is conceptually distinct from a Christian understanding in that even in death an active spiritual presence of the deceased remains, and especially in the form of his or her most negative characteristics. Navajo religion is focused upon the cultivation of health and harmony, and evil is the force that upsets them both. Yet death does not end that conflict, but instead in some sense separates out the evil, which then continues to threaten the living. Otto's assertion that ghosts are derivative of a daemonic dread—which he intended as a disparagement of their power as culture moves beyond its primitive forms—thus becomes more graphically apt in the Navajo context than he might have anticipated. The daemonic does not recede in the face of a more comprehensive concept of the sacred, but instead reinforces it; and death is not the end of life, but its accompaniment. For while to the Navajo "increase is the essence of life and of livelihood" (as John Farella puts it in *The Main Stalk,* his summary of Navajo philosophy), the ghosts of the dead loom as a palpable threat to that very aspiration.[34] The Good Shepherd church and cemetery thus bring into proximity that which traditional Navajo culture exerts itself to keep separate: namely, life and death.

In some ways, in regard to practices around death and burial, the Navajo culture has undergone significant change, both under the influence of Anglo traders and Christian missionaries, and especially in the aftermath of World War II. Through the intervention of the U.S. military, for instance, the war had the effect of introducing more Anglo/Christian burial practices such as professional mortuaries and commercially-made caskets. This evolution was most vividly represented by the establishment in 1943 of a Navajo memorial veterans' cemetery not far from Good Shepherd, which is much visited and decorated, despite the cultural reticence to do so.[35] While from the Christian point of view, the intent of the burial ground around a church is to evoke the hope of life's embrace of death, in native spirituality, the effect can instead be the opposite: an evocation of the fear that death—and its attendant ghosts—will adversely and dangerously infect life. Indeed, a recent vicar of the church reports that many Navajo are reluctant to come to the church at all, and especially for funerals, precisely because of this clash of cultural understandings.[36]

To see in these divergences only a conflict between cultures, however, would be to miss a subtler theme that also emerges: the native experience of having been able to follow two paths simultaneously (as for instance accepting death in the midst of life), whether that be spiritual, cultural, or professional. As the former vicar explains, even those Navajo who are part of the mission are quite clear in their minds that they have their Christian life, and they have their native spiritual identity—and the two are kept quite separate and distinct.[37] Hence the unqualified Anglicization of the chapel's ritual forms and the separation of native and Anglo practices, which remains intact to this day.

Perhaps one of the most powerful personal explorations of the resulting tensions is *The Scalpel and the Silver Bear,* a memoir by doctor Lori Arviso Alvord, who grew up on the Navajo reservation and went on to become its first female surgeon.[38] Her book tells of how she had to wrestle with integrating her skills as a western-trained physician with the wisdom and insight of native practices of healing. She reflects, for instance, on how her professional obligation to speak with patients about end of life decisions comes into conflict with the Navajo belief that if you speak of something, it brings it into existence: to speak of death is to enter into it. Nowhere did this conflict of cultural understandings become more tangible for Arviso than when she was in medical school and was confronted with her first cadaver for dissection in a lab. Beyond the squeamishness that any person might naturally have, she writes that "I had to combat another level of discomfort; Navajos do not touch the dead. Ever." The resolution she makes of this dilemma is to place her confidence in the fecundity of the knowledge she would thereby acquire, which would be like that of a medicine man—capable of much healing, even if at the same time fraught with much risk.

This experience of holding two traditions in tension within one's self is echoed in other personal reflections, such as *Native and Christian,* a collection of essays in which the theme of traveling two paths looms large.[39] Tweedy Sombrero, for instance (a Navajo Methodist pastor), describes her struggle with having two paths to follow, through which her Nahlee Man (or grandfather, himself a medicine man) guided her.[40] Raised by her father in such traditional practices as running each morning toward the rising sun to greet the new day given by the Creator, she also finds her way toward a vocation as a Christian pastor, a second path along which her Nahlee says "there is an obstacle all along the way."

The underlying question is the degree to which these accounts document their authors' acculturation into Anglo society, or whether the essays more powerfully represent a hybridization that defies the presumption of any one cultural hegemony. Perhaps it is here that the Chapel of the Good Shepherd becomes most instructive, for in many respects, the church building skillfully attempts to interweave the themes of native creation myths, reverence for the landscape, and Christian worship. As Meem wrote, "the whole church is an attempt to combine Christian tradition with Navajo color and symbol."[41] One particularly striking example of this cross-cultural attentiveness is a series of stations of the cross added to the church by Navajo artist Jonah Mitchell, depicting the scenes of Christ's passion in native-inspired images. Similarly, some of the mission's ordained clergy have simultaneously trained as medicine men or women even while serving the congregation. Yet while these gestures toward hybridization are honest and readily observable, the naïveté of official descriptions of the church (such as Jenkins' midcentury history of the mission, which regarded it as a surrogate for the religious life of the Navajo community), suppresses the cultural complexity of its spiritual context and the inevitable conflicts that arise in trying to hold both traditions in a syncretic tension.

Such suppression of the "two paths" is ultimately what gives rise to the unanticipated ghosts evoked by the church's proximity to the cemetery. The church is built with an implicit assumption that at least in certain critical matters such as attitudes toward life and death, the Christian worldview will supplant that of the Navajo, overlooking the fact that the cultures continue to be more parallel than convergent. In a fundraising publicity brochure from 1955, for example, Given wrote, "It is not strange that [the Navajo] are a deeply religious people, seeing the desert and mountains filled with powerful forces. For most of them, however, their religion is still the way of the old pagan gods."[42] The ghosts as they emerge and are perceived by the Navajo are thereby able to inhabit the space created by the lack of a true hybridization of the traditions. Although Meem's building is at times adept in at least proposing the idea of their intersection, in the end it may be defeated by the spectral density of the very diversity of cultures it tries to embrace. Moreover, the ghosts of the past still hang heavily in the air: to this day, the road leading from the Good Shepherd Mission around the hill to the site of the old Fort Defiance military installation continues to be named, bizarrely, Kit Carson Drive—an honorific designation maintained as though the forced Long Walk had never happened. So contrary to Otto's assertion that "ghosts have no place in our scheme of reality," the example of the Good Shepherd Mission would suggest that they may in fact assert their presence in our midst far more strongly than we allow.

AUTHOR BIOGRAPHY

**Karla Cavarra Britton** is a member of the faculty of the School of Arts, Humanities and English at Diné College, Tsaile, Arizona. She was previously a lecturer at the Yale School of Architecture and has taught on the landscape and architecture of the American Southwest at the University of New Mexico. Her research interests include the intersection of religion and modernization, and she is preparing a study of modern sacred architecture in the global context.

NOTES

1. Rudolf Otto, *The Idea of the Holy,* 2nd ed., trans. John W. Harvey (Oxford: Oxford University Press, 1931), 15–17.

2. For a useful overview of Navajo history, see

Peter Iverson, *Diné: A History of the Navajos* (Albuquerque: University of New Mexico Press, 2002).

3. Niles Carpenter, "Report of the Surveyor for the National Council: The Good Shepherd Mission at Fort Defiance," Good Shepherd Mission archives, April–August, 1940.

4. J. Rockwood Jenkins, *The Good Shepherd Mission to the Navajo*. Project Canterbury, n.d., http://anglicanhistory.org/indigenous/jenkins_navajo1956/.

5. Jenkins, *The Good Shepherd Mission*, Chapter X, n.p.

6. Arthur Kinsolving, letter to John Gaw Meem, December 31, 1949. Job Files Box 59, Folder 25, John Gaw Meem Papers, Center for Southwestern Research, University Libraries, University of New Mexico.

7. Stanford Lehmberg, *Churches for the Southwest: The Ecclesiastical Architecture of John Gaw Meem* (New York: Norton, 2005), 112. See also Chris Wilson, *The Houses and Life of John Gaw Meem* (New York: Norton, 2005); Anne Taylor, *Southwestern Ornamentation and Design: The Architecture of John Gaw Meem* (Santa Fe, N.M.: Sunstone Press, 2017); and Bainbridge Bunting, *John Gaw Meem, Southwestern Architect* (Albuquerque: University of New Mexico Press, 1983).

8. Summarized in John Gaw Meem, "Memorandum on a conference at Good Shepherd Mission," August 15, 1952. Job Files Box 59, Folder 25, Meem Papers.

9. Cynthia Hizer (vicar of Good Shepherd Mission). Interview conducted by the author June 4, 2016.

10. Meem was, for example, acknowledged for his architectural service by a resolution of the Convention of the Diocese of the Rio Grande on April 28, 1974. Correspondence and Subject Files Box 3, Folder 22, Meem Papers.

11. John Gaw Meem, "Does it make sense to be a Christian in our contemporary world?" Correspondence and Subject Files Box 6, Folder 22. Meem Papers, n.d.

12. Kate Wingert-Playdon, *John Gaw Meem at Acoma: The Restoration of San Esteban del Rey Mission* (Albuquerque: University of New Mexico Press, 2012).

13. Bunting, *John Gaw Meem*, 118.

14. John Gaw Meem, "The Architecture of New Mexico," typescript for an introductory essay for *New Mexico State Guide*, August 18, 1936, 5. Correspondence and Subject Files Box 6, Folder 19, Meem Papers.

15. Scott Sandlin, "Everything Old Is New Again," in *Un Tributo Cultural*, a special supplement to the *Albuquerque Journal* (October 15, 2000), 9.

16. John Gaw Meem, "A Contemporary Regional Style Based on the Traditional," *New Mexico Architecture* (March–April 1972): 8–9. A response to Anthony C. Antoniades, "Traditional Versus Contemporary Elements in Architecture," *New Mexico Magazine* (November–December 1971): 9–13.

17. John Gaw Meem, "Monuments of New Mexico," typescript of a lecture given at the American Institute of Architects annual conference, San Antonio, Texas, 1931, 12. Correspondence and Subject Files Box 3, Folder 24, Meem Papers.

18. John Gaw Meem, "Memorandum—Good Shepherd Mission," August 7 and 8, 1953, 3. Job Files Box 29, Folder 25, Meem Papers.

19. Meem, "Memorandum—Good Shepherd Mission," 3.

20. John Gaw Meem, letter to Davis Given, April 19, 1955, with attached description of the artist. Job Files Box 59, Folder 23, Meem Papers.

21. John Gaw Meem, "Spanish-Pueblo Architecture in Permanent Materials," May 19, 1975. Meem mentions that Frank Lloyd Wright, upon visiting the campus of the University of New Mexico, had exclaimed, "This is imitation and all imitation is base." This essay seems to be a reply to that assertion. Correspondence and Subject Files Box 6, Folder 22, Meem Papers.

22. The bishops present were from the three dioceses that include the Navajoland Area Mission of the Episcopal Church: Arthur Kinsolving (Arizona), Richard Watson (Utah), and Charles James Kinsolving III (New Mexico and Southwest Texas). "Navajo Chapel," *The Living Church* 131 (August 14, 1955): 11.

23. Jenkins, *The Good Shepherd Mission*, Supplement: *Latest News to October '55*, n.p.

24. Jenkins, *The Good Shepherd Mission*, Chapter VIII, n.p.

25. The Episcopal Church, Division of Health and Welfare Services, "A Report: Good Shepherd Mission, Fort Defiance, Arizona," August, 1953, 18. Good Shepherd Mission archives.

26. Raymond Friday Locke, *The Book of the Navajo* (Los Angeles: Mankind Publishing, 1976), 29.

27. Charlotte J. Frisbie, ed., introduction to "Navajo Mortuary Practices and Beliefs: Change and

Persistence," special symposium issue, *American Indian Quarterly* 4 no. 4 (November, 1978): 303–8.

28. Joseph Canarie, M.D. (Yale School of Medicine, formerly of the Fort Defiance Indian Health Service Hospital). Conversation with the author, October 29, 2017.

29. Gladys A. Reichard, *Navaho Religion: A Study of Symbolism* (Princeton: Princeton University Press, 1963), 42.

30. Locke, *The Book of the Navajo*, 30.

31. Reichard, *Navaho Religion*, 44–5.

32. Berard Haile, "Soul Concepts of the Navajo," *Annali Lateranansi* 7 (1943): 89.

33. Reichard, *Navaho Religion*, 48.

34. John R. Farella, *The Main Stalk: A Synthesis of Navajo Philosophy* (Tucson: University of Arizona Press, 1984), 46.

35. Stephen C. Jett, "Modern Navajo Cemeteries," *Material Culture* 28, no. 2 (1996): 5.

36. Hizer, interview.

37. Hizer, interview.

38. Lori Arviso Alvord and Elizabeth Cohen Van Pelt, *The Scalpel and the Silver Bear: The First Navajo Woman Surgeon Combines Western Medicine and Traditional Healing* (New York: Bantam, 1999).

39. James Treat, ed., *Native and Christian: Indigenous Voices on Religious Identity in the United States and Canada* (New York: Routledge, 1996).

40. Tweedy Sombrero, "Two Paths," in Treat, *Native and Christian*, 232–35.

41. John Gaw Meem, letter to Mrs. Harold Leigh McClinton, August 23, 1955. Job Files Box 59, Folder 23, Meem Papers.

42. Davis Given, "Message into the Hills," ca. 1955, Correspondence and Subject Files Box 4, Folder 40, Meem Papers.

EVELYN MONTGOMERY

# Beyond the American Foursquare

*The Square House in Period Perspective*

ABSTRACT

During the first two decades of the twentieth century the square house, now commonly called the foursquare or American foursquare, shared the consumer marketplace with the bungalow and dwellings in the colonial revival style. The form has not received the same level of attention as it did earlier in popular architecture and design media. This essay argues that the square house was popular despite its lack of formal definition because it was adaptable in size, exterior elaboration, interior plan, and cost. Designs were available to suit a range of budgets within the widely-defined middle class. The form was recognized for its cubic mass addressing the street, with openings and decorative elaboration governed by that proportion. The core of the square house was a centralized, looped circulation pattern through four main spaces located in the corners. Its period of popularity coincided with the transition from highly regimented Victorian plans, which emphasized the separation of public and private activities, to a more open arrangement with movement through contiguous spaces. The form's basic cubic mass was an ideal fit for the narrow suburban lots of the streetcar suburbs. Early examples retained many Victorian elements, while later ones featured details associated with newer styles such as prairie, craftsman, or colonial revival. The evolution of the square house mirrored the changing aesthetic preferences and domestic usage patterns in the bungalow era.

When the *Indianapolis Star* published images of notable new houses in the early decades of the twentieth century, the square house received faint praise. Bungalows were described as romantic and exotic. The colonial revival style was portrayed as offering prospective owners an affordable, stately image recalling a simpler time in America's past. Meanwhile an attractive square house illustrated in the newspaper in 1910 was described as "architecturally . . . not distinctive, being a modification of the popular square type of residence."[1] Though never receiving the critical acclaim of the more modish styles of the day, the square house nonetheless became the workhorse of middle-class domesticity even as it eluded coherent definition and was often the subject of criticism.

The author of *The Indianapolis Star* article conceded that the design of the house above "has been handled in a way to attract attention."[2] The basic cubic façade was enhanced with a combination of cladding materials, articulated brickwork to create texture, a bay window, and a large dormer. This house combined a few stylish features with a simple, sturdy shape. It illustrated the square house's ability to achieve many variations in appearance within the boundaries of its general definition.

This essay argues that the square house's versatility accounted for its popularity among early twentieth-century consumers. The form enjoyed mass appeal because it offered flexible solutions to the period's domestic needs. It could be adapted to a range of locations, budgets, styles,

and individual preferences for self-presentation. It was a modern house that offered consumers choices in how rapidly or gradually they would abandon Victorian domestic ideas. It rivaled and may have exceeded the bungalow and colonial revival in popularity among its American audiences, even though the bungalow is often seen as defining the period's domestic architecture.

Primary sources from the house's heyday (circa 1900–1930) suggest that when people spoke of the square house, they shared a common understanding of what they meant. That period term seems to refer primarily to the exterior shape and somewhat to the plan, which today we associate with the more modern label "foursquare." The term "American foursquare," not used until 1982, is a specific iteration of the form, referring to a square house with a prescribed exterior expression, including a hipped roof, full-width porch, and dormer (Figure 1).[3] This essay will use the term square house for the broader square house form, of which the American foursquare is but one possible type. It will focus on consumers, who were principally re-

sponsible for the house form's popularity during the early 1900s.

### Features of the Square House

Despite some variations, the square house form conveyed certain basic features that responded to a particular set of period needs. Part of this related to lot size and consumer expectations in the streetcar suburbs of the later nineteenth and early twentieth centuries. About fifty feet wide, these lots were too narrow for a wide house form, with a spreading footprint and grounds. They were also too wide for contiguous row houses, and beyond this the emergent suburban middle-class culture demanded a bit of land on each side. When a commodious two-story house was desired for such a lot, it was, almost by necessity, forced into cubic shape. The square house faced the street with this visible cubic form, which, when repeated, created a rhythmic streetscape. The square façade proportions determined the placement of openings and decorative elements.

Period plan books and extant square house examples show the typical house measured about thirty feet wide, with a minimum of twenty-two feet and absolute maximum of forty-five. The narrowest examples generally had the plainest appearance, fulfilling the frugal promise of a simple, unadorned box, serving the needs of modest earners (Figure 2). Wider models for larger lots sometimes stretched the square proportion beyond recognition, but such houses were still identifiable as a related form (Figure 3).

While many associate the square house form with a hipped roof, their shapes varied considerably. The popular hipped roof accentuated the square front and cubic form of the house. It may have appealed to consumers because it gave a feeling of hominess to the house's substantial form, something recognized in the period.[4] One potential builder of a square house said "the roof, of course, will be square too."[5] However, designers created square house plans with a variety of roof options. John Henry Newson offered an identical square plan with a front facing gable or a jerkin-head side gable.[6] In 1918, Milton Dana Morrill published a rectangular home plan with a choice of six roofs, from flat to Dutch; consumers could choose a roof type as if it were a fashion accessory.[7]

The preferred roof form for a square house seems to have been one that enhanced its cubic appearance, rather than distracted from it. This could be accomplished with front- or side-facing gables, jerkin-heads, or Dutch gabled roofs. In all cases proportion was the key to a successful design. When the gable faced the front, it added height and risked narrowing the form visually, while a gable to the side could widen it with the same potential loss of cubic form. Ideally, all aspects of the exterior worked together to enhance its squareness.

Square house plans also display versatility in how they fit into a standard overall form. The classic plan is based on a scheme in which rooms on each floor are arranged as four squares within a larger square in both plan and section, hence the name "foursquare." This plan centralized circulation, gave it a minimum of square footage, and created an open flow between spaces out of necessity, a common feature of the more well-known bungalow houses of the period. Wider houses might have room for a graceful center hall, but the standard square house size yielded four fifteen-foot square rooms, with no space available in between. The four primary spaces of the lower floor are the entry, parlor/living room, dining room, and kitchen. They open directly to each other without mediating hallways, and the degree of openness increased as the form matured during the 1910s.

The ideal lower-level circulation placed all communication between rooms toward the center of the plan, where children could run in a tight circle through all four main spaces (Figure 4). Jan Jennings has found such "loops," one to three per house, in designs for convenient cottages and houses at the turn of the century, "implying a more communicative way of living."[8] The maturation process of the square house certainly implies a growing acceptance of looped circulation, without which the smaller square houses would have been difficult to design.

The front two rooms were usually defined as an entry or reception hall and a parlor. They could be divided by a wall with a wide pocket

Figure 2. These are basic, minimally elaborated square houses, designed both for low cost and for very narrow lots in Chicago, Illinois. About twenty-two feet wide, they probably share the same floor plan with different roof shapes. Photograph by Evelyn Montgomery, 2015.

Figure 3. With or without side extensions, wide rectilinear houses like this one in Dallas, Texas, are clearly related to square houses but reflect greater cost and usually a more formal interior plan. Photograph by Steve Clicque, 2017.

door, or less insistently divided by a columned screen. Sometimes, the two spaces could be combined into one wide parlor or living room across the front. Such a full-width room was a popular feature of bungalows, whose open layout facilitated a friendly, easy welcome to visitors. This relaxation of more formal Victorian standards of entry was one sign of modernization found in the square house's design and links the house form to more open plans that became fashionable in later decades in American suburbs.

In most square house plans, the second floor had bedrooms in each of the four corners. This provided each room with double exposure to light and air, while also providing a shared internal access area (Figure 4). Requiring doors for the bedrooms, bathroom, attic access, and linen closets, this space was often filled with doors. Ideally, it was not a linear hall but centralized, successful if it reached the "irreducible minimum . . . it could not well be any smaller and still contain the necessary eight openings."[9] A windowless room of doors, this space provided an economical and practical allotment of square footage. Its unpretentiousness expressed the private nature of the upper floor where few guests were expected.

The decorative treatment of the exterior of the square house varied. Some square houses were rather plain, which saved on costs and presented an appearance of simplicity and thrift. These featured minimal applied decoration and windows with plain glass and few divisions. For consumers with the funds and desire for a more elaborate exterior, the square house could be finished with details associated with colonial revival, prairie, and craftsman bungalow, or any other style of the period.

A colonial revival style example might feature round fluted or plain columns as well as popular window forms associated with it. With a standard-width square house, this could require the use of only three columns, in violation of classical norms but perfectly in keeping with the common two-bay porch formation found on this house form (Figure 5). Clapboard siding and white paint were obvious choices. A craftsman option, meanwhile, featured forms more associated with the bungalow. This aesthetic was expressed as squat,

wooden, pyramidal columns on large masonry bases, a jaunty kick at the edge of the roofline, large or elaborate brackets, and the visible use of natural materials such as stone. These craftsman-inspired houses might also include rustic siding such as rough-surfaced shingles.

Many American foursquare houses used a simplified prairie aesthetic. Boxed wood columns on a full porch with a linear and typically symmetrical arrangement of windows and deep eaves gave a tall house a sense of horizontality. The texture of wall surfaces tended toward flatness, in simple wood siding, brick, or stucco covering concrete block. Often, cladding materials could be combined, with the transition occurring at the second story and adding an emphatic

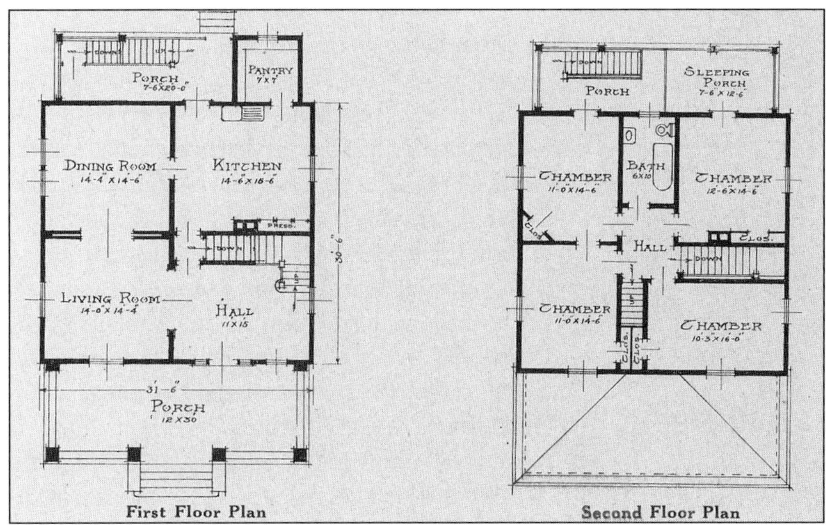


First Floor Plan    Second Floor Plan

Figure 4. Both levels of H. M. Miller's plan number 516 incorporate minimal central circulation. From H. M. Miller, *Modern Homes and Bungalows* (Roanoke, Va.: The Stone Printing and Manufacturing Company, 1918), Albert and Shirley Small Special Collections Library, University of Virginia.

Figure 5. A tall, two-bay colonial revival façade has been fitted on to this square house form, located near neighbors with prairie-style enhancements in San Antonio, Texas. Photograph by Evelyn Montgomery, 2012.

horizontal line. This material transition appeared painterly rather than sculptural, retaining a flat impression.

There was no standard aesthetic for the popular square house. Manufacturers offered a range of porch columns, railings, doors, and windows in many different styles. In their 1923 edition of *Building with Assurance* the Morgan Woodwork Organization presented fifty-six house plans in all popular forms of the period, followed by 345 pages of interior and exterior parts and decorative enhancements (Figure 6). While each plan portrayed a coherent style, doors and windows came in a variety of styles from the bungalow to the colonial. A confident consumer could combine at will. With affordable design choices offered by so many manufacturers, only social acceptability and the guidance of published design advisers limited the square house.

The plethora of exterior ornament belied the underlying logic offered by square house proponents, who rightly asserted that a plain box enclosed a maximum of square footage with a minimum of wall fabric and reduced costly corners. They noted how an iconic hipped roof saved on materials. Yet its practicality was also a challenge; commentators often voiced dislike for the basic cube and its frugal form. Even sellers of square house plans offered tepid praise for the plainest ones. Sales language for the "money's worth house," did not emphasize beauty, and the Gordon–Van Tine Company titled one plan "This Big Two-Story Home at a Bargain Price."[10] Others made their general contempt for the square house clear. A. L. Porter and W. J. Ballard offered Ideal Homes plan number 804 because "the square design still has many adherents," though they had skillfully "broken away from the plain and hard lines."[11] In Hewitt-Lea-Funck Company's *Prize Plan Book* of 1914, design number 901 "is as good a type of square house as could be devised," and it "has been given the necessary decorative treatment to relieve the square effect," in an attempt to hide its core feature.[12] In 1908, a writer at *Midwestern Magazine* observed "the rage for square houses passed over Des Moines several years ago and left some hideous things in its wake."[13] E. I. Farrington found it "needless to say that houses of this type have neither character nor charm," though he decorated one to prove that talent could overcome the form's fault of plainness.[14] A cube was seen as doomed for its lack of style, of imagination, of cultural meaning, branded as boring but economical.

Solutions to this blandness could include applied elements, windows with artistically divided lights or special glass, varying roof brackets or skirting materials. The most defining enhancement that developed was the variety of masses breaking the cube and jutting outward on the front and sides. Such protrusions could enliven the cubic form or detract from it, and many critics supported the latter strategy. Key among these protrusions is an often overlooked defining feature that may be named the stair square. It marked the location of the staircase and can be taken as an intentional exterior sign of interior circulation (Figure 7). The protrusion could be square, bowed, or occasionally triangular. Even when there was no protrusion, a window located between the levels of the upper and lower story windows marked the stair location. A side door was often located below, offering access to the

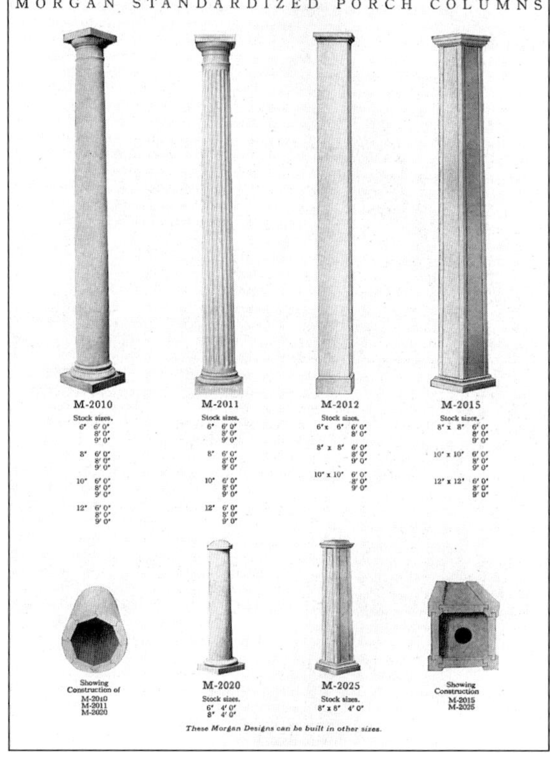


Figure 6. These columns were offered in several heights and all styles were interchangeable. Drawing by the Morgan Woodwork Organization in *Building With Assurance* (Oshkosh, Wisc.: Morgan Woodwork Organization, 1923). Author's collection.

basement and its furnace (Figure 8). Even that practical door had symbolic implications of modern technological comfort. This protrusion sometimes served a practical end, by slightly reducing the space the stairway consumed within the floor footprint. As an aesthetic element it added visual interest and was often found on houses with no other decorative additions. The stair square had a symbolic purpose, proclaiming modern interior circulation on the exterior. The center circulation pushed the stair toward the perimeter wall, and the landing broke through to the outside.

Protrusions from the cube added cost, which needed to be justified by a practical, beautifying or performative use. These were not merely aesthetic features and tools for admitting light. They could be read as signs of social class. They spoke of someone's ability and willingness to pay for domestic individuality, whether it was a homeowner who oversaw the house's creation prior to moving into it or a speculative builder or landlord who wanted to attract middle-class residents who could afford the higher costs associated with such improvements. The small, basic square house really did enclose the greatest interior space for the least expense on the exterior, but not everybody wanted to face the world proclaiming that message.

## One House Form, Many Variations

Given a range of sizes, plan options, and exterior styling elements, a consumer could craft a square house to meet individual functional and aesthetic needs and preferences. The size and level of elaboration determined the price of a house and its appeal to a broad middle class. The house's market ranged in income levels from office clerks and skilled craftsmen to successful business owners and professionals. This group had options in housing not available to the poor and working class. Their income and level of education allowed them greater access to the media, including prescriptive and proscriptive literature on the design and furnishings of the home. They had the resources to recognize the social value and potential status gained by the owner of a house that was tastefully elaborated with decorative features and supportive of proper domestic

Figure 7. The stair square side projection often has its own roof and is usually located on the same side as the entry, with the kitchen behind. Fredonia, New York, photograph by Evelyn Montgomery, 2008.

Figure 8. This concrete block square house has no stair square but does mark the stair location with a window at the landing level. West Chicago, Illinois, photograph by Evelyn Montgomery, 2015.

practices. But they also had to work within a responsible budget.

The range of home values available may be gauged through published plans. Sampled plans are from two kit-house sources: the Sears homes available from 1911 to 1913 and the Hewitt-Lea-Funck Company's *Prize Plan Book* (1914), and two plan books, *Homes of Character* by John Henry Newson (1913), and *Roberts Home Builder* by Roberts and Roberts, Portland architects (1910). The square house was well represented in all.

Of the kit-home guides, *Prize Plan Book* offered the largest houses, some exceeding 2,000 square feet. The cost per square foot was kept low by using simple shapes and only wood cladding. Final costs ranged from $1,943 to $2,757. Sears offered a greater range of sizes. The Springfield model was only 1,280 square feet. Sears' square house prices did not exceed $2,000, with a concrete block option as low as $800.

Roberts' square house plans ranged from 1,350 square feet to an unusual 2,880, with estimated construction costs of $2,000 for a small, plain one to $3,800 for the larger and more stylishly embellished model. In offering his plans, John Henry Newson recognized that degree of decoration also influenced cost. In *Homes of Character* he offered a range of estimated costs for each house, noting that greater elaboration and style elements, as well as material choices, would make a given model more impressive and costlier. He offered cost-saving advice such as choosing frame construction over masonry, and presented plans that were available in small, medium, and large sizes for different budgets. One colonial revival square house with substantial columns had a maximum construction cost of $4,500.

### The Square House in the Consumer Marketplace

By examining constructed square houses, the occupations of the consumers who owned them, and the development practices that informed the residents' choices, we can see the square house's adaptability as it was realized on the landscape. Indianapolis and Dallas are representative of cities in the northern and southern parts of the Midwest where the form is particularly common. These cities contain neighborhoods developed in the early twentieth century that are dominated by square houses.

Meridian Park in Indianapolis attracted local leaders, prominent businessmen, and a "nationally recognized fashion designer" to its building lots north of downtown.[15] Square houses are common among the varied housing stock. They tend toward elaborate exterior decoration in arts and crafts, Tudor revival, and more exotic styles (Figure 9).[16] Original square house owners in the neighborhood included physicians, attorneys, and managers and officers of downtown business establishments, including a department store, a real estate firm, a candy manufacturer, and a family investment firm.[17] With a lower income and a lot on one of the secondary streets, a traveling salesman and his wife declared they had saved for years to afford their square house.[18]

Square houses in some nearby neighborhoods, characterized by a general preponderance of small bungalows, cottages, and multifamily buildings, were smaller and less elaborate. To the west on 32nd and 33rd Streets, square houses of repetitive design and details suggest the work of a mass developer. Residents of these streets were listed in city directories as foremen, dispatchers, telephone operators, clerks, and other occupations marking the boundary between working class and lower middle class.

The Munger Place development in Dallas, Texas, was intentionally planned to attract civic and business leaders, advertised as a "strictly high-class residential district," with its racial, economic, and aesthetic homogeneity secured by the city's first protective deed restrictions.[19] Purchasers of its fifty-foot wide lots were required to build homes valued between $2,000 and $4,000. The vast majority were stylish custom square houses with a wide assortment of protrusions and ornament (Figure 10). The development's finest and most expensive street, Swiss Avenue, offered more room to spread out, and most of the houses there did so (Figure 3). The local Catholic diocese acquired an unusually narrow lot on that avenue to build a home for Bishop Joseph Lynch. To meet the $10,000 minimum construction cost required on Swiss Avenue in a compact form, they chose a deep and well-appointed square house (Figure 11). It features brick with cast-stone elements in a city dominated by wood siding. Inside, the large reception hall's stair banister is carved with a custom motif of crosses.

Munger Place's developers drew buyers by promising exclusivity and the lasting value of a quality neighborhood and fashionable houses.

Figure 9. The streetscape of Meridian Park in Indianapolis, Indiana, was enhanced by some topographical variety and creative use of exterior enhancement. Photograph by Evelyn Montgomery, 2008.

In their choice of a home, consumers wanted to secure their investment, as well as their social position (or at least its perception by their peers). Scholarship on the changing domestic landscape of the colonial and Victorian periods traces the growth of American awareness of the home as a presentation of the values and merit of the inhabitants, based on visual display and choice of style.[20] Middle-class efforts to project an appropriate image, which were influenced by the practices of the upper class, were subject to emulation by those of lesser means.[21] The growth of consumer choice easily translated into concern about making poor choices, and thus a poor presentation.[22] Sinclair Lewis used the struggle for status among the insecure middle class to great effect in works like *Babbitt*.[23] This anxiety fed a great need for information on how to make good consumer selections amid a bewildering assortment of options.[24] Expert advice was dispatched through the increasingly accessible media.

In the Victorian period, domestic advice writers encouraged readers to seek individuality, while simultaneously undercutting that advice with warnings about the dangers of displaying poor taste.[25] Bungalow-era critics targeted multiple levels of the middle class with similar warnings. *Suburban Life* was a magazine for owners of larger suburban homes. *Keith's Magazine* lured potential buyers with advertisements for innovative building products. It included readers' stories of building homes in a variety of moderate sizes and styles, with tips on economizing and on achieving the coveted "artistic" home. *American Home* entertained readers with articles about large, expensive homes, including bungalows stretched along hilltops and colonial revival houses with white columns marching across wide façades. On the pages in the back, advertisers' illustrations featured more affordable options like box bungalows and square houses. Advertisers targeted their readers' budgets. The producers of magazine content appealed to aspirations. Consumers carried the burden of meeting both in one house.

Despite the forces of the market, consumers were not passive. They were active participants,

Figure 10. Postcard, ca. 1910. A row of desirable square houses in the exclusive Munger Place development in Dallas, Texas. Courtesy of Dallas Heritage Village.

Figure 11. This Swiss Avenue home built for Bishop Joseph Lynch used expensive materials creatively arranged in the absence of space available for a wide façade presentation. Dallas, Texas, photograph by Steve Clicque, 2016.

able to effect offerings by their choices.[26] Consumers had access to multiple sources of information about current housing trends locally and across the nation. They studied printed images and published commentary in order to understand the cultural meaning of the commodities being exchanged.[27] Victorian consumers bequeathed to their descendants a sophisticated understanding of how a home's size and style choices could reflect one's social position as well as one's character, including the type of connections they might enjoy in business and leisure life.[28] For Americans in the early 1900s, the centrality of the house as the primary consumer object for making such statements was common knowledge; indeed, it was a lingering Victorian ideology few could escape.[29]

A century after that marketplace, Thomas C. Hubka included the foursquare in his book *Houses Without Names*, a study of common houses that have not been intensely studied by scholars and might lack name recognition among the general public.[30] That description fit the square house at the time of its original popularity. It was not well defined or eloquently lauded like the bungalow and colonial revival. There was no champion of the square house in its day, no philosophy for its social or domestic advantages.

In contrast, the bungalow was not just a house, it was a way to live; it was a "state of mind" with its own devotees and could confer a reputation upon its owner.[31] Domestic adviser Mable Seares called it a habit, a new way of "relaxed home-making."[32] The bungalow was "a type of house, a period of architecture, and a movement," and it carried a romantic and sophisticated mystique.[33] It was associated with exotic locales like India and California, and combined a hint of bohemianism with the security of its widespread acceptance.[34] The architects of *Roberts Home Builder* equated the bungalow style with the progress of American civilization, having reached a high point where people could recognize the value of a house that is "artistic in appearance and conveniently arranged."[35] It was seen as both modern and likely to have lasting value, unlike the styles that preceded it. The authors of the 1912 *A Book of Wildwood Plans* offered restrained craftsman styles and mocked Victorian excesses such as a "scroll-worked doorway," now broken and serving as an eternal regret for its owner.[36] Proponents of the bungalow failed to notice that their argument for its revolutionary moral and social meanings reflected a Victorian concept that equated the form and style of the house with the owner's character and beliefs.[37]

Advocates of the colonial revival style praised its clean, modern lines and the homage it paid to the nation's hearty and resourceful pioneers of democracy.[38] They encouraged the use of columns, symmetry, and white cladding outside, with piecrust tables and spinning wheels bringing the virtuous aesthetic inside. Those who studied the works of Wallace Nutting and Alice Morse Earle found a pleasantly usable past.[39] The colonial revival clearly appealed to history in rejecting Victorian excesses, as did the bungalow with its visions of British functionaries in India and the casual California lifestyle. Advocates of the colonial revival scoffed at the aesthetics of a previous generation but took pleasure in older forms as "evidence of a lost America, more innocent, more moral, more genteel."[40] In contrast, the square house had no romantic or usable past. It lacked the associational forms and values of these branded types; even so, it claimed an impressive market share despite its modest pretentions.

## The Square House Modernizes an Older Form

Versatility and lack of definition or ideology allowed the square house to fulfill specific needs in a period marked by transition, offering the consumer an adjustable degree of modernity in keeping with each buyer's domestic aspirations. Before it achieved its fully modern form the square house transitioned from Victorian expectations to those of the early twentieth century.

The square house followed small Queen Anne antecedents in addressing the problem of the narrow lots of the streetcar suburb. Such middle-class homes needed to make an attractive statement but allowed only the narrow front side to express the taste of the resident. Contemporary critics of the square house noted how its defects were magnified when rows of them were endlessly and evenly spaced on identical lots. The public must have disagreed. Images of such streetscapes were used to sell both developers' finished products and construction materials for homebuilders (Figure 12). As the cubic fronts lined up, they displayed carefully designed faces and hid most of what happened farther back. Simple beauty arose in the regularity, and gentle variety in individual building styles (Figure 13).

Orderly consistency was exactly what middle-class Victorian house designers struggled to avoid. Queen Anne characteristics such as asymmetry, multiple exterior wall plains, complex roof forms, and use of cladding colors and textures all helped to disguise regularity. The turrets and distracting roofs hid the inchoate cube.[41] The 1903 edition of *The Radford American Homes* offered a familiar example of a suburban Queen Anne form in plan 511 (Figure 14). Seen obliquely, the exterior did not seem cubic, but the front façade was thirty-three feet wide and close to that in height where the roofs begin. The inset corner porch and the four rooflines mask the cubic reading. The plan was drawn tightly into a compact, centralized form within an overall rectangular perimeter made irregular by random changes

Figure 12. The Andrews Heating Company considered this collection of square houses with various rooflines attractive enough to catch the eye of potential customers. *Keith's Magazine on Home Building* 13, no. 3 (March 1905): 168. Image of item held in the research collections of Cleveland Public Library.

Figure 13. The Oakhurst Place neighborhood in St. Louis, Missouri, is filled with houses of concrete block that demonstrate how well square house forms addressed the street and claimed the narrow lot. Photograph by Evelyn Montgomery, 2012.

in the perimeter walls. The first-floor plan incorporated the circulation and use pattern of the square house.

D. S. Hopkins' design number 169, published in 1893, came very close to an early square plan on both levels, with fewer major breaks in the flatness of the exterior walls (Figure 15). The vestigial turret, partial porch with a fanciful roof embellishment and arched openings, and the varied and intricate cladding hid the cubic form. Elaborate gingerbread trims helped disguise a house shaped like its suburban lot. Plans like these reveal that

despite purposeful and fashionable irregularity around the perimeter, the core functions of the house fit into a largely square footprint.

Both of these examples illustrate the transition from Victorian forms. Though James Massey and Shirley Maxwell have argued that initial purchasers saw American foursquares as "not Victorian, not Queen Anne, not even remotely nineteenth-century in feeling," these buildings actually expressed the gradual change from the Victorian period into the twentieth century.[42] Many examples retained Victorian details,

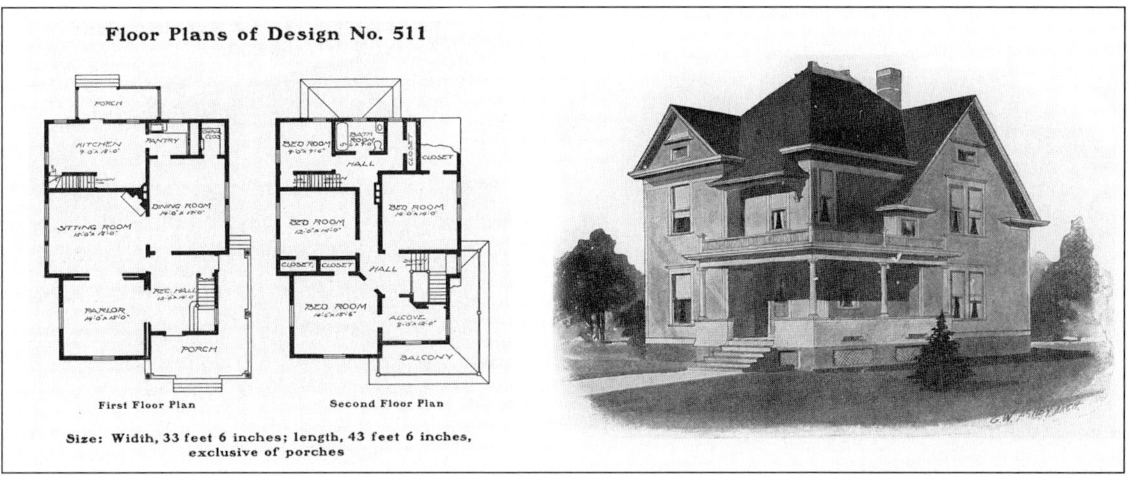


Figure 14. Both interior circulation and exterior squareness are beginning to appear in this plan from the early years of the square house. Radford plan 511 from Radford Architecture Company, *The Radford American Homes* (Riverside, Ill., 1903). Author's collection.

Figure 15. This very early plan points toward the square house. While decoration disguises the cubic exterior, the centralized plan is embraced for its practicality. Plan 169 from D. H. Hopkins, *Houses and Cottages*, vol. 7 (Muskegon, Mich.: Muskegon Publishing Co., 1893). Image of item held in the research collections of Cleveland Public Library.

as the architectural transformation was slow and uneven. Some Queen Anne houses were still being built as late as the 1910s (Figure 16).[43] It was a change similar to what Joseph C. Bigott has found in working-class Chicago cottages and bungalows, but carried out by people of greater means.[44] Even consumers who wanted to be modern could resist full and sudden changes, at first seeking only to relax Victorianism, not overthrow it.[45] The transitional square house was an example of how "new structures can be designed that adhere to a tradition's grammar, even while being novel in form," or in this case, can even change the grammar applied to a core form.[46]

The change could not proceed fast enough for some architects. John Henry Newson was pleased to note that "the Bungalow age is here." Consumers could focus on "comfort and hospitality," and a reliance on design professionals rather than "the suggestions of the cozy corner editor of a magazine."[47] He was invoking one of the more extreme Victorian decorative traditions,

but as late as 1906 *The National Builder* offered its readers instructions on how to create one.

Victorian morality and social practices lingered past 1900. In her memoir of a wealthy early twentieth-century American family, Peggie Phipps Boegner described the persistence of nineteenth-century sensibilities: "In the second half of the century, it is difficult to recognize the strong Victorian influence that still existed in the early 1900s."[48] If the wealthy found former Victorian standards to be like a straightjacket limiting the free enjoyment of life, the striving and less secure middle class must have found them even more stressful.

Many who were born to the parlor culture that Victorians so carefully built vocally rejected its stuffiness in the new century. At the turn of the century, critics in the media and popular opinion extolled new fashions and championed the relaxation of older social strictures, establishing new standards of conformity. They viewed their mothers' generation with contempt for parlors that were far too attractive and costly to be used by the family but were kept for the sole purpose of impressing guests. Readers may have shared memories of uncomfortable Sundays on horsehair sofas, whether in a farmhouse or a mansion. Post-Victorian memories of parlor childhoods were described as "grave and gay, the gaiety . . . more in a latter-day appreciation of the grotesque than in joyous recollection."[49]

Such parlor critics chose a fitting target for their attacks on the larger body of Victorian domestic propriety. Contemporaries and later historians saw the parlor and the regimented behaviors associated with it as outmoded.[50] They even tried to banish the term in favor of "living room," with its emphasis on the informality of entertaining. In popular plan publications it was a gradual process, rather than a leap, with the two terms being used interchangeably for a decade. Some plans were offered with one of each, suggesting recognition that they served different purposes, and it was not yet time to abandon the functions of the parlor.

The interior plan of the square house represents a clear marker of the move from Victorian domestic practices to the modern ones of the bungalow era. Once the requirement for a mini-

Figure 16. McGaffey House, Albuquerque, New Mexico, 1904. A vestigial turret does not detract from the cubic base form. The chimney style is a local feature. Photograph by Evelyn Montgomery, 2012.

mal façade reading of squareness was met, the interior spatial layout and circulation became a key defining feature of the form. Like the exterior, the refinement of the plan was gradual and began with those late Victorian examples. In Radford's plan 511 a circular interior access pattern was already present, with a gathering of five doors giving access to four important rooms (Figure 14). The kitchen remained less accessible in the back. As the plan modernized, the kitchen moved forward and became ever more connected to the other rooms, a consequence of fewer servants and the relaxation of the Victorian separation of public and private functions. Upstairs, the minimal, central access space shaped more like a room than a hallway emerged in the front, but a long hall leading to the bathroom in back remained a holdover from older arrangements. It may have helped isolate the small bedroom in the rear, above the kitchen, potentially a servant's room. Hopkins' design also achieved a circular path downstairs, though with that lingering separation of the kitchen (Figure 15). Upstairs, the space-saving effect of the minimal hallway was becoming more evident.

Both of these examples represented a compression of typical middle- and upper-class Victorian spatial usage into a compact form. The processes of entry, of movement of different individuals to spaces of public socializing or cozy private friendship, of the hiding of servants, and of the performance of social and private dining were all difficult to squeeze in to a small footprint. Reducing circulation was necessary, but the new plan conflicted with more slowly changing social practices. That clash began inside the front door, where Victorians used the formal entry hall to separate strangers and outsiders from the social equals and confidants of the family.[51] American domestic architecture reflected increased interest in formal entry sequences in the colonial period.[52] The Victorians perfected such ideas and overlaid the architectural strategies with a complex system of etiquette.

Bungalow philosophy plainly articulated the rejection of this Victorian ideal. Only friends entered the equitable world of the bungalow family. Stickley said it was "much more friendly, home-like and comfortable to have one big living room into which one steps directly from the entrance door" without a mediating space.[53] Henry L. Wilson, the self-proclaimed "Bungalow Man," offered some plans with reception halls in 1910, but preferred entry directly into living rooms. Bungalows were no place for "[t]he straight, cold entrance hall and the stiff, prim, usually darkened parlor."[54] The placement of bedrooms next to public rooms erased the old public/private divide, so that visitors might even catch a glimpse of a bed, an occurrence that, as Edith Wharton explained, would have shocked polite Victorians.[55]

Meanwhile, the square house allowed the option of a Victorian-style separate, formal entry hall, or one that was at least partially, if symbolically, divided from the parlor or living room by a columned screen. Later examples increasingly replaced the two front rooms with a single double-square space across the front, using a common bungalow form that offered "an impression of generous hospitality" and proclaiming the triumph of informal entry.[56]

The rejection of the entry hall was not as quick as that of the parlor, and sometimes strenuously resisted. In 1917 Aymar Embury II, a prolific commentator on domestic matters, still saw the reception hall favorably as "a coldly formal place where not too desirable guests are received, to be gotten rid of as soon as possible."[57] Margaret Greenleaf agreed, arguing that "for the stranger within our gates a less intimate place of waiting is more desirable," than the living room or a minimally segregated front hall.[58] The bungalow's vaunted openness was only a relaxation of social rules among friends, not an erasure of class-based behavior. A 1905 article in *Keith's Magazine* presented two illustrations of entry halls. Both the design praised as "the Right Thing" and the one derided as "the Wrong Thing" served the traditional entry function. The only problem with the latter was that it was fussy and outdated with Victorian textiles engulfing every surface.[59]

The center hall as a desirable form appeared in the colonial era to mark those who were more successful and refined than dwellers in compact, modest houses where visitors entered directly into the center of family life and household work.[60] The convenient and impressive center hall became a staple element of superior domestic design and was a key element of Georgian houses. It became a marker of class and refined manners. As the 1800s progressed, the Victorians hardened etiquette, dress, furnishings, and various strict rules of social association into a shield against the dangers of outsiders, pretenders, and social inferiors.[61] Victorian or modern, the small homes on fifty-foot lots of the streetcar suburbs did not have room for a center hall. The side location in smaller Victorian houses was a practical accommodation made for the compact plan. Such entries might be narrow, but they gave the right notice of their mediating purpose while presenting decorative signs of means and taste.

The standard late Victorian formal entry hall did not serve private, domestic purposes. It was not where the family lived, only where they met the public. Some Victorian houses offered an alternative: the living hall. As described by Vincent Scully, a living hall was a stylistic choice drawing on a more distant and romanticized past, where the hall was a center of domestic and social life in a castle. The Victorian version was a pale allusion, "too big for a circulation area, too small for a living space."[62] It ideally included a symbolic fireplace, elaborate woodwork, and such domestic markers as a bookcase and a seat for reading. Whether or not the family actually used it for such purposes was immaterial; it was above all a fashion statement. It belonged in larger shingle or stick style homes rather than squeezed into a narrow-lot house, but square house owners could hope to introduce other uses to a room that occupied a fourth of the lower level. Two such homeowners inquired of the advisers at *Keith's Magazine*. One wished to use the hall as a parlor, and was told by the interior design columnist that it could never achieve the character required of a parlor.[63] The other wanted to use the hall as a library and install doors to close it off from the rest of the house, an idea that was similarly rejected.[64] The letters' authors could have found support in the pages of *Beautiful Homes*, which praised a hall put to multiple uses, including a library.[65]

Clearly even the experts held varying opinions, which did not stop advice seekers from asking about what finishes, paint colors, and furniture were most correct for their square houses, with a clear fear of making an embarrassingly visible mistake. The timidity of occupants of square houses in choosing their own way to occupy their homes highlights the continuation of Victorian fears of decorative missteps. One regular advertiser in *Keith's Magazine* played upon social insecurities about masculinity, success, and domesticity with cartoons suggesting that renting was a negative social marker. By building a correct home of his own, a man could capture the affections of his true love or ensure his daughter could attend parties with the best of society.[66]

Victorians also maintained circulation separation by means of a rear stairway for servants, to help them remain unseen and avoid interaction. Household help was a domestic luxury that was increasingly unavailable after 1900, causing the period obsession with convenient arrangement as a necessity for the tired housewife. Dual staircases appear in very few published square house plans. In her study of 319 square houses in Illinois, Anita M. Schertz found only two with a second stair.[67] An extant example available for study is the Costello House, from the upscale suburb of Highland Park, Texas. Built in 1912, the house is large at 2,100 square feet, and extremely well appointed. Its reception hall includes the requisite stately stairway in dark wood. The rear service stairway is only five feet behind (Figure 17). It is distinguished by narrower width. It would have provided a less obtrusive route from the kitchen to the bedrooms above for the household staff, but the two staircases' proximity suggests that its function was at least partially symbolic.

The granddaughter of original owner Mary Costello remembers the rear stairway well, as it was the only one allowed for use by servants and children.[68] They were also restricted to the back door. She remembers her grandmother as extremely concerned with proper behavior and self-presentation in neatness, manners, and furniture. Neither her husband's modest wealth nor their status as second-generation Irish Americans would have made them socially secure in Highland Park.[69]

John Henry Newson included rear stairways in a few plans in his 1913 *Homes of Character*. Newson considered them necessary, but wasteful of valuable floor space.[70] A common substitute arrangement was a split stairway. Two lower portions, one from the entry and one from the rear service zone, met at a landing and continued on a single upper portion. This space-saving option was described as a way to maintain privacy, a coded word suggestive of the need to keep servants' activities away from family and guests.[71] It could also be seen as a tool for the servantless housewife. The Gordon–Van Tine Company offered a split stair that the housewife would appreciate for "the great number of steps saved."[72] The rear stair was another Victorian feature that disappeared or adapted to changing needs.

The square house was a work in progress during an era dominated by the faddish bungalow. Its creators—architects, local builders, domestic advisers and critics, and residents—did not give it a clear name. Instead, they explored its many possibilities. Big or small, fancy or plain, the core of a late Victorian home evolved into a modern home, capable of meeting the needs of American middle-class life after 1900. Along the way, it also met the needs of those for whom the rush to modernity was just too fast. When more romantic, less geometric styles came into fashion by 1930, they made the square house outdated. During the bungalow era, *Beautiful Home* magazine and the J. D. Loizeaux Lumber Company both published plans to convert an older house into a modern square house.[73] Then in 1959, *Popular Home* magazine published a modernization plan for a square house, removing the wall between the parlor and dining room and adding a family room and playroom to the back (Figure 18).[74]

Many square houses suffered through mid-twentieth-century periods of disinvestment and division into rental units. Those that survived are frequent objects of preservation efforts, often in designated historic districts, where they become valued as expensive products in today's consumer marketplace. Such resurgences in Indianapolis'

Figure 17. Upstairs view of staircases in Costello House, Dallas, Texas. The rear servants' staircase is on the right and is narrower. The main staircase, on the left, begins on the lower floor in the entry hall, while the servants' is closer to the kitchen. Photograph by Fred Hight, 2016.

Meridian Park and Dallas' Munger Place prove the house's lasting appeal and ability to meet changing domestic needs. Some renovated examples use a fully open interior plan to meet current living and entertaining needs or have been expanded to the back to create open family rooms, large kitchens, and giant master suites. The square house has been adapted for over a century to meet changing expectations of the performance of domestic life, spatial uses, stylistic preferences, and the etiquette of welcoming

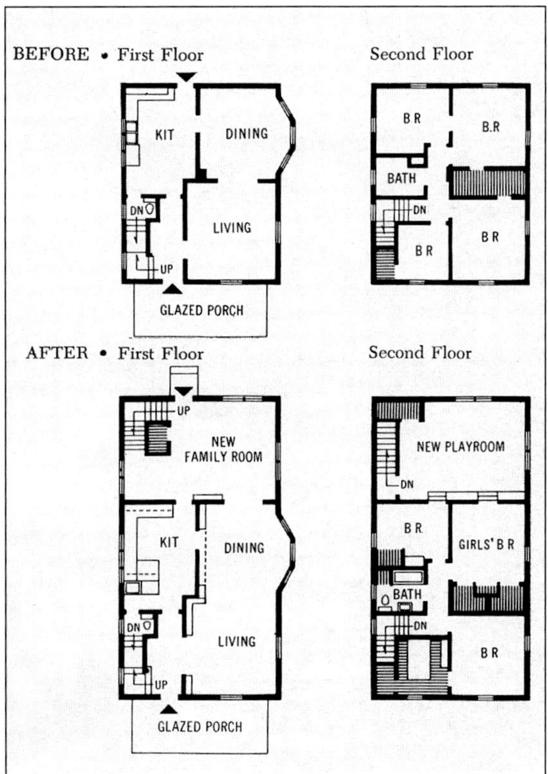


Figure 18. Before and after plans show how the renovation of this square house in the 1950s changed the lower-level spatial usage. Illustrations depict the new rooms in the latest postwar styles, with family members enjoying the idealized domestic life of the era. *Popular Homes* (no publishing information, November–December 1959). Author's collection.

visitors. Its versatility is the basis of its wide and lasting appeal to consumers.

AUTHOR BIOGRAPHY

**Evelyn Montgomery** is the Director of Curatorial Affairs at Dallas Heritage Village, an accredited outdoor museum that preserves and interprets vernacular structures from north central Texas. Her research interests focus on American houses and domestic practices in the Victorian period and the twentieth century.

NOTES

The author would like to thank Anna Andrzejewski, Cynthia Falk, Carl Lounsbury, and peer reviewers for their comments on the development of this paper. Virginia McAlester and Kenneth Hafertepe have offered invaluable encouragement. Thomas Hubka was instrumental in helping ready the article for publication.

1. "How Others Have Built," *The Indianapolis Star*, July 24, 1910, 4, Women's Section.

2. "How Others Have Built," 4.

3. The form is included, sometimes briefly and sometimes extensively, in both scholarly and popular sources on American houses. Scholarly works include: Clifford Clark, *The American Family Home, 1800–1960* (Chapel Hill: University of North Carolina Press, 1986); Alan Gowans, *The Comfortable House: North American Suburban Architecture 1890–1930* (Cambridge, Mass.: MIT Press, 1986); David P. Handlin, *The American Home: Architecture and Society, 1815–1915* (Boston: Little, Brown and Co., 1979); and Virginia Savage McAlester, *A Field Guide to American Houses*, rev. ed. (New York: Alfred A. Knopf, 2013). Popular works include John Milnes Baker, *American House Styles: A Concise Guide* (New York: W. W. Norton, 1993); John J. G. Blumenson, *Identifying American Architecture: A Pictorial Guide to Styles and Terms, 1600–1945* (New York: W. W. Norton, 1981); Rachel Carley, *A Visual Dictionary of American Domestic Architecture* (New York: Henry Holt, 1994); Mary Mix Foley, *The American House* (New York: Harper and Row, 1980); Gerald Foster, *American Houses: A Field Guide of the Home* (Boston: Houghton Mifflin, 2004); Philip Langdon, *American Houses* (New York: Stewart, Tabori & Chang, 1987); James C. Massey and Shirley Maxwell, *House Styles in America* (New York: Penguin, 1996); William Morgan, *The Abrams Guide to American House Styles* (New York: Harry N. Abrams, 2004); Lester Walker, *American Shelter*, rev. ed. (Woodstock, N.Y.: Overlook Press, 1997). Some authors have also offered alternative names for the form, such as cornbelt cube, Denver box, and American basic, which offer reference to the common use of the form in rural areas. These include Robert Schweitzer and Michael W. R. Davis, *America's Favorite Homes: Mail-Order Catalogues as a Guide to Popular Early 20th-Century Houses* (Detroit: Wayne State University Press, 1990), 161; Allan G. Noble, *Wood, Brick, and Stone* vol. 1: Houses (Amherst: University of Massachusetts Press, 1984), 125; John A. Jakle, Robert W. Bastian, and Douglas K Meyer, *Common Houses in America's Small Towns, the Atlantic Seaboard to the Mississippi Valley* (Athens: University of Georgia Press, 1988), 141. Graduate theses have also examined the form; see Thomas W. Hanchett, "The Four Square House Type in the United States" (master's thesis, University of Chicago, 1982), parts of which later appeared as an abstract in *Perspectives in Vernacular Architecture I*, ed. Camille Wells (Columbia: University of Missouri Press, 1987), 51–53; Carol Grove, "The Foursquare House Type in American Vernacular Architecture" (master's thesis, University of Missouri-Columbia, 1992); and Anita M. Schertz, "A Historic Study of American Foursquare: Implications for Historic Preservation" (master's thesis, Illinois State University, 1989). The Midwestern location of all three schools where this work was done may not be a coincidence, given the square house's strong presence in that region.

4. Grant McCracken, *Culture and Consumption, II* (Bloomington: Indiana University Press, 2005), 28.

5. "The Architect's Corner," *Keith's Magazine on Home Building* 37, no. 4 (April 1917): 296.

6. John Henry Newson, *Homes of Character* (Cleveland: John Henry Newson Company, 1913), 205–6. Newson also offered one square exterior with two plan options.

7. Milton Dana Morrill, "A Standard House Built of Concrete," *Keith's Magazine on Home Building* 39, no. 5 (May 1918): 293–4.

8. Jan Jennings, Cheap and Tasteful Dwellings: Design Competitions and the Convenient Interior, 1879–1909 (Knoxville: University of Tennessee Press, 2005), 172.

9. *Inexpensive Homes of Individuality* (New York: McBride, Winston & Co., 1911), 63.

10. Hewitt-Lea-Funck Co., *Prize Plan Book* (Seattle, Wash.: Hewitt-Lea-Funck Co., 1914), 53; *Gordon–Van Tine Homes* (Davenport, Iowa: Gordon–Van Tine Co., 1917), 33.

11. *Ideal Homes* (Spokane, Wash.: A. L. Porter and W. J. Ballard, ca. 1914), 5.

12. Hewitt-Lea-Funck Co., *Prize Plan Book*, 10.

13. "Home Building, " *Midwestern Magazine* 3, no. 2 (October 1908), 26; quoted in James E. Jacobsen, "Des Moines Residential Growth and Development, 1900–1942; The Bungalow and Square House," National Register of Historic Places Multiple Property listing, section E, 47 (Des Moines: History Pays, 2000). Mr. Jacobsen's work is one of the more nuanced investigations of the form.

14. I. Farrington, "Giving Character to a Square House," *Keith's Magazine on Home Building* 29, no. 4 (April 1913): 250–52.

15. Suzanne T. Rollins, "Meridian Park Historic District," National Register of Historic Places Inventory/Nomination Form, sec. 8, 4 (Indianapolis: Historic Landmarks Foundation of Indiana, 1989).

16. Rollins, "Meridian Park Historic District," sec. 7, 3.

17. This information was derived from field research in Indianapolis, period articles in the *Indianapolis Star*, Indianapolis Sanborn maps, and resident information from *R. L. Polk & Co.'s Indianapolis City Directory*, vols. 55–62 (Indianapolis: R. L. Polk and Co., 1909–1916).

18. "Result of a Salesman's Dreams of a Home, " *The Indianapolis Star*, August 31, 1913, 12.

19. See *Munger Place, Dallas, Texas*, by Aldredge & Knight, Munger Place Real Estate, originally published in 1905 and held in both original and reprinted versions by the Dallas History and Archives collection of the Dallas Public Library.

20. Richard L. Bushman, *The Refinement of America: Persons, Houses, Cities* (New York: Knopf, 1992).

21. See Lizabeth A. Cohen, "Embellishing a Life of Labor: An Interpretation of the Material Culture of American Working-Class Homes, 1885–1915," in *Common Places: Reading in American Vernacular Architecture*, ed. Dell Upton and John Michael Vlach (Athens: University of Georgia Press, 1986). Primary source information includes the photographs published by Jacob Riis in *How the Other Half Lives* taken in the 1880s. Many images of the apartments of impoverished New Yorkers include small decorative touches, such as hand-cut shelf frills or outdated furniture pieces such as a sideboard, enjoying pride of place.

22. See Regina Lee Blaszczyk, *American Consumer Society, 1865–2005: From Hearth to HDTV* (Wheeling, Ill.: Harlan Davidson, 2009); Susan Strasser, *Satisfaction Guaranteed: The Making of the American Mass Market* (Washington, D. C.: Smithsonian Institution Press, 1989), and various articles in *Consuming Visions: Accumulation and Display of Goods in America, 1880–1920*, ed. Simon J. Bronner (Winterthur, Del.: Henry Francis du Pont Winterthur Museum, 1989).

23. Thomas Hanchett credits Lewis with creating an ideal example of the square house admirer, Will Kennicott, the small-town doctor in *Main Street*, who values its visible stability and promise of a functional, modern heating system. See Hanchett, *The Four Square House in the United States*, 70.

24. The influence of magazines on consumers is well documented in Ellen Gruber Garvey, *The Adman in the Parlor: Magazines and the Gendering of Consumer Culture, 1880s to 1910s* (New York: Oxford University Press, 1996) and Jennifer Scanlon, *Inarticulate Longings: The Ladies' Home Journal, Gender, and the Promises of Consumer Culture* (New York: Routledge, 1995).

25. Clarence Cook, *The House Beautiful* (New York: Dover, 1995, reprint of the original, New York: Scribner, 1881), 16.

26. Herbert Gottfried and Jan Jennings, *American Vernacular Buildings and Interiors, 1870–1960* (New York: W. W. Norton, 2009), 28.

27. Daniel Miller, *Material Culture and Mass Consumption* (Oxford: Blackwell Publishers, 1994), 128; Henry Glassie, *Vernacular Architecture* (Bloomington: Indiana University Press, 2000), 70.

28. John Fiske, *Understanding Popular Culture* (London: Routledge, 2010), 11.

29. Many scholars have discovered different aspects of the strong Victorian association between the house and home and the character, morality, and social standing of respectable citizens. See Alan Gowans, *Images of American Living: Four Centuries of Architecture and Furniture as Cultural Expression* (Philadelphia: J. B. Lippincott, 1964), 287, and Mike Hepworth, "Privacy, Security

and Respectability: The Ideal Victorian Home," in *Ideal Homes: Social Change and Domestic Life*, ed. Tony Chapman and Jenny Hockey (London: Routledge, 1999), 17–29. Also see Asa Briggs, *Victorian Things* (Chicago: University of Chicago Press, 1988); Jan Cohn, *The Palace or the Poorhouse: The American House as a Cultural Symbol* (East Lansing: Michigan State University Press, 1979); Ann Douglas, *The Feminization of American Culture* (New York: Noonday Press, 1998); Harvey Green, *The Light of the Home: An Intimate View of the Lives of Women in Victorian America* (New York: Pantheon, 1983); Steven Mintz, *A Prison of Expectations: The Family in Victorian Culture* (New York: New York University Press, 1985); Marilyn Ferris Motz and Pat Browne, *Making the American Home: Middle-Class Women and Domestic Material Culture, 1840–1940* (Bowling Green, Ohio: Bowling Green State University Popular Press, 1988); Linda E. Smeins, *Building an American Identity: Pattern Book Homes & Communities, 1870–1900* (Walnut Creek, Calif.: Altamira Press, 1999); Gwendolyn Wright, *Moralism and the Model Home: Domestic Architecture and Cultural Conflict in Chicago, 1873–1913* (Chicago: University of Chicago Press, 1980).

30. See Thomas C. Hubka, *Houses Without Names: Architectural Nomenclature and the Classification of America's Common Houses* (Knoxville: University of Tennessee Press, 2013).

31. Franklin Boyd, "The Psychology of the Bungalow," *Keith's Magazine on Home Building* 41, no. 4 (April 1919): 170–71.

32. Mable Seares, "Here Are Some Excellent Examples of the Bungalow Habit," *Beautiful Homes* 1, no. 1 (October 1908): 14–15, 24.

33. Clay Lancaster, *The American Bungalow, 1880–1930* (New York: Dover, 1995), 239.

34. Scott Erbes explores the practical and imagistic arguments used to promote the bungalow in "Manufacturing and Marketing the American Bungalow: The Aladdin Company, 1906–1920," in *The American Home: Material Culture, Domestic Space, and Family Life*, ed. Eleanor McD. Thompson (Winterthur, Del.: Henry Francis du Pont Winterthur Museum, 1998), 45–69.

35. *Roberts Home Builder* (Portland, Ore.: Roberts & Roberts, Architects, 1910).

36. *A Book of Wildwood Plans* (Fort Wayne, Ind.: The Wildwood Builders Company, 1912), 17.

37. Gowans, *Images of American Living*, 287.

38. For various interpretations of this phenomena, see Richard Guy Wilson, Shaun Eyring, and Kenny Marotta, eds., *Recreating the American Past: Essays on the Colonial Revival* (Charlottesville: University of Virginia Press, 2006).

39. Earle's voluminous output gave mass readers access to history and a desire to bring trappings of the past into their own daily lives. Nutting's pictorial efforts romanticized colonial houses and rooms and popularized colonial antiques. See Susan Reynolds Williams, *Alice Morse Earle and the Domestic History of Early America* (Amherst: University of Massachusetts Press, 2013) and Thomas Andrew Denenberg, *Wallace Nutting and the Invention of Old America* (New Haven: Yale University Press, 2003), as well as original works by Earle and Nutting.

40. Cohn, *The Palace or the Poorhouse*, x.

41. Gowans, *The Comfortable House*, 87.

42. James C. Massey and Shirley Maxwell, "The All-American Family House: A Look at the Foursquare," *Old House Journal* 23, no. 6 (November–December 1995): 31.

43. Paul Diebold, *Greater Irvington: Architecture, People and Places on the Indianapolis Eastside* (Indianapolis: Irvington Historical Society, 1997), 71; Alan Gowans, *Styles and Types of North American Architecture* (New York: HarperCollins, 1993), 206.

44. See Joseph C. Bigott, *From Cottage to Bungalow: Houses and the Working Class in Metropolitan Chicago, 1869–1929* (Chicago: University of Chicago Press, 2001).

45. Daniel Joseph Singer, "Towards a Definition of American Modernism," *American Quarterly* 39, no. 1 (Spring 1987): 10.

46. Michael Ann Williams and M. Jane Young, "Grammar, Codes, and Performance: Linguistic and Sociolinguistic Models in the Study of Vernacular Architecture," in *Gender, Class, and Shelter: Perspectives in Vernacular Architecture V*, ed. Elizabeth Collins Cromley and Carter L. Hudgins (Knoxville: University of Tennessee Press, 1995), 41.

47. Newson, *Homes of Character*, 23, 25.

48. Peggie Phipps Boegner and Richard Gachot, *Halcyon Days: An American Family Through Three Generations* (New York: Harry N. Abrams, 1987), 114.

49. *Wildwood Plans*, 23.

50. The Victorians codified a movement toward stricter public behavior, which was made manifest

in domestic design. See Bushman, *The Refinement of America,* and Katherine C. Grier, *Culture & Comfort: Parlor Making and Middle-Class Identity, 1850–1930* (Washington, D.C.: Smithsonian Institution Press, 1997).

51. Kenneth Ames, *Death in the Dining Room and Other Tales of Victorian Culture* (Philadelphia: Temple University Press, 1992), 8.

52. See in particular Robert Blair St. George, "'Set Thine House in Order': The Domestication of the Yeomanry in Seventeenth-Century New England," in *New England Begins: The Seventeenth Century,* ed. Jonathan L. Fairbanks and Robert F. Trent, vol. 2 (Boston: Museum of Fine Arts, 1982), 159–88.

53. Gustav Stickley, *Craftsman Homes and Bungalows* (New York: Skyhorse Publishing, 2009), 198.

54. Henry L. Wilson, *The Bungalow Book* (Chicago: Henry L. Wilson, 1910), 3.

55. In *The Age of Innocence,* polite society is shocked by a doyen who not only has a downstairs bedroom but leaves the door open. Edith Wharton, *The Age of Innocence* (New York: Grosset and Dunlap, 1920), 26.

56. Hewitt-Lea-Funck Co., *Prize Plan Book,* 10.

57. Aymar Embury II, "The House Livable: The Living-Rooms," *Countryside Magazine and Suburban Life* 24, no. 4 (April 1917): 190. Jan Jennings suggests that architects and millwork producers joined domestic advisers in promoting the continued use of the reception hall. See *Cheap and Tasteful Dwellings,* 172.

58. Margaret Greenleaf, "Treatment of Reception Halls," *Keith's Magazine on Home Building* 28, no. 6 (December 1912): 410–11.

59. "An Entrance, and Within," *Keith's Magazine on Home Building* 14, no. 4 (October 1905): 231.

60. See Dell Upton, "Vernacular Domestic Architecture in Eighteenth-Century Virginia," in *Common Places: Readings in American Vernacular Architecture,* ed. Dell Upton and John Michael Vlach (Athens: University of Georgia Press, 1986), 315–35.

61. Karen Halttunen describes the evolution and perceived need for such behaviors in *Confidence Men and Painted Women: A Study of Middle-Class Culture in America, 1830–1870* (New Haven, Conn.: Yale University Press, 1986).

62. Vincent J. Scully Jr., *The Shingle Style and the Stick Style,* rev. ed. (New Haven: Yale University Press, 1971), 73.

63. "Answers to Questions on Interior Decoration," *Keith's Magazine on Home Building* 14, no. 1 (July 1905): 43.

64. "Architect's Corner," *Keith's Magazine on Home Building* 14, no. 3 (September 1905): 210.

65. "Hall in This Shingle House Used as Room," *Beautiful Homes* 1, no. 12 (August 1909): 7.

66. These cartoons are untitled and signed only by the anonymous "Keith's cartoonist." See *Keith's Magazine on Home Building* 23, no. 3 (March 1910): 212, 228; *Keith's Magazine on Home Building* 23, no. 4 (April 1910): 300, 315. The real estate industry joined in this effort to equate respectability with ownership; see Jeffrey M. A. Hornstein, *Nation of Realtors: A Cultural History of the Twentieth-Century American Middle Class* (Durham, N.C.: Duke University Press, 2005), 121.

67. Schertz, "A Historic Study of the American Foursquare," 86.

68. Author's interview with Mary Francis Costello Johnson at Dallas Heritage Village, November 26, 2016.

69. The house is now part of Dallas Heritage Village, relocated to save it from demolition. Highland Park is an independent city within Dallas, originating as a wealthy and socially elite suburb. See Virginia McAlester, Willis Cecil Winters, and Prudence Mackintosh, *Great American Suburbs: The Homes of the Park Cities, Dallas* (New York: Abbeville Press, 2008).

70. Newson, *Homes of Character,* 186.

71. Hewitt-Lea-Funck Co., *Prize Plan Book,* 80.

72. *Gordon–Van Tine Homes,* 117.

73. Mary Hale Lafon, "Store Room Converted into Pretty Home," *Beautiful Homes* 1, no. 3 (December 1908): 9; *Loizeaux's Plan Book No 7* (Plainfield, N.J.: J. D. Loizeaux Lumber Company), 177.

74. *Popular Home* was a small magazine published for local businesses to distribute to customers with their own name and advertisement on the front and back covers. The referenced copy of the November–December 1959 issue came from the Wynnewood Glidden Paint Center in Dallas.

MARISA GOMEZ NORDYKE

# Restyling the Postwar Prefab

*The National Homes Corporation's Revolution*

*in Home Merchandising*

ABSTRACT

In the late 1940s, American builders found themselves competing against a growing number of prefabricated housing manufacturers in a race to meet demand for detached, single-family homes in the suburbs. The National Homes Corporation of Lafayette, Indiana, and its competitors were pioneering the mass manufacture of room-sized panels that could be shipped by truck to the building site and assembled by unskilled workers. Although the production experience prefabricators gained during the war made the factory-built home's peacetime success seem certain, they were met with skeptical consumers. National Homes propelled itself to the top of the prefab industry with a three-pronged campaign aimed at banks, builders, and buyers. Advertising for National Homes, which ran in nationally circulating financial publications, building trade journals, and consumer magazines, reveals prefabricators' struggle to gain traction in a competitive housing market and sheds light on the shift within the building industry from the production of standardized economy dwellings in the 1940s to individualized homes offering the latest design trends and custom features in the 1950s. Analysis of the company's "revolution in home merchandising" enriches our understanding of the competing interests and conflicting values that shaped the postwar housing boom.

In 1946, long before he would win a Pulitzer Prize for his editorials on the U.S. involvement in Vietnam, Robert Lasch made an exciting prediction to the readers of *Popular Science*: "The day is at hand when the American family can go shopping for a house just as it shops for a car or refrigerator. Prefabrication, after fifteen years of false starts and experiment, is about to come into its own."[1] During the housing crisis of the 1930s, and again during the building boom of the postwar years, designs for a prefabricated house offering "better living" for American families that could be built cheaper and faster than conventional construction fascinated the architectural field and drew attention in popular magazines and newspapers nationwide. The prefabricated home promised to raise the standard of living for American families and revolutionize the nation's

antiquated building industry. By the late 1940s, as builders struggled to keep pace with postwar demand for detached, single-family homes in the suburbs, the number of prefabricated housing manufacturers skyrocketed.[2]

For centuries, American builders have striven to simplify the building process in order to maximize materials and lessen the cost of labor. In contrast to conventional building practices, a prefabricated house is one in which the walls, floors, and roof have been mass-produced in a factory and shipped in complete sections to the building site.[3] A critical moment in the history of prefabrication for domestic architecture was George Snow's 1832 balloon frame, which utilized a system of ready-made units to expedite construction.[4] In the second half of the nineteenth century, industrialized technology transformed many building practices. The rise of sash and blind factories, which mass-produced building elements such as doors, windows, mantels, and other woodwork, eliminated the necessity and cost of traditional joinery work on building sites.[5] The standardization of architectural elements exemplified by the balloon frame was taken a step further at the turn of the twentieth century with the introduction of mass-produced, mail-order kits configured from numbered, precut pieces.[6] Yet precut houses like those sold by the Aladdin Company of Bay City, Michigan, Pacific Ready-Cut of Los Angeles, and Sears, Roebuck & Co. still required considerable onsite assembly: wall and roof sheathing as well as subflooring had to be installed; paints, stains, and varnishes applied; and, most arduous, masonry materials for chimncys and fireplaces had to be procured from local suppliers and built onto the frame structure.[7] When the building industry collapsed and compounded the nation's credit crisis in the 1930s, public and private research institutions turned their attention to the development of a fully prefabricated and mass-produced house in earnest. Many saw in prefabrication a solution at a time when the need for quality affordable housing was acute and, in the long term, an opportunity to build a way out of the Depression.[8] Balloon framing, factory-produced architectural components, and precut houses of the nineteenth and early twentieth centuries were all important steps toward complete prefabrication and demonstrate that standardization and mass production of architectural units had, by the postwar period, been a part of American building culture for over a century.

As prefabrication grew by fits and starts in the 1940s, the National Homes Corporation of Lafayette, Indiana, quickly established itself as the "General Motors" of the industry.[9] The company was led by brothers James and George Price. James Price got his start as a builder-dealer for Foster Gunnison's prefabricated housing company, Gunnison Housing Corporation.[10] Competition between the two companies would help fuel the industry's growth in the two decades following the war.

Foster Gunnison was among the pioneers of the prefabrication industry. In 1934, he was brought on by the chairman of the General Electric Company, Owen D. Young, to steer its newly-formed subsidiary—Houses, Inc.—in the effort to develop a commercially viable mass-produced house. Houses, Inc. did not undertake production itself, but rather funded research on prefabricated housing and provided financial backing to upstart manufacturers.[11] Inspired to start a company of his own, Gunnison left Houses, Inc. in 1935, rented a plant in New Albany, Indiana, and founded Gunnison Magic Homes. The company manufactured modest, low-cost houses for middle- and working-class families.

Gunnison initially met resistance from homebuyers. But when the Ohio River flood of 1937 significantly damaged the city's housing stock, the company won a contract to erect twenty homes for the New Albany Housing Authority as part of the relief effort. An additional twenty houses were built conventionally. Gunnison's models compared favorably to the conventional homes in cost, erection time, and design, lending the young company much-needed credibility with local residents. The company soon began marketing its houses to communities throughout Indiana, Ohio, and Kentucky.

The promise of the market for prefabricated homes led former Gunnison executive Donald Lowman to found the National Homes Corporation in 1940. Lowman brought the Price brothers on as dealers and in 1944 James Price took over as president.[12] Under his leadership the company became the nation's biggest producer of factory-built homes. That same year, Gunnison's operation attracted the attention of the U.S. Steel Corporation. Eyeing potential uses for steel in peacetime, U.S. Steel purchased a controlling interest in the company under the belief that the prefabricated housing industry would be a leader in the anticipated postwar building boom. Indeed, Gunnison Homes found significant postwar success, maintaining its status as an industry leader into the 1950s.[13] Yet even with the backing of one of the nation's largest and most powerful corporate monopolies, the company struggled to keep pace with National Homes.

National Homes manufactured room-sized

panels and roof sections that could be shipped by truck to the building site and assembled by unskilled workers. It was not, however, the company's construction system that distinguished it from its competitors. Like Gunnison and, in fact, the majority of postwar prefabricators, National Homes utilized a system of load-bearing "stressed-skin" plywood panels developed by the United States Department of Agriculture (USDA) Forest Products Laboratory (FPL) in the 1930s. FPL experiments with synthetic resins and panels for airplane fuselages during World War I yielded the development of bent plywood and ultimately the stressed-skin panel.[14]

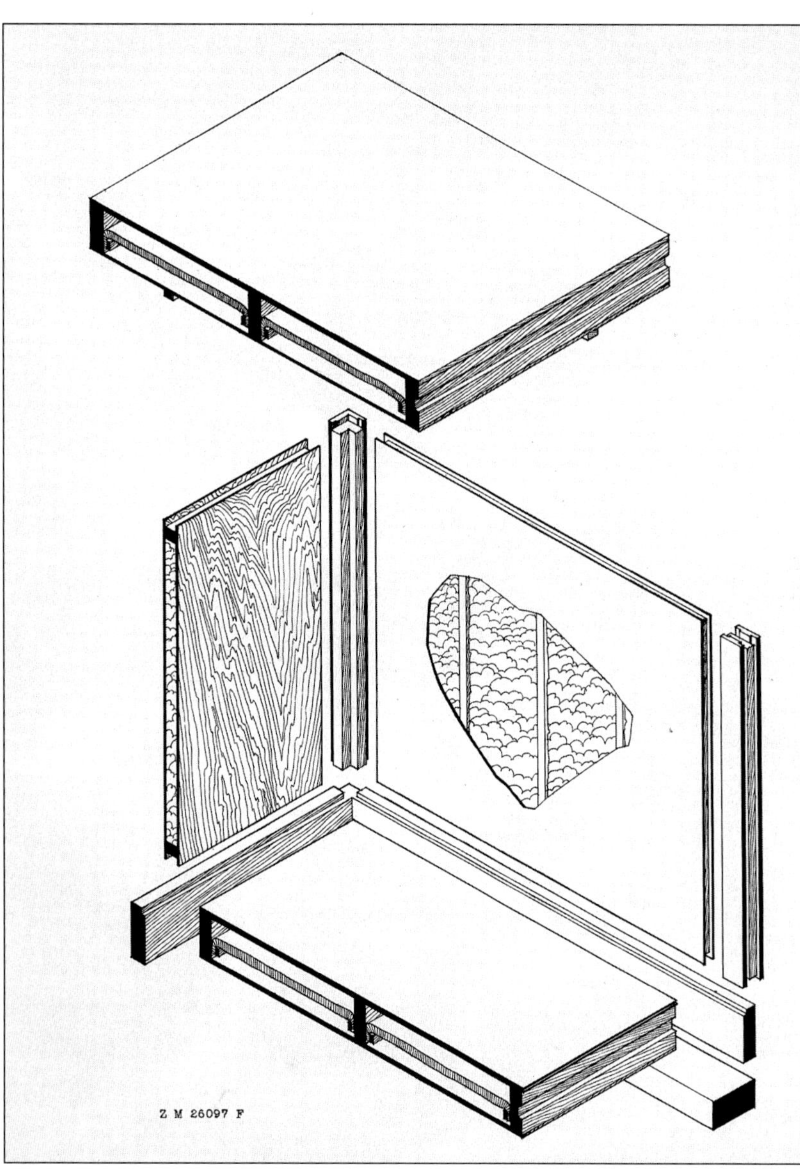



Each four-by-eight foot panel was composed of two standard-sized sheets of plywood glued to a wooden box girder, with a thickness to match stock doorframes (Figure 1). By bonding the plywood to the framing members with glue, rather than nailing it, the panel acted as a single structural unit. Because the plywood sheathing was no longer dead weight, the panels used smaller, more economical framing members than conventional wall construction. In addition, the space between the plywood sheets allowed for electrical wiring and insulation that could be installed in the factory. When compared to traditional frame construction, stressed covering allowed a superior range of strength and rigidity values with a minimum of material.[15] The FPL built several test houses between 1935 and 1937 and aided manufacturers, including Foster Gunnison, in adopting the system. By 1949, an estimated 75 percent of the nation's prefabricated housing manufacturers were utilizing technology originally developed at its laboratory.[16]

Experts agreed that prefabricated panels were structurally superior to conventional construction; stressed technology was stronger, stiffer, and lighter.[17] But unless a prefabricated house could yield cost savings, measure up to conventional aesthetic standards, and offer attractive amenities, the fact that panelized plywood walls offered sturdier construction for a fraction of the material mattered little to homebuyers.[18] In a comprehensive analysis of prefabricated systems in production in 1943, the *Architectural Forum* concluded: "success or failure of the movement is dependent more upon the development of merchandising methods—on which little conclusive experience exists and which is now virtually at a standstill—than upon the technological developments."[19] National Homes' unified marketing campaigns coordinated at the national and local levels proved critical to the company's success, breaking new ground in home merchandising within the prefabricated housing industry and the residential construction industry as a whole. Although the company looked to conventional builders as a model for many of its merchandising strategies, it executed these methods on a scale far larger than that of even the most successful conventional builders. Moreover, the campaigns exemplify prefabricators' struggles to overcome consumer resistance (underpinned by negative experiences of temporary war housing) and steep competition from merchant builders who were themselves developing new and innovative onsite methods to save costs and speed construction.[20]

Advertisements for National Homes, which appeared in industry trade journals, shelter and women's magazines, financial publications, and local newspapers, reveal the company's evolving marketing strategies. Between 1948 and 1960, the company carefully refined its messages in an effort to win the confidence of banks, builders, and buyers. In their design, National Homes' lines reflect an increasing emphasis on amenities and customization characteristic of an era of planned obsolescence. The design and marketing of the houses manufactured by National Homes offers insights into the shifting status of prefabrication within the building and finance industries and sheds light on deeply-held notions of domesticity in postwar American culture.

### Building an Industry

Despite enthusiasm for the factory-built house during the Depression in both the popular press and professional discourse, the prefab industry produced less than ten thousand houses in the 1930s.[21] Prefabricators lacked critical ingredients for commercial success: capital and organization. Large-scale mass production of any product, especially whole houses, required heavy investment upfront on the part of entrepreneurs. They then faced the formidable challenge of marketing, selling, financing, and erecting the houses.

In the 1940s, government contracts for temporary war housing were a boon for prefab housing, moving it out of the stage of experimentation and into that of mass production. The mandate was that war housing be demountable. This favored panelized systems like those produced by National Homes, which could be transported cheaply and erected and disassembled quickly.[22] National Homes won several government contracts, ultimately manufacturing 7,500 houses for army camps and war-plant workers (Figure 2).[23] As the national imagination turned to the postwar

home, the future looked bright for prefabricators in terms of wholesale production. Citing tens of thousands of prefabricated units manufactured for war housing, the *Architectural Forum* declared that "measured by purely quantitative standards, the prefabricated house has arrived."[24] But government contracts for highly standardized minimum dwellings did not prepare manufacturers for open competition in a postwar housing market. The *Forum* questioned prefabrication's ability to meet peacetime needs on a qualitative basis, expressing doubt over the prefab's potential to command consumer appeal: "The present production of military aircraft is no more evidence that the airplane will supplant the auto. In terms of the peacetime housing market, we may be no closer to the manufactured house than we were when the war began."[25] Similar concerns surfaced in the pages of the trade journal *American Builder*. Criticism centered on the fact that while the war provided prefabricators valuable experience in production, it did nothing to test the industry's ability to market and deliver its products.[26]

In many ways, war housing sullied the reputation of prefabricated buildings. Buyers' previous housing experiences may have been the single biggest factor influencing their postwar buying decisions.[27] During the war, some Americans got their first experience of living in a prefabricated dwelling. Much of the temporary housing constructed during the war, prefabricated or not, was hastily built, cramped, and characterized by shoddy, substandard construction. As a result, postwar sales of prefabricated homes made slow gains. Harry H. Steidle, president of the Prefabricated Home Manufacturers Institute (PHMI), laid the blame on "buyer resistance" stemming

Figure 2. Erie Gardens defense housing manufactured by National Homes for workers at the Erie Ordnance Depot, Port Clinton, Ohio, 1940; photograph ca. 1942. Courtesy of Ottawa County Museum, Port Clinton, Ohio.

from the public's perception of prefabricated homes as temporary.[28]

Steidle's assessment was correct. A 1946 *Fortune* magazine survey found only a third of respondents willing to consider living in a prefabricated house, and only if they could get nothing better. When asked what they so disliked about factory-built homes, the most common answers included that prefabs were "not substantial enough," "not strong enough," "not permanent," and "lacked individuality."[29] As Lasch's editorial on the industry in *Popular Science* concluded, if postwar prefabricators were indeed determined to build an industry on the scale of the automobile industry of the 1920s, their chief task must be to convince the public they could produce "sound permanent homes."[30]

The bad taste of wartime prefabrication lingered long on consumers' lips. A 1950 study in the *Journal of Marketing* confirmed *Fortune*'s findings from four years earlier, reporting those surveyed were better acquainted with the disadvantages of prefabs—real or imagined—than with their benefits. Poor construction and quick depreciation along with poor appearance and "too standardized" topped respondents' lists of complaints.[31]

While professional journals like *American Builder* and the *Architectural Forum* evaluated the potential hurdles to the industry's postwar success, the promise of prefabrication became a government mandate under federal Housing Expediter Wilson Wyatt. President Truman charged Wyatt with solving the housing crisis and gave him emergency powers to do so. Among the key pieces of Wyatt's sweeping plan to generate 1.2 million housing units in 1946 and another 1.5 million in 1947 was a recommendation that the government "give vigorous assistance" to manufacturers of prefabricated housing.[32] Wyatt was willing to go as far as extending new companies 100 percent loans if necessary.[33] Lasch predicted that, with Wyatt's help, manufacturers would soon be far out-producing "hammer-and-saw methods."[34] Similar expectations surfaced in an article on "assembly-line homes," which appeared in the *Science News-Letter*: "The factory mass-production methods that so successfully produced giant airplanes, ships and fighting tanks for war are now turning out ready-made homes in increasing numbers for veterans and other home-lovers."[35] The article was so optimistic about prefabrication it even predicted that it would come to dominate the small home field and eventually replace the conventionally-built house altogether.

As it turned out, 1946 to 1947 was a period of boom and bust for the fledgling prefab industry. Upstart manufacturers eager to take advantage of material priorities granted by Wyatt's Veterans' Emergency Housing Act (VEHA) struggled to acquire adequate production facilities and negotiate restrictive local building codes.[36] What's more, they faced sharp criticism from the National Association of Home Builders (NAHB) and others who felt government controls were restricting the potential of the free market to meet demand for low-cost housing. The NAHB was bitterly opposed to what they considered "favoritism" by the government toward manufacturers of a product that had yet to prove its marketability. Furthermore, they claimed that stockpiling supplies for prefabricators aggravated a shortage of materials desperately needed by conventional builders.[37] Wyatt's resignation in November of 1946 seemed to spell doom for an industry only just beginning to gain its footing. Within a month, material priorities extended to prefabricated housing manufacturers were cancelled.[38] The industry was dealt a double blow when the market guarantee established by the VEHA was allowed to expire at the end of 1947.[39]

Meanwhile, the colossal and highly publicized failure of the Lustron Corporation of Columbus, Ohio, undermined public faith in prefabrication.[40] In 1946, Carl Strandlund of the Chicago Vitreous Enamel Product Co. proposed production of fully prefabricated economy houses built with a structural steel frame covered by a skin of enameled steel panels to Housing Expediter Wyatt. Marketed as "the house America has been waiting for," the company projected it could manufacture a whopping thirty thousand houses per year.[41] Wyatt was impressed.[42] Over the next three years, Lustron received $52 million in government loans and an unprecedented guarantee from Wyatt to cover the cost of the first fifteen thousand houses to roll off the assembly line.[43] But the venture seemed doomed from the beginning; Lustron was plagued by production problems, an insufficient dealer network, and slow sales. The company finally managed to get into production in 1948, but lagged far behind production goals and was soon losing a million dollars a month.[44] When the government was forced to foreclose on the company in 1950, Lustron had manufactured only 2,498 houses.[45] Most damaging to the prefabrication industry, the saga had played out in the pages of major newspapers, business magazines, and architectural journals across the country.

As Lustron floundered, conventional builders picked up the slack. The emerging prefab industry was largely unprepared to meet the wartime advances made in the realm of conventional building. Although war-housing contracts propelled the prefab from theory to practice, it was, in fact, conventional builders who capitalized most on their wartime experiences. As the 1944 study *American Housing: Problems and Prospects* concluded, the war had produced the large-scale local builder, not the "big central prefabricator, as had been expected."[46] A shining example was California housing developer David Bohannon, who in 1944 had pioneered new construction practices at San Lorenzo Village on the outskirts of San Francisco. The "California method" brought the assembly line to the building site: an onsite sawmill precut lumber for each house which was assembled into kits, then, like the precut houses pioneered by the Pacific Ready-Cut company at the turn of the century, each kit would be sent to a specific lot for assembly by unskilled workers. The San Lorenzo Village project broke war-housing production records (1,300 houses in just seven months) and caught the attention of merchant builders across the country, including Levitt & Sons of New York.[47]

Postwar builders named the use of power tools, precutting, and preassembly among their top cost-saving measures.[48] Large-volume merchant builders like Fritz Burns on the West Coast and the Levitts in the East fabricated homes onsite by relying on specialized work crews and borrowed assembly techniques from the factory, allowing them to realize projects faster and cheaper than ever before—and on an unprecedented scale.[49] As government support for the prefab industry crumbled and financing for new homes tightened, prefabricators were forced to deploy new tactics to gain traction in an increasingly competitive housing market.[50]

## A Revolution in Home Merchandising

Prefabricators thus emerged from World War II facing even fiercer competition from conventional builders than they had during the Depression. What's more, although war housing provided manufacturers valuable experience in streamlining production and transportation, questions about how to finance and market the prefab house loomed large. The economic success of mass-produced housing depended on a steady flow of orders. In turn, manufacturers needed to be sure their models met Federal Housing Administration (FHA) standards and would be approved by banks for financing. An article for the *Harvard Business Review* noted that many manufacturers, impatient to get into production, had given scant consideration to how they would negotiate "the laborious process of making individual retail sales."[51] Even by 1948, most manufacturers were only beginning to grasp that "tooling up" for sales, not production, was their biggest challenge.[52] The National Homes Corporation soon established itself as an industry leader, swiftly developing a regional network of builder-dealers to handle sales, site preparation, and construction, as well as a mortgage arm to streamline purchasing by offering financing to builders. In what the trade journal *PF: The Magazine of Prefabrication* would later characterize as a "revolution in home merchandising," the company also made marketing and advertising a top priority.[53]

National Homes promised builders a steady supply of materials, easy and efficient assembly, and brand-name recognition that would boost their sales. To ensure rubber-stamped financing for its models, they would need to qualify for FHA-insured loans. In exchange for guaranteeing up to 90 percent of a mortgage, the FHA set standards for materials, structural systems, and design. The government standards were so universally accepted that they often determined eligibility even for a conventional mortgage.[54] FHA regulations were therefore a major influence on the form, style, and marketing of the postwar prefab.

Of five hundred prefabricated systems the FHA examined in 1944, it deemed less than half eligible for insured mortgages.[55] National Homes was among the first manufacturers to secure FHA backing by working with engineers at the Forest Products Laboratory and Purdue University's Housing Research Project to demonstrate its panels met structural requirements. Complying with government standards was a prerequisite to their subsequent success.[56] To support the launch of its line of FHA-approved Thrift Homes in 1948, the company deployed a three-pronged strategy targeting lending institutions, builders, and consumers.

**Winning Favor with Banks and Builders**

A 1951 study found the industry's most successful manufacturers were dividing their advertising efforts between dealer recruitment and establishing approval with financial institutions and investors.[57] Ads targeting banks stressed manufacturers' financial stability and the sound construction of their product. In many ways, the purpose of the ads was to educate banks on prefabrication. Once it had FHA approval, National Homes turned its attention to assuring lending institutions it offered secure investments.

National Homes ran advertorials in the *Wall Street Journal* made to look like news articles, which recounted the company's wartime success and asserted its status as an "undisputed leader" in the housing field.[58] Pointing to the popularity of its Thrift and Super Thrift models, ads boasted National Homes was even outperforming conventional builders. The company's efforts were supplemented by the campaigns of the Prefabricated Home Manufacturers Institute—part of an overall effort to persuade lending institutions to look favorably on the prefabricated house and the industry that manufactured it.[59] As the company gained increasing acceptance among lenders, National Homes turned its attention to recruiting the dealers who would sell and erect its models.

To bolster the claim that its homes would "COST LESS to build" and "yield MORE PROFIT," advertising targeted at builders stressed security, guaranteed sales, and expanding markets (Figure 3).[60] Ads played on builders' anxieties, stressing the uncertainties of a homebuilding industry plagued by shortages of materials and labor. Assessing builders' failure to meet Wyatt's goals for new construction of single-family homes in 1946, *American Builder* blamed "a major bottleneck" in materials supply, but one that might soon ease.[61] Still, costs were high, as materials flowed down a long supply chain from the lumber mill to the job site.[62] Looking ahead to 1947, the forecast was clouded with potential setbacks: "[The] shortage of skilled labor looms as the greatest obstacle to increased building activities in the coming months."[63] In addition, the elimination of wage controls and hints that housing would soon shift from a seller's to a buyer's market promised to compound the problem.[64] Selling a mass-produced, factory-built home that required limited onsite assembly had the potential to help builders combat rising material costs while cutting labor costs, which amounted to roughly a third of the cost of the conventionally-built house.[65]

Advertising intended to recruit dealers for National Homes mused on builders' many woes: "Will the new restrictions on financing get you down? How about shortages of materials? Labor? Home buying prospects who are shopping for bargains?"[66] In response, National Homes offered security, especially to the small builder who built only ten to twenty houses per year. As a large manufacturer that could buy materials in bulk, the company promised to eliminate inventory and purchasing problems and provide a *"steady supply* of houses to erect."[67] Ads for National Homes backed up these promises by continually emphasizing the company's dominant position as the prefabricated housing industry's highest volume producer, running the tagline "Nation's Largest Producers of Prefabricated Homes" at the bottom of ads throughout the early 1950s.

Security also meant quick erection and fewer headaches on the job site. Although the rationalization of onsite fabrication through mechanization and precutting had given conventional builders a considerable edge over their prewar counterparts, close supervision of workers on the building site remained critical to maintaining a low bottom line.[68] National Homes campaigns claimed that erecting prefabs would not only minimize the amount of labor required to build a house, but could reduce material waste by cutting errors in half.[69] Indeed, conventional builders who converted to prefabrication found such promises held up in the field. Chicago-area builder Bob Nixon reported to *House & Home* that building prefabs had improved his workflow by providing workers a reliable schedule and had cut down on goofing off on the job site.[70]

Builders of National Homes would also find security in sales that were, the company claimed, virtually guaranteed. The fact that National Homes led the prefabricated housing industry not just in production but also in direct advertising to consumers became a central feature of ads recruiting builders. In the 1950s, the company's advertisements touted that its models were already "presold" by "the biggest ad campaign in the field."[71] In fact, the "tremendous prestige" of National Homes received far more attention in its advertising than the actual product being manufactured.[72] Beyond the general assurance that its Thrift Homes were "tops in quality, beauty, comfort, value," detailed descriptions of the designs featured in the Thrift and Super Thrift lines were omitted.[73]

Rather than suggesting they offered a product superior in design or construction, National Homes appealed to builders' desire for commercial success, wooing potential dealers with "an ever-increasing market further enhanced by a million-dollar national advertising and promotion program."[74] As an ad for their 1953 line boasted, National homes were sensationally restyled and sensationally *promoted* (Figure 4).[75] The ad went on to list all the major publications the company was currently running campaigns in: *Good Housekeeping, Living for Young Homemakers, McCall's, Fortune, Better Homes & Gardens, Coronet, This Week Magazine,* the *Saturday Evening Post, Newsweek,* and *Life.*

This approach set National Homes apart from other manufacturers of prefabricated housing as well as most conventional builders. While manufacturers typically furnished booklets, catalogs, and sales manuals to their builder-dealers, those whose distribution networks had only a regional reach found national campaigns a waste of their advertising dollars. Although National Homes would not open plants outside the Midwest until 1950, in Horseheads, New York, and 1955, in Tyler, Texas, the company placed ads in national magazines as early as 1947—building brand-name recognition by marketing directly to buyers—and they wanted potential dealers to know it. The company claimed to run more advertising in popular magazines than all other prefabricated housing manufacturers combined (Figure 5).[76]

Figure 3. This National Homes ad recruiting builder-dealers features the company's manufacturing plant rather than a model house and promises increased profits through factory production. *American Builder* 72, no. 3 (March 1950): 197. Courtesy of Simmons-Boardman Publishing Corp.

Figure 4. This ad for the "sensationally restyled" 1953 line boasts of the company's full-color ads running in leading consumer magazines. *American Builder* 74, no. 11 (November 1952):144. Courtesy of Simmons-Boardman Publishing Corp.

Figure 5. As the postwar housing shortage subsided, National Homes promised builders that its regular advertising in popular magazines, nationally-coordinated open houses, and collaboration with architect Charles Goodman would "pre-sell" its models to consumers. *American Builder* 77, no. 3 (March 1955): 91. Courtesy of Simmons-Boardman Publishing Corp.

National Homes' direct marketing to consumers was largely targeted to women, taking advantage of the dramatic rise in subscription rates to home magazines after the war.[77] This strategy was welcomed by builders, who urged the prefab industry to provide promotional materials with less technical detail and more sales appeal for female buyers.[78] National Homes made it clear feminine appeal was a top priority. As one ad proclaimed: "'Sell the *wife*—and you've sold the house!' Every builder knows how true this is."[79] From 1952 on, nearly all of the company's ads carried the *Parents' Magazine* seal, and later the *Good Housekeeping* guarantee (Figure 6). Builders were pleased.[80] One satisfied National Homes dealer explained that "the greatest asset to the small builder is the public acceptance of nationally advertised products. . . . When we advertise, people know the name of our house, even if they have never heard of us."[81] National Homes' marketing program also received accolades in the pages of *House & Home,* which affirmed its national media campaigns were giving the prefabricated house the prestige it had often lacked in the past.[82]

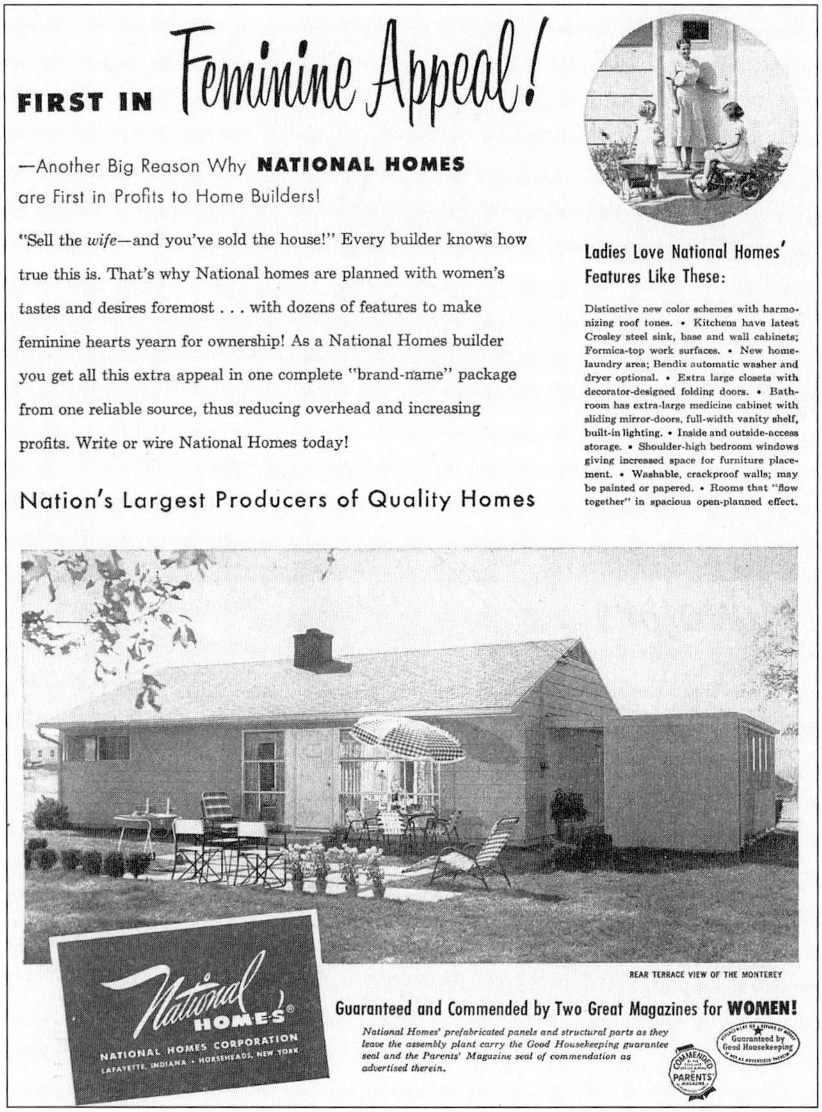

National Homes' consumer-oriented marketing program bolstered claims that the company could offer its dealers guaranteed sales. Even better, the ads claimed, these sales would be transformative for a builders' business. Alongside "Snapshots from the National Homes Album of Progress," which depicted the evolution of the company's models going back to its founding in 1940, copy boasted its sales had topped fifty thousand homes, an impressive figure to even the large-volume merchant builder.[83] Another ad described a "typical" experience of a National Homes dealer: nearly four thousand visitors to a model house opening and thirty-eight homes sold in a single day.[84] In yet another, a sweeping aerial shot of the Mt. Vernon Park subdivision in Fort Wayne, Indiana captured hundreds of newly erected Thrift Homes—convincing proof of the successes that awaited converts to prefabrication.[85]

Although testimonials like these described exceptional cases, many of the benefits of becoming a National Homes dealer the company claimed were legitimate. The final element of advertising to builders focused on helping them reach buyers in new markets. Early campaigns framed the company's Thrift and Super Thrift lines as a way for builders who generally focused on more custom work to break into the booming low-cost market. By the early 1950s, when the worst of the housing crisis was over and builders found themselves looking for ways to sell homes to families who were already adequately housed, National Homes responded by expanding its lines into new price brackets.[86]

Conventional builders had seized on the concept of upward mobility as way to keep sales of new homes strong. As James A. Jacobs has explained,

the industry aimed "to educate and induce millions of American families to trade up to a product, and a life, believed to be of higher quality than what they already enjoyed."[87] Prefabricators, too, recognized the necessity for consumers to "trade up." In addition to leading the prefab industry in both production and direct marketing to consumers, National Homes was in the forefront of the "new trend in Spacious Living."[88] By 1953, the company had moved beyond the minimum dwelling and was offering a "fully diversified housing program."[89] The 1953 National Homes line ranged from two-bedroom economy models of seven hundred to nine hundred square feet priced between $5,000 and $6,100 to "de-luxe" options offering two thousand square feet of indoor-outdoor living space and four bedrooms priced between $12,500 and $17,000.[90]

In the 1950s many builders abandoned conventional construction in favor of prefabrication, while others chose to build both conventionally and with prefabs. Small volume builders, especially, benefited from prefabricators' coordinated advertising campaigns, interim financing options, and architectural design services. Yet sales of prefabricated houses lagged far behind that of conventional homes. For giants of the industry like the Levitts and Kaiser Community Homes, which had the ability to buy materials in bulk at a discounted rate and sophisticated site-fabrication operations, there was little benefit from prefabrication. In either case, the builder was still saddled with the considerable task of grading and preparing the site, as well as coordinating the installation of utilities and construction of streets.[91] By the middle of the decade, only about ten percent of new, non-farm housing starts were prefabricated.[92] More than banks and builders, homebuyers proved to be National Homes' hardest sell.

### Depression-Era Marketing

National Homes' marketing to consumers differed markedly from the prewar promotion of prefabricated houses. In 1933, the model houses featured in the Homes of Tomorrow exhibition at the Century of Progress World's Fair in Chicago presented a synergy of technological progress and modern design in which science and technology made life easier and more elegant. The brochure for the Good Housekeeping Stran-Steel House offered scenes of chicly dressed women excitedly inspecting the home's steel framework and posing in its elegant interiors (Figures 7 and 8). Later, as if to drive home the point the Stran-Steel House would be "a home in which modernism has at last been made livable," the lady of the house is caught luxuriating in a palatial bathtub.[93] In contrast, promotional materials for the American Rolling Mill Company's frameless steel house focused on construction and load-bearing tests. In one photograph, factory assembly is guided by "the glare of the welder's torch," in another, an imposing pair of Percheron draft

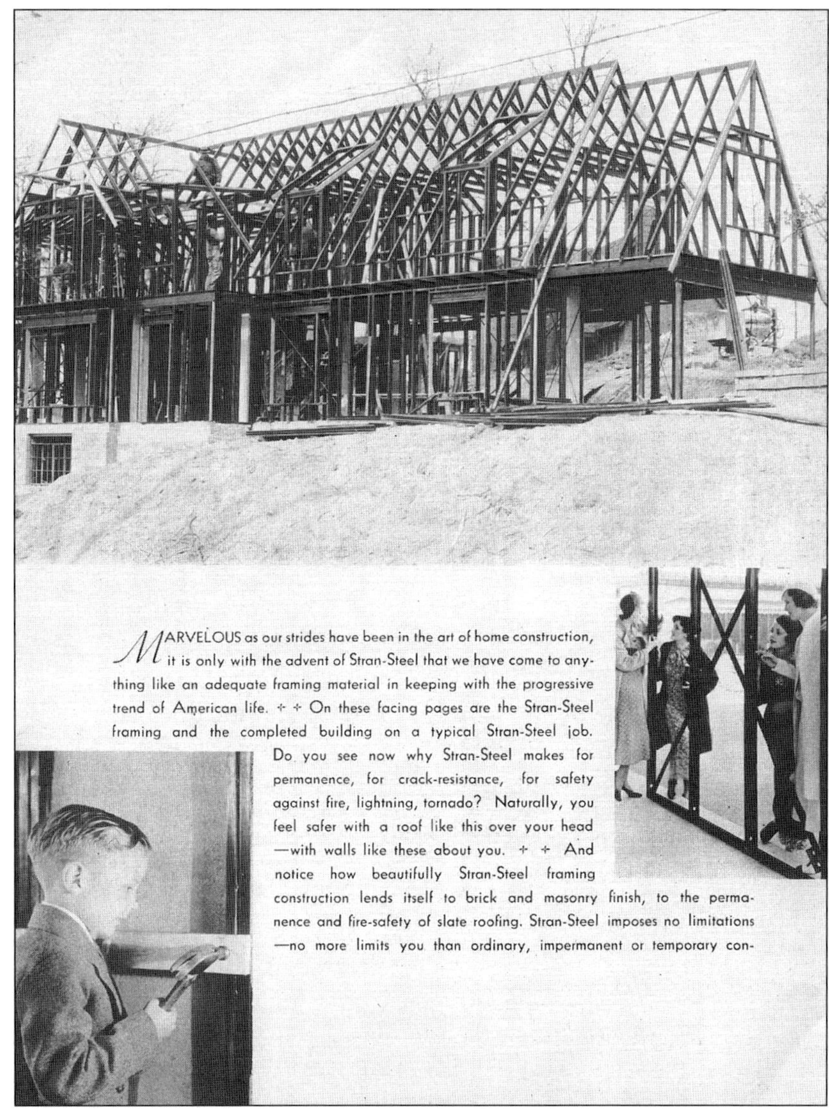



Figure 7. Ladies inspect Stran-Steel framing. *Homes for Modern Living* (Detroit: Stran-Steel Corporation, 1934), n.p. Century of Progress International Exposition Publications, Crerar Ms 226, Special Collections Research Center, University of Chicago Library.

horses have been driven atop a floor panel to demonstrate its strength (Figure 9).[94]

After the Fair, ads for American Houses' Motohome sought to capitalize on prefabrication's novelty by highlighting demountability (Figure 10). Should a family move, they would simply

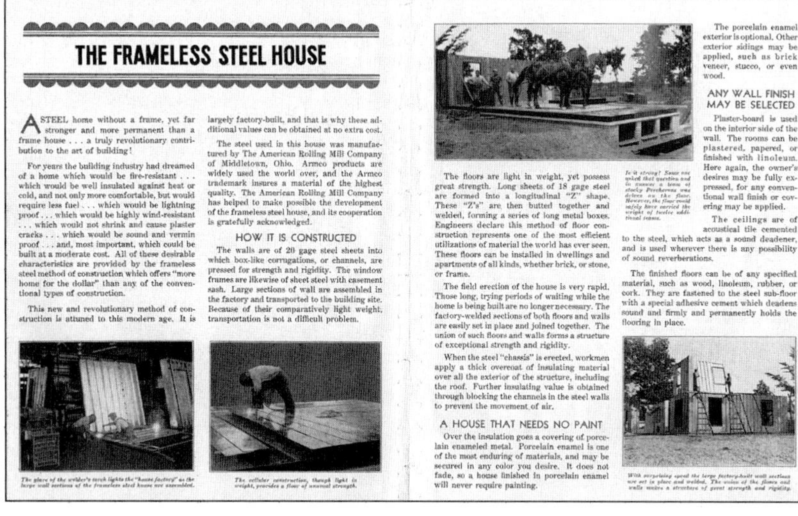

Figure 9. A brochure for the American Rolling Mill Ferro Enamel Steel House features factory assembly of steel wall and floor panels alongside a stunt demonstrating their superior strength. *A New Idea in Home Construction! Frameless Steel* (Cleveland: Insulated Steel, Inc., 1932), np. Century of Progress International Exposition Publications, Crerar Ms 226, Special Collections Research Center, University of Chicago Library.

"unbutton" their home and take it with them. Such outrageous claims were paired with marketing gimmicks executed on a grand scale. Motohome prototypes were staged in department stores across the East Coast.[95] Then, Sarah Delano Roosevelt, mother to the president, presided over an unveiling—or rather an unwrapping, for the model was covered in cellophane—at Wanamaker's New York City store. She dedicated it to the women of America.[96] Homebuyers, however, had difficulty envisioning the Motohome's streamline moderne styling and metal walls in American suburbs teeming with craftsman bungalows and colonial revival cottages.

Like war housing, early promotional efforts ultimately prejudiced the public against the prefabricated house. Looking back on the industry's precarious beginnings three decades on, housing expert Glenn Beyer directly attributed the industry's stalled success to "the fact that the pioneers in prefabricated housing developed designs that were highly controversial and revolutionary."[97] In the 1930s, the novelty of the factory-built house was thought to be its primary selling point. In a complete reversal, postwar manufacturers found themselves reassuring prospective buyers their mass-produced home would be anything but radical.

Lasch assured the readers of *Popular Science* that manufacturers had resolved to make factory-built housing as indistinguishable from conventional homes as possible, "[dedicating] themselves to pitched roofs, fake shutters, window boxes and similar earmarks of the cozy cottage that word 'home' evokes in so many imaginations."[98] Whereas early prefabrication had been characterized by boxy, flat-roofed designs based upon "ruthlessly functional" plans, manufacturers now recognized that "public taste in the mass market responds more heartily to the unsophisticated appeal of Cape Cod and Midwest Colonial."[99] American Houses serves as a pointed example. By 1938, having managed to sell only about a hundred fifty Motohomes, the company dropped the futuristic name and completely reimagined the design. After the war, American Houses was named among the "big three" in the prefabrication business, alongside Gunnison and National Homes. It was by then manufacturing colonial revival cottages constructed with panelized plywood walls and finished with clapboard siding.[100] The prefab of the 1930s, sheathed in novelty and styled for modernity, was reconfigured to meet market realities.

**A Real Home for Real Living**

Although postwar prefabs were made to look like conventional houses, the stigma of the Depression era and war housing was hard to shake. In light of the widely-held belief among consumers that factory-built homes were poorly constructed, temporary, and oppressively standardized, manufacturers were exceptionally hesitant to describe their product as "prefabricated."[101] Builders too avoided the term. Ernest Fritsche, a prominent Ohio builder, admitted that "we are not so cocky *yet* to come out and shout this is a prefabricated house. We point out it has the same materials that go into conventional building." Fritsche described his strategy of continually making comparisons between site fabrication and off-site fabrication to "mellow the sting attached to the word 'prefabrication.'"[102] He aimed to give potential buyers the sense that he was merely a step ahead of old-fashioned, conventional builders. National Homes' overarching strategy was therefore to downplay prefabrication. Language alluding to the industrial origins of its models almost never appeared in the company's consumer-oriented advertising. Instead, ads emphasized quality, durability, and sound investment, assuring consumers a lifetime of security. "A Real Home for Real Living" and "Homes of Superior, Permanent Construction" were favored slogans throughout the 1940s (Figure 11).

Tightly cropped renderings and photographs worked in concert with the ads' reassuring rhetoric, drawing on cultural iconography deeply ingrained in the American conscience. As Dianne Harris has explored, depictions of homes in postwar advertising often drew on conventions dating back to the mid-nineteenth century.[103] Renderings of the Thrift Home depicting tidy landscaping and window boxes brimming with flowers recall the classic Downing cottage (Figure 12). Picturesquely sited in a shady grove, the

Pre-Fabricated Houses, Shipped Direct From Factory, Make Auspicious Debut



The dwelling pictured above may be a typical home of the future, if pre-fabricated houses meet with general public approval, and whole houses may some day be moved from city to city in great vans like that shown below.

THE pre-fabricated house—long a dream in industrial circles—has at last made its bow to the American public. In the east, a number of these ultra-modern dwellings are on exhibition.

Within five years, it has been predicted, a prospective home owner will be able to look over miniature models, choose and order the one he wants, and have his house delivered and set up for him, at a startlingly low price.

In the near future, great factories may be turning out the standardized parts for these houses in large quantities. Each house would be so light and compact that it could be loaded on one big van, carried to its destination and installed, all within a couple of weeks.

The pre-fabricated house may revolutionize the housing industry as the automobile did transportation; it all depends on how the average purchaser reacts to the new type of houses.

One hurdle pre-fabricated houses face is that of appearance. While they offer a variety of de- chine-made, and may lack the individual touch sought by the average homemaker.

On the other hand, mass production permits them to be sold cheaply. And there are other advantages, revealed in the following description of one of the experimental houses on display in New York, one which might very well approximate the Home of the Future.

THIS particular dwelling resembles an ordinary stucco bungalow. Inner and outer walls are panels of composition asbestos cement, with insulation between.

Its flat roof may be used as a sun deck by day. At night, since it is fireproof, comfortable bonfires might even be lit on it.

The house has no cellar. It is to be built on a continuous concrete foundation extending below the frost line, with a three-foot air space between ground and floor.

The inside suggests a suite of modern apartment house rooms. Interiors are fitted with washable fabric covering; closets are cedar lined. Floors are of compressed ates windows of the steel casement type.

ONE of the unusual features of this five-room house is a so-called domestic "moto-unit." Resembling four or five kitchen cabinets stuck together, its gleaming front projects into the kitchen, where it presents to the housekeeper a built-in sink, dishwasher level with sink, laundry tub, electric refrigerator and gas (or electric) range. Above is built-in closet space, indirect lighting, and electric clock.

On the back of the moto-unit is the heavier machinery—water heater, furnace, and an air conditioner that receives the air from outside, washes it, and distributes it, heated or cooled, throughout the house.

There is an exhaust to draw off from the kitchen poisonous cooking vapors. A bathtub, shower, and small lavatory extend from the unit into a bathroom adjoining the kitchen.

The house itself is of steel and aluminum. With a monkey wrench and screw driver, it can be "buttoned up" or "unbuttoned." New parts or additional rooms are simply ordered from the factory, and can be adjusted in double-quick time.

The whole house can be taken apart, transported to some other location, and put together at a slight cost.

It is too early yet to gauge the public response to these "take apart" houses, but if they do become popular, the appearance of the average American town is ev-

Figure 10. This promotional article advertising the American Houses Motohome ran in syndicated newspapers across the country. It promised a fully demountable house that could be disassembled with just a monkey wrench and screwdriver. Originally published in the *Canyon News*, Canyon, Texas, July 4, 1935, 2.

Figure 11. When advertising to consumers, National Homes used the slogans "A Real Home for Real Living" and "Homes of Superior, Permanent Construction" to push back against the popular perception that prefabricated homes were poorly built and temporary. *Better Homes and Gardens* 26, no. 6 (February 1948): 152.

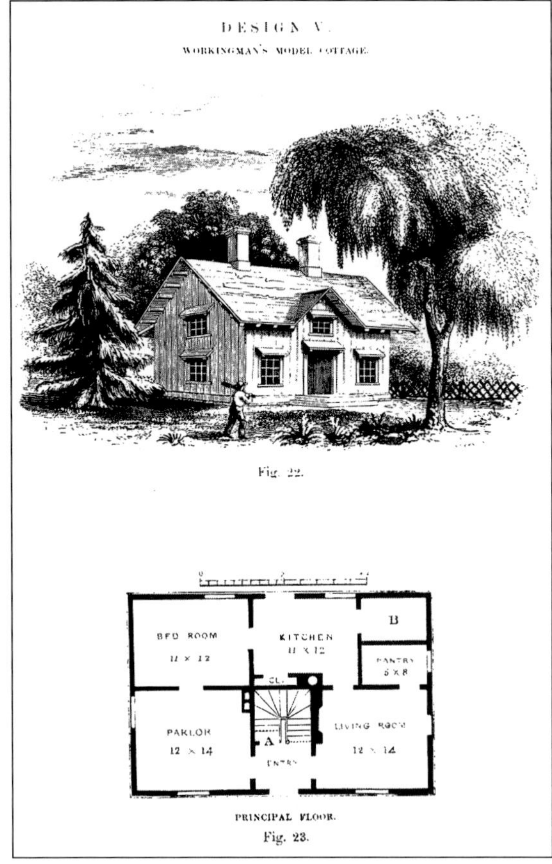

Figure 13. This advertisement for the Thrift Home
implicitly suggests "better living" takes place in nature and
downplays the model's industrial production by picturing
it in a rural setting far from the factory floor. *Better Homes
and Gardens* 27, no. 6 (February 1949): 173.

setting is one of pastoral domesticity. In a 1949
advertisement, which ran in *Better Homes and
Gardens*, the Thrift Home is set on a secluded lot;
a wooded mountainside slopes up from the back-
yard and a creeping vine has begun to overtake
the edge of the garage (Figure 13). By embedding
the prefabricated house in nature, the ad visually
and metaphorically distances it from the factory,
severing it from its industrial origins.

A visual trope favored by National Homes in
the early 1950s pictured a mother and two young
children in the center of the scene (Figure 14).
Gone are the glamorous ladies entertaining in
evening gowns featured in promotional literature of the 1930s. In their place a young mother
stands on the front stoop, lovingly watching her
curly-headed brood amuse themselves with tri-
cycles and baby dolls. The children's faces were
consistently turned away from the camera's gaze,
allowing the prospective buyer to imagine those
of her own children, or future children. In this

way, the ads offered a cheerful and relatable set of images that made the promise of a "real home" for "real living" seem attainable.

No amount of print advertising, however, could substitute for giving prospective homebuyers the chance to inspect the product in person. As manufacturers and dealers sought to normalize the prefabricated house, they drew on the merchandising practices of conventional builders. Merchant builders used model homes to demonstrate high-quality construction, debut new types of plans, and showcase amenities. While speculative builders had been relying on model houses as selling aids since before the war, merchandising the model house grew in importance and sophistication in the postwar period. Much of the trade literature of the period is devoted to staging and styling the model home. Builders relied on models to generate excitement with discriminating second- and third-time homebuyers. Models also served as a sign of professionalism by verifying the builder's credibility.[104] For builders selling prefabs, erecting a model house was a critical part of establishing not only their own credibility, but also the manufacturer's. In fact, manufacturers reported the model house was their dealers' most important selling aid.[105] Buyers liked to see what they were getting before they placed an order, and houses looked more attractive and impressive in person than in photographs. In addition, open houses typically drew large crowds and thus generated favorable publicity. Most importantly, a well-staged model house could go a long way toward overcoming consumer bias and unsettling preconceived notions of "prefabricated" housing.[106]

National Homes provided a slew of selling aids to its dealers to help them promote model house openings, including scripts for television and radio commercials, publicity releases, road signs and pennants to attract traffic, and full-color brochures. In addition, the company offered "complete furniture selections, stylishly done by leading interior decorators to maximize the space and glamorize the room arrangement in the home."[107] National Homes also provided training for builders' sales staff and, if requested, would send in its

Figure 14. In the 1950s, National Homes models became the backdrop for tableaus of wholesome domestic life. *Better Homes and Gardens* 30, no. 11 (November 1952): 49.

own personnel. Visitors would be guided through the house by National Homes "hostesses," stationed at key vantage points to emphasize the best features of the model. At the end of the tour, the sales staff walked prospective buyers through displays featuring additional National Homes models, and "equally important," a community map indicating the location of schools, churches, shopping centers, and offices.[108]

## National Homes and the New Look in Housing

Although its high profile magazine ads set National Homes apart from smaller manufacturers, local newspaper advertising used to promote open houses consumed the majority of dealers' marketing budgets.[109] Builders who erected prefabs as well as those who undertook conventional construction found newspaper advertising proved the best way to reach the greatest number of potential buyers. Before World War II, new homes were generally publicized in traditional classified advertisements that disclosed only the most important features of the house, such as the construction materials and number of rooms. In the postwar era, as newspaper advertising became the primary means by which merchant builders enticed buyers to visit outlying suburbs, ads for new homes took on a new appearance. They increased in size and content and generally included photographs, architectural renderings, and detailed lists of amenities.[110]

National Homes provided dealers with copy and layouts for their ads, thereby crafting a consistent message to buyers at the national and local level. A typical example, promoting an open house in the North College Hill neighborhood of Cincinnati, reveals how advertising mediated consumer reception of the prefabricated house (Figure 15). The ad features a photograph of the model with the heading "Let Us Show You the New Look* in the 1950 National 'Thrift Home.' "[111] The phrase "new look," which reappears four times throughout the ad copy, is unapologetic in its appeal to changing fashion. After Christian Dior introduced the "new look" in lady's fashion in 1947, advertisers eagerly announced the "new look" in refrigerators, televisions, electric ranges, and sewing machines.[112] Already by 1950, National Homes recognized that the desire for the new, now, and next, which was driving mass consumption of automobiles and consumer durables, might be harnessed to fuel demand for better housing. National Homes' use of the phrase "new look" by National Homes to describe its Thrift Home framed domestic space not as something to be modified and remodeled, but to be upgraded. Furthermore, modern marketing methods recognized that consumers preferred to identify with a class image higher than their own rather than with a reflection of their actual lives.[113]

In this case, the vignette of the smartly-dressed couple in the upper corner of the ad played on the notion that homeownership was the key to upward mobility, by suggesting social ascendance could be unlocked through the purchase of the latest Thrift Home model. In much the same way as appliances, automobiles, and designer dresses, the postwar house had become yet another luxury item which homebuyers, as consumers, could acquire to indicate status and craft identity.[114]

As the housing industry transitioned from a seller's to a buyer's market and prefabricators and builders alike met with increasingly discerning homebuyers, National Homes sought to boost sales by exploiting consumers' devotion to nationally-recognized, brand-name products.[115] While advertising for the company's early lines provided only general descriptions of its models, by 1952 its ads promised Thermopane picture windows, Crosley kitchens with Formica countertops, and Bendix washers and dryers. A campaign for the 1956 line in *Better Homes and Gardens* boasted an "all-electric" kitchen, outfitted with the latest Frigidaire garbage disposal and GE washer/dryer and promised "year-round comfort" with the installation of "two-great brand names—Delco for heating, Frigidaire for cooling."[116] Offering brand-name products helped National Homes compete with conventional builders and gain credibility with consumers.

The company was also keen to capitalize on branding potential for its own product, the detached, single-family home. During the interwar years single-family housing became increasingly standardized through FHA codes and regulations, and was packaged financially through streamlined, long-term mortgages.[117] With the standardization and commodification of the American home well underway, by 1948 marketing experts recognized the special advantage consumer faith in "brand-name" products could offer prefabricators. The *Harvard Business Review* advised that establishing brand recognition with consumers, by helping to build an association with quality, could be the key to prefabricators' success in the single-family home market.[118] To dispel the lingering association between prefabrication and war housing, establishing a positive reputation with consumers was particularly important. Merely relying on the promise of a lower price than conventionally-built homes would only serve to reinforce consumers' perception of prefabricated housing as cheap, poorly constructed, and impermanent. What the prefab industry needed was a complete rebranding. The article therefore urged manufacturers to focus on establishing a reputation for quality rather than relying on price as the prefabricated home's distinguishing characteristic.[119]

In the 1950s, the importance of building brand recognition with homebuyers emerged as a major concern within the prefabricated housing industry. *PF* predicted that buyers would increasingly invest in homes manufactured by large and well-known companies, who could "back the quality of their label."[120] Indeed, by the middle of the decade, prefabrication had changed the nature of the housing industry; residential construction, the journal announced, had become "essentially a 'brand-name' business."[121] In part as the result of extensive and costly advertising campaigns run by National Homes, prefabricated housing manufacturers were establishing name recognition with homebuyers for the first time.

The birth of "brand-name" housing not only demonstrated the application of modern marketing methods to an industry often faulted for its conservatism; it also worked in a practical way to better serve homebuyers. Brand-name models afforded consumers a standard of comparison that would be difficult to establish through conventional building.[122] Moreover, National Homes' reputation lay in the hands of the dealers who sold their models and the crews who erected them. Maintaining a high valuation of the National Homes name in the eyes of consumers meant producing a consistent, high-quality product and carefully selecting retailers who would be competent in the erection of each model. Although the company was well on its way to becoming a household name, National Homes still faced tough competition from conventional builders who were far better equipped to respond to increasing consumer demand for custom options.

Figure 15. National Homes advertisement promoting the "New Look" in the 1950 Thrift Home, originally published in the *Cincinnati Enquirer*, March 11, 1950.

### Restyling the Postwar Prefab

In the mid 1950s, manufacturers of prefabricated housing would finally succeed in emulating the automobile industry, at least in terms of merchandising. As an editorial published in *PF* pointed out, Ford wasn't selling basic Model T's anymore.[123] Consumers wanted all the extras, whether they were buying new a sedan or building a ranch home. An era of renewed prosperity was dawning, codified by design historian Thomas Hine as the age of "populuxe." Populuxe culture extended to Americans "an invitation to indulge in the luxuries" and heightened their expectations of comfort, enjoyment, leisure, and affluence.[124] The era's material culture often encapsulated a multiplicity of contradictions—the modern and traditional, the eye-catching and the tasteful, the machined and the handcrafted.[125] An emphasis on "restyling," initiated with the "new look" campaign, defined advertising for National Homes lines in the 1950s. The company also expanded its offerings beyond the low-cost starter-home, increasingly emphasizing variety, flexibility, and amenities. Slogans like "Tomorrow's Homes . . . Today!" and "Easy to Own!" promised consumers immediate gratification, while descriptions of National Homes models as both "compact" and "luxurious" suggested a light pocketbook need not place limits on better living.

In 1954 National Homes introduced its Custom and Pacemaker lines, which would be vigorously promoted through a "nation-wide open house week." National advertising campaigns prompted potential buyers to check their local real estate pages for information about when and where to view the company's latest models (Figure 16). Local "tie-in" advertising complimented the national campaign. National Homes provided builders with a schedule for newspaper advertising, radio, and TV spots, and suggestions for publicity stories. In addition, the company coordinated with manufacturers to acquire furnishings and supplied builders with booklets illustrating exactly where in the model each item should be placed.[126]

This cross-country open house scheme was almost certainly conceived as a way to compete with conventional builders for the public's attention. In what Jacobs has characterized as a "marketing coup for the housing industry," the NAHB had introduced an annual National Homes Week in 1948. This weeklong festival of housing, for which builders across the country held simultaneous open houses to introduce the latest trends in domestic design, was a "supercharged period of self-promotion" that took advantage of the era's consumption-driven culture while unifying the vast spectrum of builders who operated independently from (and in competition with) one another as producers of a single product: the detached, single-family home in the suburbs.[127] Prefabricators like National Homes, eager to capitalize on the cultural commodification of domestic space, modeled their merchandising on methods successful with conventional builders.

Ads for the National Homes open house week promised visitors "so much more in new designs" and implored, "seeing is believing."[128] The Custom and Pacemaker lines not only of-

Figure 16. Ads like this one invited homebuyers to inspect the National Homes 1955 "Custom-Line," designed by Charles Goodman, at a nationwide open house week. *Better Homes and Gardens* 33, no. 3 (March 1955): 192.

fered more in the way of customization than any of the company's previous options, they also incorporated popular new architectural features like lunch bars linking kitchen and dining areas, split-level floor plans, and sliding glass doors connecting living spaces inside and outside the home (Figure 17). Buyers could walk through the model house, then flip through the National Homes catalog, select a floor plan, add porches, garages, or carports, and customize colors and finishes (Figure 18). In this way, the company's mass-produced homes provided an affordable option for middle-class buyers seeking the "custom" look of upscale neighborhoods.

The company's merchandising program built upon American consumers' belief in homeownership as a marker of status and the cultural imperative to make one's home one's own by offering color-styling by prominent interior decorator Beatrice West and "architect-designed" models by Charles Goodman. Goodman had earned popular and professional acclaim for his contemporary ranch homes in the bourgeoning suburbs of Washington, D.C., just after the war.[129] In his custom houses the architect integrated structure and site with attention to the framing of views, connections between interior and exterior through extensive glazing, decks, and terraces, and the incorporation of natural materials and rich textures.[130] The thirty-two floor plans he designed for National Homes' 1955 line "put a bargain price tag on many of the best features of modern custom design," making it possible for builders to incorporate these types of features into the modestly-priced tract home.[131]

The line was distinguished by two general styles: the Ranch and the Ranger (Figure 19). Beyond the use of vibrant accent colors in shades of blue, yellow, green, orange, and red for doors and decorative panels surrounding windows, the Ranch models were fairly unremarkable economy houses offering two to three bedrooms and a combined living and dining area. Like many tract homes of the era, Ranch designs featured low-slung hipped roofs and picture windows. In contrast, the Ranger models exemplified Goodman's efforts to bring modernist design to the mass market through sweeping rooflines with

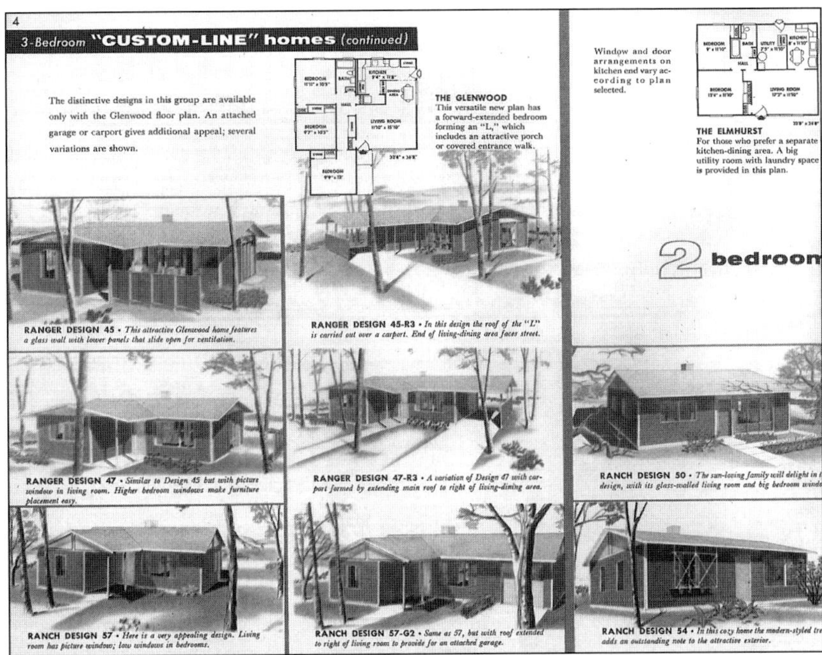

Figure 17. The three-bedroom Glenwood floorplan, available for the Ranger line, featured a lunch bar connecting the kitchen to the dining area, an expansive floor-to-ceiling window in the living room, and an optional carport or attached garage. *1955 "Custom-Line" and "Pacemaker" Houses by . . . National Homes* (Lafayette, Ind.: National Homes Corporation, 1955), 4.

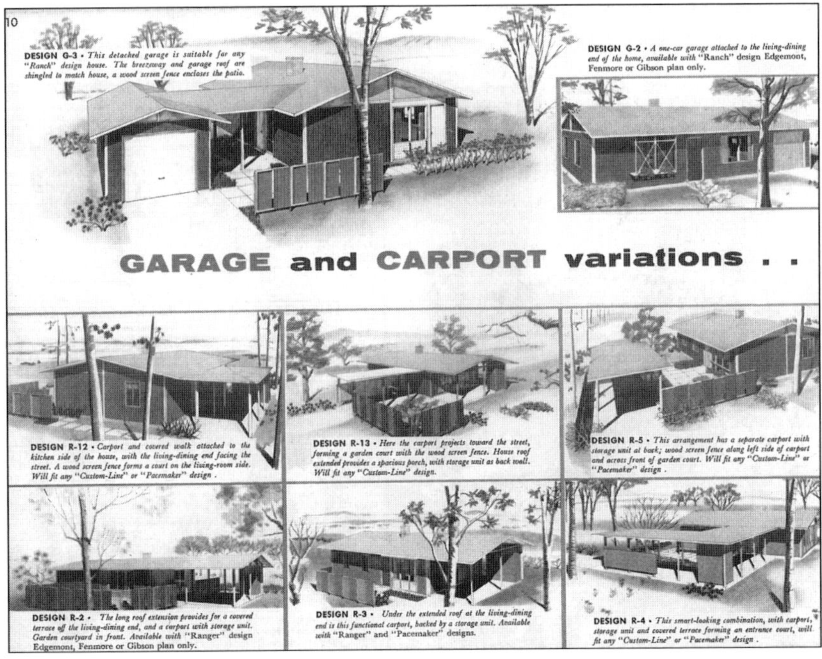

Figure 18. Charles Goodman's designs for the 1955 line offered a variety of customizable garage and carport options. *1955 "Custom-Line" and "Pacemaker" Houses by . . . National Homes* (Lafayette, Ind.: National Homes Corporation, 1955), 10.

deep overhanging eaves, interpenetrating interior and exterior spaces, floor-to-ceiling glazing, and covered walkways connecting garages and carports to the main block of the house.[132] Trellises, breezeways, and porches with contemporary styling complimented the houses' modernist form. Taken together, the two design categories reveal the company's effort to offer something for every buyer, ranging from the conventional to the contemporary. Moreover, the variety of finishes and floorplans available within each style prioritized individuality and made it possible (at least in theory) to achieve site specificity with mass production. National Homes wasn't alone in this approach; competing lines, like Madison, Wisconsin, based builder Marshall Erdman's U-Form-It system and American Houses' Design-It-Yourself options, also sought to capitalize on the cultural potency of customization in postwar America.[133] By diversifying its lines and reframing the prefabricated house as fully customizable, National Homes further distanced prefabrication from the standardization associated with factory production.

**Tomorrow's Homes . . . Today!**

Prefabrication made steady gains in the two decades following the war—National Homes alone had sold over 250,000 homes—but never came to dominate the single-family home market as proponents had predicted. Prefabrication's success was plagued by the twin problems of consumer resistance to factory-built homes and competition from conventional builders.[134] The war may have launched National Homes into mass production, but its status as an industry leader was hard won. The battles the company waged to win over banks, builders, and buyers in peacetime played out in its high-profile advertising campaigns.

In 1965 the Prefabricated Home Manufacturers Institute (PHMI) ceased publication of its journal; the housing crisis of the immediate postwar years had passed and many manufacturers had turned to the production of component parts such as roof trusses and partition systems. Ever abreast of industry trends, National Homes transitioned its plants to the production of com-

ponent parts under the umbrella of National Building Systems.[135] Over the course of the next two decades the company further diversified its activities, reestablishing itself as a design-build firm focused on large-scale construction projects ranging from apartment complexes to retirement living centers.[136] Although the company remained operational into the 1980s as National Enterprises, Inc., the closing of its original plant in Lafayette, Indiana, in 1974 marked the end of its production of fully prefabricated homes.[137]

National Homes' efforts to recruit builder-dealers highlights the volatile character of the postwar housing industry, adding complexity to our picture of the postwar building boom. Likewise, the company's appeals to banks underscores the restrictive role government regulations and conservative lending institutions played in stalling technological developments in the building industry and dictating postwar design. Finally, the "revolution in home merchandising" led by National Homes, with its unprecedented emphasis on direct marking to consumers, illuminates Americans' deep attachment to the notion of home as both permanent and personal.[138] The company's marketing strategies also shed light on the cultural impediments that prevented the prefabricated house from achieving the success that had long been heralded. Where the first pitches for prefabs in the 1930s had touted new technology paired with images of better living through science, postwar advertising painted the prefab as utterly conventional. As a 1947 advertisement for National Homes argued, "the prefabricated or factory-built home is not fantastic wizardry as many have been led to believe. It presents no miracle contraptions, it is not the dream palace that many editorials have painted it."[139] National Homes was careful to mediate the technological innovation that made "Tomorrow's Homes . . . Today!" possible with romanticized representations of traditional American home life. The company's advertising downplayed factory production by replacing images of homes rolling off assembly lines with scenes of Downing-esque domesticity and family living (Figure 12).

As Jacobs has observed, in the two decades following World War II, "the detached single-family

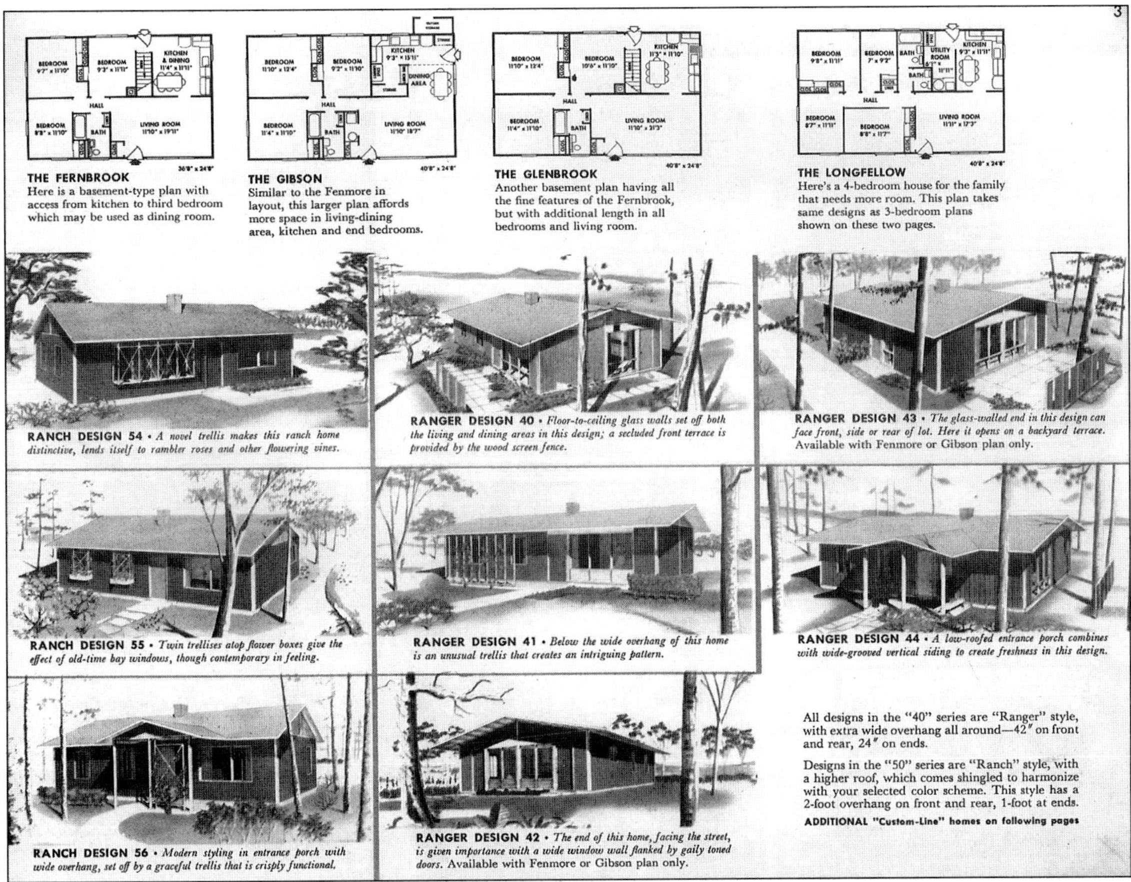



Figure 19. National Homes expanded its offerings to include a range of options, from the traditional Ranch to the more contemporary Ranger, as part of its Custom-Line. *1955 "Custom-Line" and "Pacemaker" Houses by . . . National Homes* (Lafayette, Ind.: National Homes Corporation, 1955), 3.

house attained preeminent status among consumer products available for mass consumption in the United States."[140] As conventional builders pursued new avenues in home merchandising to drive home sales, including enhanced and expanded print advertising, nationally-coordinated festivals of housing showcasing model homes, and the rapid introduction of new house types, manufacturers of prefabricated housing followed suit. Better than any of its competitors in the prefab industry, National Homes capitalized on a postwar culture driven by the desire to "trade up." Defining slogans announcing the "new look" in housing and promising "Tomorrow's Homes . . . Today!" along with the company's reliance on brand names to drive home sales—from refrigerators and washing machines to the houses themselves—mark a key point in the commodification of domestic space over the course of the twentieth century (Figure 20). What's more, the company operated on a scale bigger even than the largest and most successful

Figure 20. National Homes adopted the slogan "Tomorrow's Homes . . . Today!" to persuade both builders and homebuyers it could offer the newest, least expensive, and best quality house on the market. *The All-New 1952 National Homes "Super Thrift"* (Lafayette, Ind.: National Homes Corporation, 1952).

merchant builders. In coupling promises of permanence and security with the new, now, and next, National Homes' campaigns illustrate the competing interests and conflicting values that have shaped American suburban landscapes.

AUTHOR BIOGRAPHY

**Marisa Gomez Nordyke** is a PhD candidate in the Buildings-Landscapes-Cultures program in the Department of Art History at the University of Wisconsin–Madison. Her dissertation, "Fabricating the American Dream: Stressed-Skin Technology and the American Home, 1930–1965," traces the development and use of the stressed-skin panel for prefabricated housing to address broad changes in building practice and domestic space.

NOTES

1. Robert Lasch, "What to Look for in Prefabs," *Popular Science* 149, no. 2 (August 1946): 66.

2. Before World War II, manufacturers of prefabricated houses numbered about thirty. The fledgling industry had produced less than 10,000 homes, amounting to only 1 percent of single-family, non-farm houses built during the Depression. This statistic comes from Burnham Kelly, *The Prefabrication of Houses* (New York: Technology Press of the Massachusetts Institute of Technology and John Wiley and Sons, 1951), 50. Spurred by government contracts for emergency war housing, the number of manufacturers jumped to 200 by 1942 according to *Architectural Record* 76, no. 2 (February 1942): 83. Kelly estimated the total number of prefabricated housing units to be approximately 200,000. By the end of 1946, with the help of the Veterans' Emergency Housing Act, the number of manufacturers reached 280. But many new enterprises ultimately failed. By the end of 1947, the number of manufacturers again dipped below 100. Kelly, *The Prefabrication of Houses*, 60, 71.

3. My definition is based upon that published by the Prefabricated Home Manufacturer's Institute in 1947. The definition was republished in Glenn H. Beyer and Theodore R. Yantis, *Practices and Precepts of Marketing Prefabricated Houses* (Washington D.C.: Housing and Home Finance Agency, Office of the Administrator, Division of Housing Research, 1952), 1.

4. For the development of the balloon frame, see Paul E. Sprague, "The Origin of Balloon Framing," *Journal of the Society of Architectural Historians* 40, no. 4 (December 1981): 311–19. While the invention of balloon framing is often cited as the beginning of the simplification of the building process, the process in fact originated in the colonial period as settlers faced with a shortage of skilled labor began experimenting with new, simplified framing techniques. Over the course of the seventeenth century, builders modified traditional English framing practices to erect dwellings more quickly and at less cost. Willie Graham, "Timber Framing," in *The Chesapeake House: Architectural Investigation by Colonial Williamsburg,* ed. Cary Carson and Carl R. Lounsbury (Chapel Hill: University of North Carolina Press, 2013), 206–14.

5. Daniel D. Reiff has detailed the rise of prefabricated architectural components in the nineteenth century. See Reiff, *Houses from Books: Treatises, Pattern Books, and Catalogs in American Architecture, 1738–1950, a History and Guide* (University Park: Pennsylvania State University Press, 2000), 120–22.

6. Two master's theses provide in-depth analysis of the ready-cut industry in the first decades of the twentieth century. Carolyn Patricia Flynn has explored the economic processes of industrialization that transformed construction of single-family homes from a craft-based process to an industrially-based one, giving particular attention to the ready-cut system's contribution to the standardization and rationalization of homebuilding. See Flynn, "Pacific Ready-Cut Homes: Mass-Produced Bungalows in Los Angeles, 1908–1942" (master's thesis, University of California–Los Angeles, 1986). Scott Steven Erbes has noted that mail-order kit manufacturers like the Aladdin Company promised to save consumers time and money through the prevention of waste by pre-cutting in the factory, the reduction of labor costs through assembly by unskilled workers, and the elimination of the middleman (lumber dealers, wholesalers, etc.). See Erbes, "The Ready-Cut Dream: The Mail-Order House Catalogs of the Aladdin Company, 1906–1920" (PhD diss., University of Delaware, 1990). In addition, Amanda Cooke and Avi Friedman have examined the production, distribution, marketing, and financing of Sears pre-cut homes. See Cooke and Friedman, "Ahead of Their Time: The Sears Catalogue Prefabricated Houses," *Journal of Design History* 14, no. 1 (2001): 53–70. More recently, Richard Harris has ad-

dressed the contributions and struggles of manufacturers of mail-order houses, with particular attention to the strategies by which kit companies tried to win over contractors. See Harris, "The Talk of the Town: Kit Manufacturers Negotiate the Building Industry, 1905–1929," *Journal of Urban History* 26, no. 6 (November, 2010): 868–96.

7. In the case of Sears, the most famous of the mail-order kit companies, carpenters (or a handy homeowner) were required to finish all the lumber on site. Reiff, *Houses from Books*, 188.

8. In addition to the U.S. Forest Products Laboratory, these institutions included the National Bureau of Standards, which conducted testing of new materials and structural systems; the Farm Security Administration, which built prefabricated farmsteads for sharecropper families and migrant workers in the 1930s and emergency housing during the war; the Tennessee Valley Authority, which produced demountable, sectional trailer houses; the Alfred Farwell Bemis Foundation at the Massachusetts Institute of Technology, the first privately subsidized (nonprofit) research center to improve housing with a focus on prefabrication; the Housing Research Division of the Pierce Foundation, in Raritan, New Jersey, which undertook research on new materials and construction systems; and the Purdue University Housing Research Project in West Lafayette, Indiana, which erected a range of test houses at its Housing Research Campus to evaluate new structural systems and published informational pamphlets for homeowners on technical developments in housing on behalf of Better Homes in America.

9. The Price brothers are quoted in *Barron's Weekly* as referring to themselves as the "General Motors of housing." John Chamberlain, "Spurt in Prefabs: The Factory-Built Dwelling Has Arrived in the U.S.," *Barron's National Business and Financial Weekly*, March 14, 1955, 3.

10. The name of Foster Gunnison's company changed several times in its first few years. Begun as Gunnison Magic Homes, the name changed to the Gunnison Housing Corporation in 1937, and again in 1944 to Gunnison Homes, Inc. See Kelly, *The Prefabrication of Houses*, 42. Finally, in 1953, the name changed to U.S. Steel Homes. Despite the name change, Gunnison's legacy lived on and builders continued to refer to "Gunnison Homes." See for example, "200 Homes Built, Sold and Occupied in 2 Years—That's Why We Build Gunnison Homes," *American Builder* 76, no. 6 (June 1954): 114–15.

11. For an account of the beginnings of Houses, Inc. and Gunnison Magic Homes, see Kelly, *The Prefabrication of Houses*, 40–43.

12. Gordon J. Chapman, "Marketing of Prefabricated Homes in the East Northcentral States," (PhD diss., Indiana University, 1951), 16.

13. In 1952, Gunnison's production output topped 7,500 units. This put it well ahead of its competitors in the prefab industry, most of whom produced less than 1,000 annually. For a snapshot of the industry see "What's New on the Market—1953 Models Show Progress in Product Design," *House & Home* 2, no. 5 (November 1952): 94–101.

14. F. J. Champion, *The U.S. Forest Products Laboratory* (Madison, Wis.: Forest Products Laboratory, 1960), 3.

15. George W. Trayer, *Forest Products Laboratory Prefabrication System: A New Departure in All-Wood Housing* (Madison, Wis.: Forest Products Laboratory, 1935), 2.

16. This statistic was recorded in R. F. Luxford, *Prefabricated House System Developed by the Forest Products Laboratory* (Madison, Wis.: Forest Products Laboratory, 1958), 1.

17. "'Reengineering': The Measure of Progress," *Architectural Forum* 78, no. 6 (June 1943): 91.

18. Because nearly all newly constructed homes in the postwar period would be purchased with Federal Housing Administration (FHA) insured mortgages, and thus met the FHA's minimum standards for construction, buyers felt assured that a new home was reasonably well built. James A. Jacobs has shown that, more than the type of construction, buyers were interested in spatial planning and amenities. See Jacobs, *Detached America: Building Houses in Postwar Suburbia* (Charlottesville: University of Virginia Press, 2015), 54.

19. "Reengineering," 96.

20. "Merchant" builder refers to builders who built speculatively. In trade literature of the period, these builders are also referred to as "operative" builders. Merchant builders, as group, were extremely varied in their production output. The smallest built fewer than ten houses per year, while "large-volume" builders put up over fifty houses per year. For discussion of the

various types of builders constructing single-family homes in the postwar period, see Jacobs, *Detached America*, 33.

21. Miles L. Colean, *American Housing: Problems and Prospects* (New York: Twentieth Century Fund, 1944), 147.

22. "Wood," *Architectural Forum* 78, no. 4 (April 1943): 71.

23. "Factory-Built Homes Do Better and Better," *Business Week*, February 10, 1951, 64.

24. "Reengineering," 89. The lengthy consideration *Architectural Record* devoted to the future of the prefabricated housing industry reflected the enthusiasm for planning for postwar living that, as Andrew Shanken has shown, captivated the architectural profession almost from the start of the war. See Andrew M. Shanken, *194X: Architecture, Planning, and Consumer Culture on the American Homefront* (Minneapolis: University of Minnesota Press, 2009).

25. "Reengineering," 89–90.

26. "Local Prefabs Out in Front," *American Builder* 65, no. 3 (March 1943): 41.

27. Barbara Miller Lane, *Houses for a New World: Builders and Buyers in American Suburbs, 1945–1965* (Princeton, N.J.: Princeton University Press, 2015), 187.

28. Max Hall, "Factory-Built Homes Lag Far Behind Goal," *The Evening Review*, September 12, 1947.

29. "The Fortune Survey," *Fortune* 33, no. 4 (April 1946): 275.

30. Lasch, "What to Look for in Prefabs," 71.

31. Robert Ferber and Hugh G. Wales, "The Market for Prefabricated Housing," *Journal of Marketing* 16, no. 1 (July 1951): 19. In the first major study of the industry, *The Prefabrication of Houses*, published in 1951, Burnham Kelly asserted that the prefab home's poor reputation stemmed chiefly from the "minimum-standard" dwellings erected as emergency housing during the war. Kelly, *The Prefabrication of Houses*, 90. For further discussion of the stigma of war housing attached to the prefabricated house, see Glenn H. Beyer, *Housing and Society* (New York: McMillan Company, 1965), 222.

32. L. B. Wheildon, "National Housing Emergency, 1946–1947," in *Editorial Research Reports 1946*, vol. II (Washington, D.C.: CQ Press, 1946), 855–76, available from http://library.cqpress.com/cqresearcher/document.php?id=cqresrre1946121700. See also "Text of Wyatt's Plan for New Homing This Year and Next, and Truman's Indorsement [sic] of It," *New York Herald Tribune,* February 9, 1946, 6A.

33. Wheildon, "National Housing Emergency, 1946–1947." Clashes between Wyatt and the Reconstruction Finance Corporation, which would fund the loans to prefabricators, ultimately led to Wyatt's resignation.

34. Lasch, "What to Look for in Prefabs," 66.

35. A. C. Monahan, "Assembly-Line Homes," *Science News-Letter* 49, no. 12 (March 23, 1946): 186. The *Science News-Letter* was a biweekly publication on innovations in the fields of science and technology published by the Society for Science and the Public. It remains in publication under the name *Science News.*

36. For the rapid expansion of the prefabrication industry in 1946 see Kelly, *The Prefabrication of Houses,* 71; "Prefabrication Gains Stature During Past Year," *American Builder* 68, no. 12 (December 1946): 105; and "Expect Bigger 1947 Total of Pre-Fab Homes," *Chicago Daily Tribune,* January 4, 1947, 19. Prefabricators who dreamed of national distribution were greatly hindered by thousands of local building codes that excluded new materials and structural systems. Building codes were also used to protect the interests of conventional builders and tradesmen. For the role of building codes in preventing innovation and maintaining the status quo in the building industry, see Robert Lasch, *Breaking the Building Blockade* (Chicago: University of Chicago Press, 1946), 105.

37. See "NAHB Directors Determine Association Policy Towards Wyatt Housing Program," *American Builder* 68, no. 4 (April 1946): 35; and "Builder Charges Favoritism to Unknown Prefabricators," *Chicago Daily Tribune,* November 2, 1946, 21.

38. Samuel A. Tower, "New System Set for U.S. Housing," *New York Times*, December 24, 1946, 1.

39. Kelly, *The Prefabrication of Houses,* 69. See also, "Wyatt's Program Has Guaranteed a Market Maximum of 200,000 Prefabricated Houses," *Wall Street Journal,* April 4, 1946, 5.

40. For histories of the Lustron Corporation see Tom Wolfe and Leonard Garfield, "'A New Standard for Living': The Lustron House, 1946–1950," in *Perspectives in Vernacular Architecture III,* ed. Thomas Carter and Bernard L. Herman (Columbia: University of Missouri Press, 1989), 51–61; Douglass Knerr, *Suburban Steel: The Magnificent Failure of the Lustron Corporation, 1945–1951* (Columbus: Ohio State University Press,

2004); and Thomas T. Fetters, *The Lustron Home* (Jefferson, N.C.: McFarland & Company, Inc., 2006).

41. Wolfe and Garfield, "The Lustron House," 51.

42. Wyatt was quoted as labeling the scheme "sensationally" good. Edson Blair, "Washington: Both Sides of the Curtain: Inside Reports on Latest Developments in National Affairs," *Barron's National Business and Financial Weekly,* December 2, 1946, 48.

43. Wolfe and Garfield, "The Lustron House," 54.

44. "What's Stalling Lustron?" *Business Week,* October 29, 1949, 25.

45. Knerr, *Suburban Steel,* 3.

46. Colean, *American Housing,* 147.

47. Elaine Stiles, "Every Lot a Garden Spot: 'Big Dave' Bohannon and the Making of San Lorenzo Village," available from http://www.sanlorenzoheritage org/history/stiles.htm.

48. "Merchant Builder Survey," *Architectural Forum* 92, no. 4 (April 1950): 94. For the impact of new technologies and assembly methods on postwar merchant builders, see "Labor-Saving Tools and Equipment Mean Much to the Builder in Today's Market," *American Builder* 71, no. 5 (May 1949): 76.

49. Colean, *American Housing,* 147. Richard Longstreth provides an in-depth discussion of the influence of the West Coast housing projects erected during the war and immediately following as well as the Levitts' determination to pursue site fabrication over prefabrication. See Longstreth, "The Levitts, Mass-Produced Houses, and Community Planning in the Mid-twentieth Century," in *Second Suburb: Levittown, Pennsylvania,* ed. Dianne Harris (Pittsburgh: University of Pittsburgh Press, 2010), 123–74.

50. In 1948, Congress revised liberal postwar lending practices by introducing new restrictions on government-backed mortgages. Kelly, *The Prefabrication of Houses,* 73.

51. William K. Wittausch, "Marketing Prefabricated Houses," *Harvard Business Review* 26, no. 6 (November 1948): 696.

52. Wittausch, "Marketing Prefabricated Houses," 709.

53. Reflecting back on his company's early days, George Price observed: "From the very start, marketing of homes was made as important a part of our operation as production." See George Price, "Revolution in Home Merchandising," *PF: The Magazine of Prefabrication* 5, no. 5 (May 1957): 14.

54. Beyer and Yantis, *Practices and Precepts of Marketing Prefabricated Houses,* 41.

55. Colean, *American Housing,* 147.

56. The results of these tests are held in the FPL archives. See Materials Testing Laboratory, Purdue University, "Loading Tests of Prefabricated Wall Panel Sections, National Homes Corporation, Lafayette, Indiana," February 17, 1947.

57. Chapman, "Marketing of Prefabricated Homes in the East Northcentral States," 90.

58. "National Homes Corporation Looks FORWARD!" *Wall Street Journal,* September 10, 1951, 2.

59. See for example the PHMI advertisements "In HOUSING, the Swing Is to PREFABRICATION," *Wall Street Journal,* December 17, 1951, 16.

60. "National Homes COST LESS to Build—Yield MORE PROFIT to Builders!" *American Builder* 72, no. 3 (March 1950): 197.

61. "Building Outlook Improved for 1947," *American Builder* 69, no. 1 (January 1947): 58.

62. For the high cost of materials see Lasch, *Breaking the Building Blockade,* 88–93.

63. "Building Outlook Improved for 1947," 58.

64. Experts were predicting this shift as early as 1949. See "Merchant Builder Survey," 115; and "Labor-Saving Tools and Equipment Mean Much to the Builder in Today's Market," 76.

65. Lasch, *Breaking the Building Blockade,* 93.

66. "You May Find Your Future in This Book," *American Builder* 72, no. 10 (October 1950): 155.

67. "National Homes Lead with New Trend in Spacious Living," *American Builder* 75, no. 3 (March 1953): 137; "Brand-new Dealer Sells 28 National Homes," *American Builder* 73, no. 4 (April 1951): 199.

68. "Close supervision" on the job site was the top cost-saving measure given in the "Merchant Builder Survey," 94.

69. "National Homes . . . Are Easier to Sell . . . Easier to Erect," *House & Home* 1, no. 2 (February 1952): 35.

70. "These Builders Joined 'Em," *House & Home* 2, no. 5 (November 1952): 103. According to the article, George Nixon (a past president of the National Association of Home Builders) had been convinced by his son Bob to start building prefabricated houses in an effort to expand into the low-cost house market.

71. "Brand-new Dealer Sells 28 National Homes," 199.

72. "You, Too, Get 'So Much More' from National Homes!" *American Builder* 77, no. 3 (March 1955): 91.

73. "Brand-new Dealer Sells 28 National Homes," 199.

74. "National Homes Dealerships Offer GOOD Business Opportunities Some Territories Now Open," *American Builder* 73, no. 5 (May 1951): 193.

75. "Sensationally Restyled . . . Sensationally Promoted!" *American Builder* 74, no. 11 (November 1952): 144.

76. "You, Too, Get 'So Much More' from National Homes!" 91. While ads for Gunnison Homes did appear in popular women's magazines during the 1950s, they ran far less consistently than advertisements for National Homes. National Homes had a more significant presence in both trade journals and popular magazines.

77. Dianne Harris found that subscriptions tripled and even, in some cases, quadrupled between 1945 and 1960. See Harris, *Little White Houses: How the Postwar Home Constructed Race in America* (Minneapolis: University of Minnesota Press, 2013), 67.

78. Theodore Russell Yantis, "The Marketing of Prefabricated Houses" (PhD diss., Ohio State University, 1955), 137.

79. "First in Feminine Appeal!" *American Builder* 75, no. 8 (August 1953): 156.

80. Yantis, *The Marketing of Prefabricated Houses,* 137.

81. "These Builders Joined 'Em," 103.

82. "Prefabrication Has Something for Everyone," *House & Home* 7, no. 6 (December 1954): 103.

83. "Now . . . 50,000 National Homes!" *American Builder* 75, no. 7 (July 1953): 169. The NAHB's classifications for merchant builders help contextualize National Homes' production output in relation to the broader housing industry. The NAHB classified builders who erected between ten and forty-nine houses annually as "medium-volume" and those who erected over fifty houses annually as "large-volume" builders. NAHB, *Housing Almanac: A Fact File of the Home Building Industry* (Washington, D.C.: National Association of Home Builders, 1957), 15–16. National Homes' production was exceeded only by the most exceptional builders; in 1950 the company's Indiana plant manufactured thirty homes a day, whereas the Levitts put up thirty-five each day. "Company Started with $12,500 Top 'Pre-Fab' Markets," *New York Times,* January 22, 1950, 191; "Built 4,945 Homes in '50: Levitts Average 35 Houses on Each Working Day Last Year," *New York Times,* January 13, 1951. The company's production capacity increased significantly with a $1.5 million expansion of its Indiana plant and the opening of two additional plants in New York and Texas, bringing production up to 275 homes per day. "National Homes Builds Southern Plant," *PF: The Magazine of Prefabrication* 3, no. 3 (March 1955): 39.

84. "Brand-new Dealer Sells 28 National Homes," 199.

85. "Builds Over 1,000 National Homes," *American Builder* 73, no. 6 (June 1951): 181.

86. For further discussion of this problem see Jacobs, *Detached America,* 80; and Samuel Dodd, "Parade of Homes: Salesmanship and the Postwar American Housing Industry," *Journal of Design History* 28, no. 4 (November 2015): 2.

87. "National Homes Lead with New Trend in Spacious Living," 137.

88. Jacobs, *Detached America,* 61.

89. "Now . . . 50,000 National Homes!" 169.

90. "Here Are the New Prefabs Whose Values Every Builder Must Meet," *House & Home* 4, no. 5 (November 1953): 103; John S. Cooper, "Prefab 'Mansions': Factory-Built Houses Take a Turn Toward Bigness and Luxury," *Wall Street Journal,* May 5, 1952, 1.

91. Longstreth, "The Levitts," 136. For the debate over the savings of prefabrication in building trade literature, see for example "Prefabs Held Small Builders' Answer to Today's Problem of Cutting Costs," *American Builder* 74, no. 3 (March 1952): 34; "Prefabricated Houses—Should the Builder Fight 'Em or Join 'Em?" *House & Home* 2, no. 11 (November 1952): 89–90; and "Small-town Builder Does BIG BUSINESS with 'PF' Homes," *PF: The Magazine of Prefabrication* 3, no. 2 (February 1955): 18, 20–21.

92. David Thaler, "Report on Prefabrication: Sales Continue to Rise, but Competition, Public Image Pose Twin Problems," *American Builder* 86, no. 12 (December 1964): 41.

93. *Homes for Modern Living* (Stran-Steel Corporation, 1934), n.p.

94. *A New Idea in Home Construction! Frameless Steel House* (Cleveland: Insulated Steel, Inc., 1932), n.p.

95. "Loeser's Motohome Opening Tomorrow," *Brooklyn Daily Eagle,* July 14, 1935.

96. "Mother of Roosevelt Unwraps a Bungalow," *Brooklyn Daily Eagle*, April 1, 1935.

97. Beyer and Yantis, *Practices and Precepts of Marketing Prefabricated Houses*, 221.

98. Lasch, "What to Look for in Prefabs," 66.

99. Lasch, "What to Look for in Prefabs," 66.

100. The early history of American Houses, Inc. is recorded in Kelly, *The Prefabrication of Houses*, 41–42. *Business Week* named American Houses, Gunnison Homes, and National Homes as the "big three" in the prefabricated housing industry. See "Factory-Built Homes Do Better and Better," 64.

101. The study by Beyer and Yantis found that only 14 percent of manufacturers used the term "prefabrication" in their advertising. Beyer and Yantis, *Practices and Precepts of Marketing Prefabricated Houses*, 11.

102. "Fritsche Makes Customers His Best Salesmen," *PF: The Magazine of Prefabrication* 1, no. 1 (September 1953): 23.

103. Harris, *Little White Houses*, 86.

104. Dodd, "Parade of Homes," 7.

105. Beyer and Yantis, *Practices and Precepts of Marketing Prefabricated Houses*, 11.

106. Beyer and Yantis, *Practices and Precepts of Marketing Prefabricated Houses*, 12.

107. "Top Marketing Advice," in *National Homes Corporation: 25 Years of Leadership* (Lafayette, Ind.: National Homes Corp., 1965), n.p.

108. "Successful Selling Techniques," in *National Homes Corporation: 25 Years of Leadership*, n.p.

109. Chapman, "Marketing of Prefabricated Homes in the East Northcentral States," 90.

110. Jacobs, *Detached America*, 39–40.

111. "Let Us Show You the 'New Look' in the New 1950 'Thrift Home,'" *Cincinnati Enquirer*, March 11, 1950, 2.

112. See for example: "For Cold Storage: There's a 'New Look' to Refrigerator Containers," *New York Herald Tribune*, February 15, 1948, SM33; "One Quick Glance and You Can Tell . . . It's Television with a 'New Look,'" *New York Herald Tribune*, April 18, 1948, H5; "Exciting New 'Push-button' Range," *Good Housekeeping* 127, no. 4 (October 1948): 132; "Before You Buy . . . Compare the NEW Free-Westinghouse Sewing Machines," *Good Housekeeping* 134, no. 5 (May 1952): 226.

113. Roland Marchand, *Advertising the American Dream: Making Way for Modernity 1920–1940* (Berkeley: University of California Press, 1985), xvii.

114. See Monica Penick, "The Pace Setter Houses: Livable Modernism in Postwar America" (PhD diss., University of Texas at Austin, 2007), 24; and Lizabeth Cohen, *A Consumer's Republic: The Politics of Mass Consumption in Postwar America* (New York: Vintage Books, 2003), 202.

115. Experts were predicting this shift as early as 1949. See "Merchant Builder Survey," 115.

116. "Take a Look at the New Nationals," *Better Homes and Gardens* 34, no. 4 (April 1954): 271.

117. For a detailed analysis of this process, see Richard Harris, "The Birth of the Housing Consumer in the United States, 1918–1960," *International Journal of Consumer Studies* 33 (2009): 525–32.

118. Wittausch, "Marketing Prefabricated Houses," 701.

119. Wittausch, "Marketing Prefabricated Houses," 702.

120. "'PF' Homes on Parade," *PF: The Magazine of Prefabrication* 2, no. 11 (November 1954), 21.

121. T. Bert King, "The Buyer Gets a Break," *PF: The Magazine of Prefabrication* 4, no.1 (January 1956): 22.

122. This point was made by J. Williams Brosius Jr., a dealer for National Homes. See J. Williams Brosius Jr., letter to the editor, *PF: The Magazine of Prefabrication* 4, no. 3 (March 1956), 10.

123. Harper Richards, "Housing Industry Needs Better Merchandising," *PF: The Magazine of Prefabrication* 3, no. 1 (January 1955): 14.

124. Thomas Hine, *Populuxe* (New York: Alfred A. Knopf, 1986), 11.

125. Hine, *Populuxe*, 53.

126. National Homes' first nationally-coordinated open house was held in February 1953. Beginning in 1954, the company's nationwide open house week was held each September to help launch the upcoming year's line of homes. "How Merchandising on Local and National Level Builds Volume," *American Builder* 75, no. 2 (February 1953): 137.

127. Jacobs, *Detached America*, 49.

128. "You Get So Much More from National Homes," *Better Homes and Gardens* 33, no. 3 (March 1955): 192.

129. Most significant of these was Hollin Hills, which received sustained attention in professional journals and popular magazines over the course of its development between 1949 and 1958. See Elizabeth Jo Lampl, "Charles M. Goodman and 'Tomorrow's

Vernacular,'" in *Housing Washington: Two Centuries of Residential Development and Planning in the National Capitol Area,* ed. Richard Longstreth, 229–53 (Chicago: Center for American Places at Columbia College Chicago, 2010).

130. Lampl, "Charles M. Goodman and 'Tomorrow's Vernacular,'" 233–34.

131. "Here are the new prefabs whose values every builder must meet," 103.

132. Lampl has noted that Goodman was "proud to be called a 'production house architect'" and derived greater gratification from designs replicated in the mass market than one-off projects completed for the wealthy. Lampl, "Charles M. Goodman and 'Tomorrow's Vernacular,'" 234.

133. Anna Vemer Andrzejewski, "Selling Suburbia: Marshall Erdman's Marketing Strategies for Prefabricated Buildings in the Postwar United States," in *Making Suburbia: New Histories of Everyday America,* ed. John Archer et al., 281–301 (Minneapolis: University of Minnesota Press, 2015).

134. Prefabricated housing accounted for only 20 percent of non-farm, single-family housing starts in 1964. Thaler, "Report on Prefabrication," 41.

135. During the 1950s, National Homes pursued an aggressive plan of expansion, opening up new plants to serve the East Coast and Southwest, and later by buying up smaller manufacturers across the country, including on the West Coast. The most prominent, and oldest, of those acquired by National Homes was American Houses, Inc. See, "National Homes Announces Merger," *Manufactured Homes* 7, no. 8 (August 1959): 39.

136. Steve Kerch, "Once Powerful Builder Tries Fast Lane Again," *Chicago Tribune,* July 19, 1987, N1.

137. "National Homes Corp. To Close Plant Making Prefabricated Houses," *Wall Street Journal,* November 8, 1974, 24.

138. George Price, "Revolution in Home Merchandising," 13–14.

139. "Facts About National Homes," *The Republic,* August 29, 1947. National Homes' efforts to reframe the prefabricated house as a practical solution to postwar living was part of a movement within the building industry that pushed back against the "miracle house" rhetoric of the 1930s. As Shanken has noted, in the 1940s American Builder "laced its pages with anti-dreamhouse commentary" and played a significant role in promoting traditional aesthetics for new homes. See Shanken, *194x,* 169.

140. Jacobs, *Detached America,* 80.

TRAVIS MCDONALD

# *Research Notes:* Understanding the Physical Poetry of a Parallel American Dream

Anne Spencer (1882–1975) was an African American high school librarian in Lynchburg, Virginia, who became nationally known, if not by her own choosing, as a poet of the Harlem Renaissance during the 1920s. The 1903 house Anne built with her husband Edward is now a National Register property and Virginia Landmark house museum, known principally for its personal and eclectic interior and flower garden, which evolved over a sixty-two-year period. This essay considers how to interpret this remarkable yet little-known historic site, which represents an artistic and architectural creation that is inextricably based on, and exhibits, the ephemeral characteristics of flowers and poetry.

Fieldwork at the Anne and Edward Spencer house prompts questions about how and why we record what we record. The site defies typical interpretations, and even the wide-net approaches found in VAF's *Invitation to Vernacular Architecture.*[1] In this case many of the fields through which architectural history is now studied overlap: ethnicity, gender, class, race, sociology, feminism, and economics. A Venn diagram of intersecting subjects at this site would thicken with the major themes of architecture, art, interior decorating, decorative arts, craftsmanship, material culture, gardening, and poetry. The diversity of new fields and the range of subjects within those fields have led to a broader but more fragmented view of architectural history. Dell Upton characterized architecture as "the art of social story-telling, a means for shaping American society and culture."[2] That is surely the more public macro lens though which to see the Spencer site.

Upton also acknowledged that in some cases architecture was "a vehicle of individual aesthetic expression."[3] This is the more challenging and private micro lens through which to see Anne Spencer's artistic creation. Particularly challenging to confront is how the ephemeral and ever-changing essence of Anne Spencer's garden found expression both in her poetry and in her interior decorations and furnishings (Figure 1). Anne managed to describe the colors, smells, and textures of flowers in words, writing, "Earth, I thank you / for the pleasure of your language."[4] She effectively used poetry to capture the nuances of nature, but describing the poetry of colors, patterns, and textures of an interior setting, inspired by the same ephemeral beauty of nature, challenges our typical interpretive conventions.

Literary and artistic shrines can evoke the autobiographical nature of a writer's or artist's home and garden, yet few have the symbiotic spirit and presence of poetry, flowers, art, and architecture that define the Spencer house and garden. While Anne Spencer's poetry and gardening have been studied to an extent, the house itself had been minimally documented before I took on what I thought would be the modest task of recording the interior and advising on restoration issues.[5] The authenticity of the house rests on the fortunate circumstance that it was left virtually intact as a museum when Anne Spencer died in 1975. In *Half My World: The Garden of Anne Spencer,* Rebecca Frischkorn and Reuben Rainey describe Anne Spencer's garden and poetry as "subtle, original, richly nuanced, and carefully crafted." I soon began to realize that this was equally true

Figure 1. Anne Bannister Spencer in a 1901 wedding photograph. Courtesy of Anne Spencer Memorial House Foundation.

for the architecture, decoration, and furnishings of her house.[6] This site and story are even more unusual and significant for the way all these familiar themes are overlain by the filters of social, cultural, educational, political, and racial contexts of an African American family's pursuit of happiness in a small traditional Southern city in the early twentieth century. The liberating equality and dignity achieved through this family's accomplishments was private and public, local and national, unique and popular. Understanding this site as an autobiographical domestic creation poses one set of fieldwork questions. Another is how the site fits into a larger social, cultural, and architectural landscape, particularly in terms of race. In other words, how does it reflect the many studies and interpretations of the iconic single-family house in America?

### The Creation of Anne Spencer's Identity

Anne Bannister Spencer was born in 1882 on a rural plantation in Henry County, Virginia, to Joel Bannister, a former slave, and Sarah Scales, who was the daughter of a prominent slave owner and one of his slaves.[7] After her parents separated, Anne's mother moved to the coalfields of Bramwell, West Virginia, to find work. Anne boarded there with a prominent black family who informally taught her to read at the age of nine. Sarah's ambition for her daughter led Anne to enter the Virginia Theological Seminary and College in Lynchburg in 1893 at the age of eleven. She graduated six years later with a liberal arts education in history, literature, math, science, Latin, French, and German. Anne received a four-volume set of the writings of Ralph Waldo Emerson shortly after graduation. It "became a major influence on her life and work as a poet."[8]

Anne returned to Bramwell as a pioneering African American teacher, working there for several years before moving back to Lynchburg to teach for the Seminary. In 1901 she married former Seminary student Edward Spencer (Figure 2). After raising three children, Anne served from 1923 to 1945 as the first female librarian at the segregated Dunbar High School in Lynchburg. If for no other reason, Anne would be remembered as the well-educated librarian who inspired many students through her erudition and the extensive personal library she shared with the school children. But these are her backstory accomplishments, and not those for which she is publicly remembered.

Anne and her husband lived in what now appears to be a fairly conventional 1903 Queen Anne–style house on a suburban neighborhood street with a restored garden in the back yard (Figure 3). What makes the house and neighborhood different is that it was an African American enclave surrounded by a white neighborhood. The area was formerly Camp Davis, a Civil War campground that later became a Freedman's Bureau refuge for freed slaves. Beginning in the 1870s African Americans bought part of this land and developed houses, businesses, and churches. Warwick Spencer and his sons Edward and Warwick Jr. developed part of Pierce Street as "Spencer Place," constructing a number of houses.[9] The house Edward and Anne constructed at 1313 Pierce Street, next to Warwick's house, stood in this fashionable African American neighborhood. The neighborhood now forms the National Register's Pierce Street Renaissance Historic District, boasting eight Virginia state historical markers in its two block area that pay homage to the significant African American educators, musicians, physicians, athletes, architects, aviators, civil rights pioneers, and civic leaders who lived here during the twentieth century. This "American dream" suburban neighborhood looked like many contemporary white neighborhoods in the segregated city. It was racially separate but architecturally equal. How unusual was this in Lynchburg, or elsewhere, for the time? Did living in this neighborhood make a difference for African American families as opposed to those who lived in older neighborhoods of "hand-me-down" houses left by white families moving to the suburbs?[10]

While the Spencer's house looked typical on the exterior, inside was a unique artistic creation (Figures 4 and 5). Edward served as Lynchburg's first African American parcel postman, a position that led him to collect bits and pieces of discarded architectural parts he discovered around town for use in the house and garden.[11] His finds were innovatively reused throughout the house, on the staircase, in windows, on the roof, for the metal wainscot, in the attic billiard room, as radiator covers, in the entry hall alcove, for kitchen windows and cabinets, in the garden, at the cottage, pasted on walls, on floors, as wall panels, around fireplaces, and for doorways (Figures 6 and 7). These in turn became the canvas for Anne's artistic talents, inspired by the bold and flamboyant combination of colors and textures in the garden. The "constant revisions, enlargements, re-crafting, and refinements" that characterized Anne's poetry and gardening for seventy years mirror, and are mirrored, in the 1903 house.[12]

The interior spaces display a chronological and stratigraphic record on floors, walls, and ceilings of ever-changing colors, textures, wallpapers, and textiles. Anne painted flowers and designs on walls and furniture. Cutout portions of wallpapers or textile fabrics are glued and mixed with other forms and designs on walls and

Figure 2. Anne and Edward Spencer with two of their grandchildren, Billie and Barbara Stevenson, in the 1930s. Courtesy of Anne Spencer Memorial House Foundation.

Figure 3. The 1903 Spencer house. Photograph by Travis McDonald, 2017.

furniture (Figure 8). Her good friend and former neighbor, African American modernist architect Amaza Lee Meredith, contributed to the decor with murals and tilework. Anne's poem "Lines to a Nasturtium" was hand-painted on a kitchen cabinet by Meredith (Figure 9).[13] Anne's poetry was written on walls, kitchen cabinets, in the phone booth, and on every conceivable paper or cardboard surface. A painted mural, "The Cocktail Party," was wry social commentary reserved for an upstairs bedroom wall.[14] Chinese papers and fabrics of bright colors sometimes determined the room scheme. Another bedroom featured a small tribute to Anne's Native Indian heritage with a map by African American artist Louise E. Jefferson pasted on the wall. In that same room, painted Mexican furniture coexists

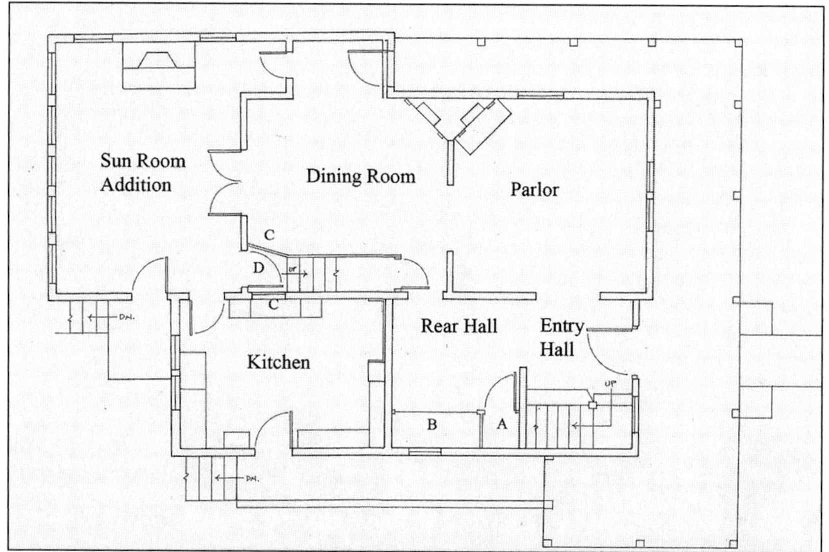

Figure 4. First-floor plan. The original rear hall was altered when a telephone booth (A) and window alcove (B) were created. The house was expanded with the sun room addition overlooking the rear garden. At that time the double doors from the parlor to the dining room were moved to the new doorway to the sun room. With the addition, the doorways at C from the rear stairs (D) to the kitchen and dining room were closed. Drawing by Travis McDonald.

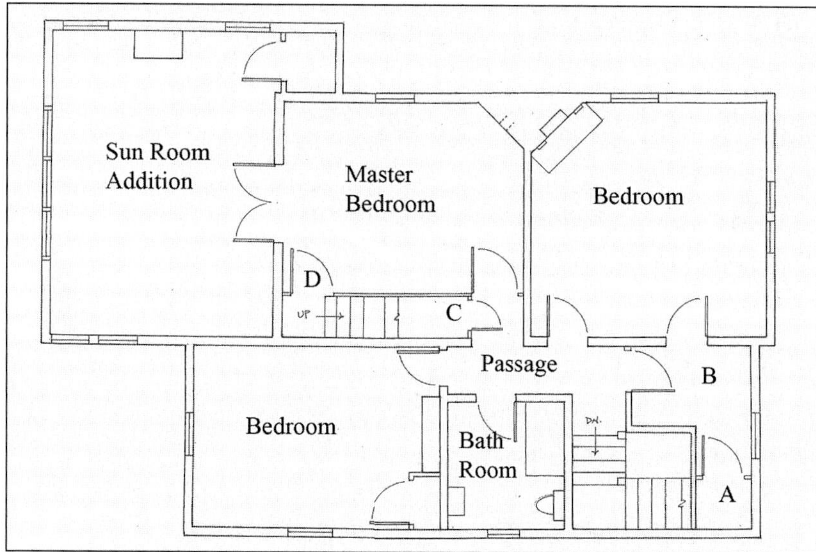

Figure 5. Second-floor plan. A closet (A) was added in the space (B) that was most likely a nursery room. The back stairs at C lead down and the stairs at D lead up to the attic room. The sun room addition overlooking the back garden provided more space for family. Drawing by Travis McDonald.

with Anne's hand-painted furniture and decorative arts objects that match the room's final color scheme. A portrait of Anne's grandfather, a plantation owner who had fathered Anne's enslaved grandmother, references a different heri-

tage. The dining room suite must have been the one expensive and up-to-date commodity indulgence, an arts and crafts set of Stickley pieces in a floral design (Figure 10).[15] Edward created his own space in the attic where he played billiards with friends. The attic later became the domain of many grandchildren who came to visit. The house expanded in the 1950s with a family sunroom overlooking the garden that provided extra informal space for visitors and guests. The upper story of the addition was another light-filled room overlooking the garden, providing extra bedroom space for a growing family. Probably at the time of the addition the exterior took on a more craftsman look when wood shingles were placed over the weatherboards. The house was a lively conversation of eclectic forms, finishes, and furnishings, incorporating Victorian, Edwardian, Queen Anne, gothic revival, renaissance revival, art deco, art nouveau, chinoiserie, aestheticism, and arts and crafts. This bespoke dwelling reflected the popularized suburban ideal and the important social aspect of property ownership and architectural pride. Anne wrote: "We have a lovely house—one that money did not buy—it was born and evolved slowly out of our passionate, poverty-stricken agony to own our own home [our] happiness."[16]

In *Architecture and Suburbia*, historian John Archer suggests that the "American Dream House" is elusive, but tied to a mix of personal and private opportunities and goals related to the long history of the individual dwelling and development of the individual self.[17] Dell Upton reiterated the importance of that "American icon," the single-family house, that claims "a place for the individual and the family in time (history) and space (community)."[18] But this was not a typical family or a typical house. Anne's personal, eclectic taste was inspired by popular home and garden arbiters of fashion, including *Better Homes and Gardens, House Beautiful, American Home, House and Garden, Country Life, Garden and Home Builder, The Delineator, Arts and Decoration*, and *Home Garden*.[19] The poetic ensemble of textures, colors, fabrics, materials, art, and furnishings of the house interior, related to and inspired by the garden, makes this unique personal creation hard to define and interpret. But to analyze the building and landscape without knowledge of Anne's poetry, her gardening, and her social and political activism, would miss key factors that explain the building's and its owner's historical significance. Anne's poetry was derived from nature, from the outdoor "rooms" and seasonal changes of the garden, and from the characteristics of individual flowers and plants. This peaceful and beautiful oasis became the intimate setting and context that shaped the relationship between family, friends, colleagues, artists, writers, and national civil rights leaders.

In searching for a framework to make sense of the confluence of these cultural spheres, I turned to Henry Glassie's pioneering work to try to understand such intangible factors as I felt unequipped to consider. Glassie's ethnological approach to understanding vernacular houses relied on interviews with builders and occupants to learn the social process of a dwelling.[20] While historians had interviewed Anne Spencer before she died in 1975 and her house and garden have been faithfully preserved and restored, an ethnological approach along the lines of Glassie's would provide a useful starting point for a richer understanding of the site, if its creators were still alive.[21] Glassie believed the exterior of a house appeals to the intellect and is more rational, while the interior "comforts the body and delights the senses—soft seats and titillating array of textiles, patterns, and colors. The weary bones find rest, the eye finds excitement. As a device for communication, unfolding from the householder's interests and taste, the interior stimulates engagement."[22] This seemed an accurate description for the feeling inside the Spencer house, with the "engagement" even extending into the garden "rooms." Glassie describes a phase of cultural transformation in vernacular houses as the "commodity" stage. This was the moment when houses themselves became commodities "and people were assigned the difficult task of shaping their personalities out of things made by other people."[23] This seemed especially true of the Spencer house. Was this another example of the single-family house that is said to reflect an individual portrait of its occupants? Did the

Figure 6. Parlor. Window architraves painted with metallic gold paint with symmetrical moldings and corner blocks are typical throughout the house. Recycled parts include the radiator cover and the mirror. The floor has a second period covering and the walls, formerly papered, are now stenciled. Anne's eclectic taste is seen in an oriental style desk, art nouveau vases, an art deco statue, and nineteenth-century furniture. Photograph by Travis McDonald, 2016.

Figure 7. Rear of the entry hall. The floral wallpaper with birds is the third generation of paper on this wall and is matched by other pink wallpaper and green and pink woodwork. The mirror and the parts that make up the window alcove are recycled pieces. Reflected in the mirror is the open door of the booth created for an early telephone, one of the most up-to-date conveniences in the house. The second-generation floor covering is an arts and crafts–style linoleum imitating tiles featuring flowers and animals. Photograph by Travis McDonald, 2015.

Figure 8. Second-floor bedroom. The final decorative scheme in this room is dictated by the red, green, and yellow colors of the Chinese wallpaper. Woodwork and walls are bright yellow, floors and ceiling are bright orange, and one door and the headboard are covered with the same recycled wallpaper. Photograph by Travis McDonald, 2016.

Victorian ideology hold true here that the interior of a home and its garden was the province and domain of the woman, or was the Spencer house different in some way?

### Anne's Outdoor Tapestry

Anne referred to her garden as "half my world" and mentioned the Greek god Antaeus as a reference to her strength coming from contact with the earth.[24] As a woman of color, she could not benefit from the early garden clubs in Lynchburg but taught herself from popular home and garden magazines. Her early influences, she said, were roaming the woods and streams as a young girl and she and Edward would collect native plants for the garden (Figure 11).[25] Anne created a compact series of garden "rooms," including the rose garden, the cottage garden, the arbor garden, and the pool garden, each defined by recycled architectural parts, including an African Ebo tribe metal head given to her by W. E. B. Du Bois and used for a fountain at the lily pond. Anne's garden cottage, her personal and creative sanctuary retreat, built by Edward with reused parts, was named Edankraal, a combination of Ed and Anne, and kraal, an Afrikaans word connoting a cultural recognition of the past and a

safe enclosure (Figures 12 and 13). There she could retreat when tired, frustrated, sad, or satisfied. The other significant intellectual retreat in the Lynchburg area was Thomas Jefferson's Poplar Forest, which Anne might have known about but probably never saw. Anne's small intimate cottage, just 240 square feet, served a similar purpose as Jefferson's, an intellectual "sanctum sanctorum" where her literary muse found strength and inspiration surrounded by the nurturing nature of the garden. The garden also functioned as a family and social space, and as an outdoor salon for her notable guests. Anne wrote of her garden, "This small garden is half my world. I am nothing to it—when all is said, I plant the thorn and kiss the rose, But they will grow when I am dead."[26]

Rebecca T. Frischkorn and Reuben M. Rainey's book on the Spencer garden, *Half My World,* describes the centuries-old connection between garden sanctuaries and poetry, saying "Often the engaging presence of the garden itself, its processes of growth, decay, and transformation, its sounds, textures, tastes, fragrances, and visual delights, touch the deepest levels of the human spirit and quicken the poetic imagination. The language of the poet is infused with the alchemy of the garden. The garden both shelters and cultivates the poet."[27] Anne and Edward Spencer's architectural creation was no less alchemy; the genius of the place was a fusion of poetry, gardening, and architectural settings that reflected the complex intellect of its creators. This statement about Anne's outdoor world seems a perfect metaphor: "A garden is a tapestry of relationships between those who design and care for the garden, those who visit and appreciate it, and the garden itself."[28] It was both a private and personal sanctuary and a safe, stimulating refuge for visiting public figures in the midst of public and racial strife.

Unlike the house, the garden needed restoration after Anne's death, which was lovingly and expertly carried out under the direction of Jane White and the Lynchburg Hillside Garden Club in 1983–85 (Figure 14). White's *Lessons Learned from a Poet's Garden* details the challenging nuances of this garden restoration based on physical evidence, photographs, and documents.[29] Anne's garden resembles a cottage garden in many ways and had elements of both formal and natural aspects. As in the interior, Anne had drawn ideas from magazines, but her gardening style was all her own. Certain features could be considered vernacular African American forms (but are not obviously so): the imaginative use of recycled materials, brilliant flower colors, the use of native plants, and as an intimate family and neighborhood space.[30] The Spencer garden can now be experienced as the indispensable natural realm through which to understand and interpret Anne's poetry and her choices in interior decoration. On a more public level, as devices for communication and for stimulating engagement, Anne and Edward's personally-shaped spaces, both inside and out, served as the setting for nationally-significant intimate and humanistic conversations, albeit unrecorded, that finally define the sociopolitical civil rights role of Anne Spencer.

From the 1920s onward, Anne and Edward Spencer were part of the private hospitality network of African Americans, both friends and strangers, who happened to be traveling through Lynchburg and could not stay or eat at segregated white establishments. Although they were not listed in the famous *Negro Motorist Green Book* guides published for African American travelers, the Spencers' house and garden were well known and prized by an upper echelon of visitors. Notable African Americans stayed with the Spencers by circumstance, and many made a determined pilgrimage to this neighborhood and house, including Langston Hughes, Paul Robeson, W. E. B. DuBois, Adam Clayton Powell, James Weldon Johnson, Sterling Brown, Thurgood Marshall, Marian Anderson, Zora Neale Hurston, George Washington Carver, Mary McLeod Bethune, and the Reverend Martin Luther King Jr.

We can only image the conversations. One of the most important guests was the writer and poet James Weldon Johnson, who had come to Lynchburg on behalf of the NAACP and brought Anne into a more active role in civil rights when he established one of the earliest chapters of that organization in her living room. Anne also cam-

Figure 9. Kitchen. Recycled parts include the window sash (bright yellow), the reoriented louvered blinds (light green), the cabinets, and the padded double door from a former movie theater. The wooden wainscot is a bright green, the ceiling is light green, the final wall treatment is a patterned contact paper, the floor is a third-generation linoleum covering. Anne's poem "Lines to a Nasturtium" is hand-painted by Amaza Lee Meredith on floral wallpaper covering the cabinet door. Photograph by Travis McDonald, 2015.

paigned for more black teachers in black schools and became a powerful voice seeking to improve the legal, social, and economic lives of local African Americans. Anne's commitment "was strengthened by what she described as 'a colossal reserve of constructive indignation.'"[31]

It was while staying with the Spencers that Johnson discovered Anne's poetry, theretofore written privately for herself. About half of her

Figure 10. Dining Room. The Stickley suite, in an oriental style with flowers, includes the dining room table and chairs, a small side table, the buffet side board, and a cabinet with gold leaf and floral panels. The stained wood wainscot features recycled metal panels painted metallic gold. Above the sideboard is a recycled floral wallpaper. Two other walls have hand-painted panels of flowers. All the walls had an earlier patterned wallpaper. On the right side of the rear wall is the filled doorway that originally led to the rear staircase and kitchen. Recycled gothic style trim with multicolored tile covers a radiator (just visible on the right) that used to be in front of the rear window but now separates the dining room from the sunroom addition. Photograph by Travis McDonald, 2016.

poems expressed thoughts about nature and her garden, drawing heavily upon her Emersonian philosophy. She also admired the work of Robert Browning, John Keats, and Emily Dickinson. Some of her poems served as outlets for her opinions about national and local Jim Crow racism. Johnson encouraged Anne to submit her poems for publication. Her first published work in 1920, at age thirty-eight, appeared in

Figure 11. Anne Spencer in the garden, 1947. Courtesy of Nancy Marion.

the NAACP journal *The Crisis*. Johnson sent one of Anne's poems to his editor, H. L. Mencken, who published it and thus began her public literary life as part of the Harlem Renaissance, with over thirty published poems. Her work appeared in Johnson's *The Book of American Negro Poetry* (1922), in Alain Locke's *The New Negro* (1925), and in Countee Cullen's *Caroling Dusk: An Anthology of Verse by Negro Poets* (1927). Her poem "Requiem" appeared in her good friend Langston Hughes's *The Poetry of the Negro, 1746–1949* in 1949. It refers to the death of a poet and the body returning to the earth.

Notably, Anne was the only Virginian, and the only African American woman, to be included in the first edition of the *Norton Anthology of American Poetry* (1973). Anne said of her poetry, "I write about things I love. I have no civilized articulation for the things I hate. I proudly love being a Negro woman-—it's so involved and interesting. We are the *Problem*—the great national game of TABOO." Anne's close friend Langston Hughes wrote: "On Anne Spencer's table there lies an unsharpened pencil—As though she has left unwritten—Many things she knows to write."[32] In her book on Anne Spencer's poetry, Nina V. Salmon commented: "To call Anne Spencer a Harlem Renaissance poet is as generic as calling one of her nasturtiums a flower. She was as unique and multifaceted in her field as a nasturtium is in the garden."[33] Anne's reputation was further enhanced by trips to New York City, Washington, D.C., and Atlanta, where she cultivated friendships within the Harlem Renaissance milieu.

### Finding Meaning in Anne Spencer's Creation

Poetry is the one part of this complex artistic equation for which Anne Spencer is well known. Understanding Anne's poetry in relationship to the garden and the interior of her home is more of an intuitive and sensory experience than something easily defined, with layers of interconnected forms and meanings. My first experience with visiting, and then recording, the Spencer house was from the somewhat straightforward approach of seeing it as an example of the public history venue of the historic house museum. I knew from bringing my annual field school participants to the site that it was usually a class favorite, beating out the likes of Monticello and Montpelier with a powerful authenticity. It felt like being in your grandmother's house where she had just stepped out. The stratum of interior finishes was intriguing, but also intimidating to understand.

Slowly the many intersecting layers of furnishings and finishes that reflected literary and gardening connections stymied my frame of reference. I felt that the micro level of meaning, analyzing the decorative overlays, still required a unique approach. Perhaps I could find an answer here to macro-level questions about an African American middle-class architecture. But could this site be analyzed in typical fields of vernacular study, or did it need a different ethnic and racial analytical framework? I felt uncomfortable that by suggesting it needed a special approach I was somehow denying the Spencer's dignity and attainment of the American dream by putting it in a "separate-but-equal" category.

Upton's broad sweep of American architecture clearly documented what architectural historians have long realized—that the major published mainstream histories of American houses missed a large segment of the population.[34] The aspirations of ethnic groups and class distinctions were skewed by urban reformers' moralistic attitudes that held the poor were "people who needed behavioral modification, people for whom the mechanisms of consumption were irrelevant or even out of place."[35] Even our contemporary urban planners seem to misunderstand the diversity they claim to champion. So how did the nineteenth-century importance of the single-family house and the cult of domesticity relate to the Spencer house? Gwendolyn Wright's 1981 *Building the Dream: A Social History of Housing in America* frames important questions about domestic space. Her work focused on ordinary houses and middle-class people as they reflected the domestic cult of the model American house.

Wright only touched on African Americans in this work, but her discussions of the following themes do give us framework for a set of relevant analytical questions we might be asking. These include the progressive reform movement

Figure 12. Edankraal retreat. This small structure of local greenstone was built with recycled architectural parts. The meaning of the cutout feature on the roof is a puzzle, showing a woman watering a child on the ground while holding an implement that engages with a cat. Photograph by Travis McDonald, 2016.

Figure 13. Edankraal. The small interior of Anne's retreat contained photographs of family and friends, books, eclectic furnishings and objects, a small wood stove, and her desk. Two walls of windows overlooked the garden that inspired her poetry. Photograph by Travis McDonald, 2016.

by women in the 1890s; the rise of "domestic science" taught in schools; the public health movement for domestic hygiene; the arts and crafts movement in housing and furnishings; the social and technological emphasis on bathrooms and kitchens; the Federal Housing Act of 1949; slum clearance and the rise of public housing; and the practice of real estate redlining in suburban development. All of these themes could be explored through the Spencer house and neighborhood, alongside the larger question of how they relate to other African American houses and neighborhoods that were not the leftover older intercity areas whites abandoned for the suburbs. Archer examines examples of African American middle-class suburbs but states: "The implicit condition for the success, nevertheless, was the persistence, even hardening, of racial

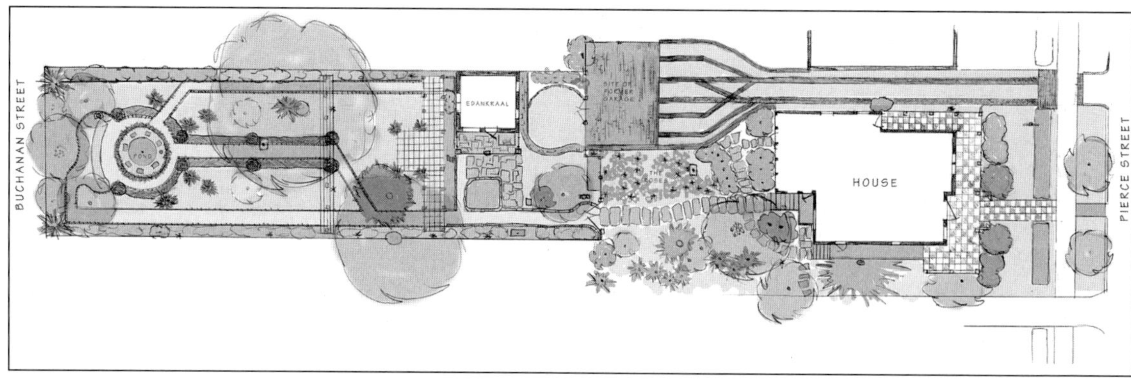



Figure 14. Plan of restored garden, 2011. The sequence from the house is through the rose garden, the wisteria pergola, the grape arbor, the cottage garden, and the lily pond garden. Recycled parts and bird houses on tall poles were used throughout the garden. Courtesy of Jane Baber White.

segregation: African Americans' *class* aspirations and achievements were allied with their continuing isolation as a *racial* group."[36]

I wondered if there were any vernacular studies that might have addressed the social and cultural aspects of middle-class African American dwellings.[37] My survey of published articles from *Perspectives in Vernacular Architecture* and *Buildings & Landscapes* from 1982 to the present revealed only three articles (out of 297) that principally addressed this subject. M. Jeff Hardwick's article on the African American houses in Langston, Oklahoma, is an interesting example of what African Americans built when they shaped their own town and community as part of the Indian Territory land rush in the 1890s.[38] When a later generation of residents upgraded from dugouts and log cabins in the twentieth century, they primarily chose the bungalow from popular American house forms. This was a more modern and progressive style, as opposed to the popular romanticized colonial revival models, which did not appeal to African Americans for obvious historical reasons.[39] Hardwick remarked that breaking down the monolithic "American experience" into separate ethnic examples serves to create narratives that emphasize separation and exclusion from popular cultural forms. He thought that "appropriation and participation in popular culture by African Americans presents a troublesome topic for scholars searching for 'authentic' forms of African American culture."[40] Studying the house forms in Langston, the author concluded, revealed that this example was neither a singular nor a monolithic phenomenon of cultural production; this seemed like a conundrum of an answer.

The other two articles, both by M. Ruth Little, were more to the point and answered my primary questions on the larger level of architectural history.[41] Little began with the same assumptions architectural historians had: that African American buildings, besides the well-known shotgun houses, exhibited ethnic traditions even into the twentieth century. She pointed out that other ethnic groups, so well represented in vernacular studies, had shed any cultural forms by the twentieth century. She also suggested that most African Americans would be surprised to learn their architecture was somehow ethnic and that "most assume that their buildings represent an architecture vocabulary that is shared by whites."[42] Little's study was based on a multicity survey of African American neighborhoods in North Carolina. She asked the same inevitable basic question: is African American housing different from white housing? Her answer was tempered by the realization that a direct comparison could not be made unless the same agencies had been at work, in other words, the same freedom and forces of choice in location, developer, builder, and economy. She determined that out of three categories of African American housing (rental housing, hand-me-down housing, and owner-built housing), it was the last type that could be compared with white neighborhoods to determine architectural aesthetics. In a number of examples, Little records that middle-class African American houses of "free agency" resembled the same Victorian, neocolonial, bungalow, Spanish colonial, Tudor, craftsman, and even Sears and Roebuck mail-order houses that were in comparable white suburban neighborhoods. Whether in self-segregated or code-segregated neighborhoods, the separate-but-equal architecture of free agency represented a proud upward mobility for the African American middle and professional classes. Black leaders saw home ownership as "race progress" that could "earn full participation in southern society by property ownership, exemplary citizenship, and the 'moral, social, religious and general development of the community.' "[43] Little concluded that African Americans, given the same agency, were acculturated into mainstream American culture at the same rate as other ethnic and racial groups. On a level playing field, there "is no longer white or black architecture, but simply middle-class architecture."[44] The Spencers can be considered middle class by a number of measures, but in terms of education and lifestyle aesthetics in their time and place, they might be considered upper class and exceptional. It would be interesting to know how other middle-class African Americans of the twentieth century defined their status through material culture. Lizabeth Cohen found that the white working classes did not follow the advice of progressive era reformers to favor architectural simplicity and shy away

from Victorian aesthetics of material culture. Instead, "the old style well suited their desire to adapt to mass produced goods, just as it had for the middle class several generations earlier."[45] This is certainly true of the Spencers' eclectic and artistic furnishings. Unfortunately, apart from the scant research on house styles, scholarship lags behind on the material culture of middle-class African American families in owner-occupied houses, not to mention working-class African Americans in any type of housing (Figure 15).

Little summarizes a Jim Crow–era debate within the African American community that pitted Booker T. Washington's accommodation policy against W. E. B. Du Bois's confrontation policy. Apparently they both agreed that successful African American communities were part of the solution. In his 1903 *The Souls of Black Folk*, W. E. B. Du Bois states that the domestic legacy of slavery, represented by African Americans still living in similar cabins, reinforced white attitudes toward standards of character and cleanliness, and legitimized segregation policies.[46] Five years later in his book *The Negro American*

Figure 15. Anne and Edward Spencer in the rear of the garden seated in front of the lily pond featuring "Prince Ebo's" fountain head, 1937. Courtesy of Anne Spencer Memorial Foundation.

*Family*, Du Bois saw successful African American neighborhoods in North Carolina as the definition of progress.[47] He undoubtedly thought the same of the Pierce Street enclave when he stayed in the Spencer house, which easily matched contemporary white suburban houses in its modern, up-to-date conveniences.

Glassie remarked that the ethnographic alternative to the familiar experiences of fieldwork would "alert us to what we cannot know when all we have to study is an empty house in ruins."[48] In the case of the Spencers' creation, it is the opposite that challenges conventional analysis, the extraordinarily rich visual, literary, and cultural clues are there to be deciphered. This is not an empty house in ruins but one empty of translation. If only we could talk to Anne Spencer we could exchange our inadequately parsed understanding with glimpses of her innermost creative impulses. Can we use vernacular studies, in Glassie's definition, as "one of the tools we use when we face architectural objects with a wish to crack them open and learn their meanings?"[49] What seems impossible is to relate the "subtle, original, nuanced, and carefully crafted" stratigraphic layers of paints, wallpapers, and finishes to eras of poetry, gardening, or personal events in the life of this remarkable couple. How might our "tools" still find meaning in this exceptional case of ephemeral cultural landscapes?

Glassie's definition of "vernacular" also meant a transition from the unknown to the known, "accommodating cultural diversity . . . it welcomes the neglected into study in order to knowledge the reality of differences and conflict."[50] The reality of differences in this challenge seems to be a conflict in judging something that is still considered separate and equal, singular and monolithic. I still grapple with the answers, but this is not my task. I have raised the questions and noted the challenge as it suggests a different approach from normative vernacular architectural fieldwork and recording, and cultural landscapes still to explore. In this particular case it will require an academic lifetime or two of interdisciplinary work to do justice to this one small place of personal achievement, happiness, and legacy in Lynchburg, Virginia.[51]

AUTHOR BIOGRAPHY

**Travis McDonald** is Director of Architectural Restoration at Thomas Jefferson's Poplar Forest.

NOTES

For colored versions of some images in this article, see the online issue at http://www.jstor.org/r/umnpress.

1. Thomas Carter and Elizabeth Collins Cromley, *Invitation to Vernacular Architecture* (Knoxville: University of Tennessee Press, 2005).

2. Dell Upton, *Architecture in the United States* (Oxford: Oxford University Press, 1998), 11.

3. Upton, *Architecture in the United States*, 11.

4. Nina V. Salmon, *Anne Spencer: "Ah, How Poets Sing and Die!"* (Lynchburg, Va.: Warwick House Publishing, 2001), 11.

5. The only other architectural description is a 1976 National Register of Historic Places nomination form that described the house in general terms. Virginia Historic Landmarks Commission Staff, Anne Spencer House (National Park Service, National Register of Historic Places, 1976), available from http://www.dhr.virginia.gov/registers/Cities/Lynchburg/118–0061_Spencer,Anne,House_1976_Final_Nomination.pdf.

6. Rebecca T. Frischkorn and Reuben M. Rainey, *Half My World: The Garden of Anne Spencer, A History and Guide* (Lynchburg, Va.: Warwick House Publishing, 2003), 27.

7. This history comes from the Anne Spencer House Museum website, from Frischkorn and Rainey; Salmon; and Stewart Plein, "The Poet Anne Spencer and Her Two Virginias," undated online paper available at www.academia.edu/22842078/The_Poet_Anne_Spencer_and_Her_Two_Virginias

8. Frischkorn and Rainey, *Half My World*, 13.

9. An excellent history of this neighborhood is found in W. Scott Breckenridge Smith, *National Register Nomination, Pierce Street District* (Richmond: Department of Historic Resources, 2014).

10. There is no doubt that the life the Spencers made advanced the lives of their children. Their third child, Chauncey Spencer, was an early African American aviator who made a flight in 1939 from Chicago to Washington in an old biplane and convinced Senator Harry Truman to admit men of color into the Army Air Corps. He was a founding member of the National Airmen's Association of America, which became the

Tuskegee Airmen. His flight suit is in the Smithsonian National Air and Space Museum.

11. Edward was also a partner in Calloway's grocery store on the same block as the Spencer house and operated it with his brother Warwick after William Calloway died in 1907. When Edward died in 1964 a *Lynchburg News* editorial praised him as "one of the city's most respected, exemplary citizens . . . generous, kindly, honorable and with a sensitive intelligence, such men live on in memory." Quoted in Frischkorn and Rainey, *Half My World,* 26.

12. Frischkorn and Rainey, *Half My World,* 27.

13. Meredith (1895–1984) spent part of her childhood a few doors down from the Spencer house. She received her master's degree in art from Columbia University in 1934 and later taught art at Dunbar High School where Anne Spencer worked, and eventually founded the Art Department at Virginia State University, where she designed her own Bauhaus-style home, "Azurest South." She also founded an upscale black development, "Azurest North," at Sag Harbor, Long Island, New York.

14. This was perhaps related to a book in Anne's library: *The Cocktail Party: A Comedy* by T. S. Eliot. Shaun Spencer-Hester, Anne's granddaughter, says that her grandfather pasted the canvas mural on the wall to keep his wife from getting up at night and writing poetry on the wall.

15. The label on this multi-piece set is Quaint American Furniture, Stickley Brothers, Grand Rapids, Michigan.

16. Quoted in the Anne Spencer House Museum brochure.

17. John Archer, *Architecture and Suburbia: From English Villa to American Dream House, 1690–2000* (Minneapolis: University of Minnesota Press, 2005), xv.

18. Upton, *Architecture in the United States,* 17.

19. This list is compiled from the catalog of Anne Spencer's papers at the University of Virginia. See final endnote.

20. Henry Glassie, *Vernacular Architecture* (Bloomington: Indiana University Press, 2000), 19.

21. J. Lee Greene, *Time's Unfading Garden: Anne Spencer's Life and Poetry* (Baton Rouge: Louisiana State University Press, 1977). Greene's interviews with Anne Spencer are invaluable for insights into her poetry and some of her gardening. Unfortunately they do not shed much light on her thoughts regarding her interior work.

22. Glassie, *Vernacular Architecture,* 66.

23. Glassie, *Vernacular Architecture,* 152.

24. Frischkorn and Rainey, *Half My World,* 27.

25. Frischkorn and Rainey, *Half My World,* 30.

26. Salmon, *Anne Spencer,* 59.

27. Frischkorn and Rainey, *Half My World ,* 11.

28. Frischkorn and Rainey, *Half My World,* 45.

29. Jane Baber White, *Lessons Learned from a Poet's Garden: The Restoration of the Historic Garden of Harlem Renaissance Poet Anne Spencer* (Lynchburg, Va.: Blackwell Press, 2011).

30. Frischkorn and Rainey, *Half My World,* 30.

31. Frischkorn and Rainey, *Half My World,* 25.

32. Salmon, *Anne Spencer,* 24.

33. Salmon, *Anne Spencer,* 1.

34. Upton, *Architecture in the United States.*

35. Upton, *Architecture in the United States,* 243.

36. Archer, *Architecture and Suburbia,* 301.

37. One reader of this manuscript suggested Stephanie Shaw's *What a Woman Ought to Be and Do* (Chicago: University of Chicago Press, 1996); Howard Rabinowitz's *Curating America: Journey Through Storyscapes of the American Past* (Chapel Hill: University of North Carolina Press, 2016); or work by Kimberlé Crenshaw regarding intersectionality.

38. M. Jeff Hardwick, "Homesteads and Bungalows: African American Architecture in Langston, Oklahoma," in *Perspectives in Vernacular Architecture, VI,* ed. Carter L. Hudgins and Elizabeth C. Crowley (Knoxville: University of Tennessee Press, 1997), 21–32.

39. Hardwick remarks that the Langston College president's house was even more of a modern statement being in an art deco style.

40. Hardwick, "Homesteads," 29.

41. M. Ruth Little, "The Other Side of the Tracks: The Middle-Class Neighborhoods that Jim Crow Built in Early Twentieth Century North Carolina," in *Perspectives in Vernacular Architecture, VII,* ed. Annmarie Adams and Sally McMurry (Knoxville: University of Tennessee Press, 1997), 268–80; M. Ruth Little, "Getting the American Dream for Themselves: Postwar Modern Subdivisions for African Americans in Raleigh, North Carolina," *Buildings & Landscapes* 19, no. 1 (2012): 73–86. The first article by Little was used for this research.

42. Little, "Other Side of the Tracks," 268.

43. Little, "Other Side of the Tracks," 271.

44. Little, "Other Side of the Tracks," 277.

45. Lizabeth A. Cohen, "Embellishing a Life of Labor: An Interpretation of the Material Culture of American Working-Class Homes, 1885–1915," in *Common Places: Readings in American Vernacular Architecture*, ed. Dell Upton and John Michael Vlach (Athens: University of Georgia Press, 1986), 275.

46. W. E. B. Du Bois, *The Souls of Black Folk* (1903; reprint ed., Greenwich, Ct.: Fawcett Publications, 1961), 106.

47. W. E. B. Du Bois, *The Negro American Family* (Atlanta, Ga.: Atlanta University Press, 1908), 65. Quoted in Little, "Other Side of the Tracks," 277.

48. Glassie, *Vernacular Architecture*, 69.

49. Glassie, *Vernacular Architecture*, 21.

50. Glassie, *Vernacular Architecture*, 20.

51. In 2008 the papers of Anne Spencer were purchased by the University of Virginia and include 4,175 items of correspondence, photographs, manuscripts and notebooks of poetry, short stories, articles, and prose works, fragmentary notes, financial and legal papers and volumes, and topical files. A checklist of her books, also at the university, was cataloged separately in 2014. This author has not seen this collection, which is detailed as to scope and content online as "A Guide to the Papers of Anne Spencer and the Spencer Family," in the Special Collections at the University of Virginia, Collection Number 14204. The full historical and cultural significance of Anne Spencer will await someone who can devote considerable time to this very rich collection.

# Reviews

**Clifton Ellis and Rebecca Ginsburg, editors**

*Slavery in the City: Architecture and
Landscapes of Urban Slavery in North America*

Charlottesville: University of Virginia Press, 2017.

ix + 186 pages, 30 black-and-white illustrations.

ISBN: 978-0-8139-4005-2, $32.50 HB

ISBN: 978-0-8139-4006-9, $32.50 EB

Review by Lydia Mattice Brandt

Atlantic and American historians have sought to unravel slavery's monolithic narratives since the dawn of social history studies a generation ago. But rarely do researchers investigate the institution in an urban context beyond a handful of major southern cities. A slim new volume from University of Virginia Press, *Slavery in the City: Architecture and Landscapes of Urban Slavery in North America,* offers compelling evidence that the lives of enslaved Africans and African Americans in places other than Richmond, Charleston, and New Orleans are indeed hidden in plain sight. Its eight essays push beyond the familiar fields and big houses of the plantation to small Tennessee towns and Texas' very edges to prove that "many of the urban environments that are familiar to us today are the legacy of [slavery's] violence, as well as of ingenuity, courage, and perseverance" (10).

*Slavery in the City* argues that urban material culture is key to this more comprehensive understanding of slavery's impact. Beginning with an introductory essay that is almost too generous to traditional history's paucity of attention to urban slavery, the book's editors, Clifton Ellis and Rebecca Ginsburg, clearly espouse their commitment to fieldwork. The essays that follow arc from those rooted firmly in the documentation of structures and landscapes to studies about peoples' movements between buildings. Two pioneers of the vernacular architecture movement, Edward A. Chappell and John Michael Vlach, launch the book with comparative typological investigations of slave housing in the Chesapeake, Jamaica, and northern settlements like Comack, New York. Their essays root the book in the materials and dimensions of buildings, using physical evidence to speak of the intentions of their builders and the perceptions of their otherwise undocumented users. They identify the ways in which the institution of slavery "weaponized" even the very places where enslaved Africans and African Americans laid their heads and built their families (65). Material culture thus confirms the futility of any attempt to argue that urban slavery was any less brutal than agricultural slavery.

The book continues with essays that focus on single case studies but vary in the methodologies they use to recover the experiences of the enslaved. Clifton Ellis translates painstaking documentary and archeological research into a highly readable essay on Annapolis. He ultimately concludes that the *lack* of distinct spaces for enslaved people indicates the fluidity of slavery in late eighteenth-century Annapolis, complicating the previous essays' arguments for the importance of physical evidence. Gina Haney follows with an essay that also finds much in what is not there. Her bold combination of feminist scholarship's "standpoint theory" and sensory history delivers an evocative look at how something as natural as shifts in daylight affected spaces for white and black Charlestonians.

The volume's final essays epitomize vernacular architecture's gospel of the local. Each looks closely at how a specific place's landscape, geography, economics, size, and/or culture shaped the lives of enslaved people—and how they, in turn, attempted to carve out their own spaces there. Based in demographics, Charles H. Faulkner's dense essay locates free and black residents in Knoxville, Tennessee. He concludes that African Americans lived relatively autonomously from their masters or white neighbors, allowing for the development of distinct cultures confirmed by archeological artifacts. Lisa Tolbert paints a very different picture of the small town of Franklin, Tennessee, where blacks and whites lived so close to one another that enslaved residents effectively "had multiple masters" (147). She creatively uses records of a salacious murder to argue that in towns where everybody knew everybody, all whites had eyes and ears on all enslaved African Americans at all times.

While both Faulkner's and Tolbert's essays offer examples of the very particular landscapes produced by places of different sizes, Kenneth Hafertepe presents the placelessness of antebellum Texas. Reconstructing long-gone homesteads with Sanborn maps, printed and photographic images, and first-hand accounts, Hafertepe argues that most white settlers brought ideas of how to spatially organize race with them to the frontier. The generous grids of Texas cities also ensured that while ideological barriers separated blacks and whites, there were few physical boundaries that confined or controlled the daily lives of enslaved people—a very different scene than Gina Haney casts of Charleston in the same period.

The book contributes new analysis and case studies to long-running themes, especially African and African American resistance and the ways enslaved people developed lives separate from those of their masters. With their fine-grained studies of two very different cities, Haney and Tolbert address the ambiguities of autonomy and resistance most successfully. They enliven their essays with individual voices to give a sense of how complicated the tight knots of black and white lives could be. Differences between real and perceived control were subtle from the perspectives of both the oppressed and the oppressor. This is where the book is at its best and has the most potential to change the way scholars think about slavery: it directly addresses the ways in which the experiences of enslaved people in cities differed from those in rural contexts.

Unfortunately, the book's dearth of images impacts the efficacy of its elegant essays. Its format denies the book's central claim on the importance of material evidence. Chappell's essay, the result of decades of painstaking documentation, lacks a single illustration of a building in Annapolis, one of its three study locations. A map that is illegible as printed accompanies Ellis's impressive web of documentary sources, robbing his analysis of the full strength of its geographic conclusions. Small, black-and-white scans diminish Hafertepe's resourceful approach to visual sources, denying the reader the opportunity to look closely as the text encourages them to do.

Despite its visual deficiencies, the book is a tremendous step forward in the study of slavery and antebellum landscapes in North America. Its concluding essay suggests a handful of avenues for future scholarship, but the content of the essays promise even more. Ellis's and Faulkner's essays map the spatial proximity between free and enslaved black populations, leading this reader to ask questions about those relationships, perceptions of racial divide by both blacks and whites, and the impact of those disparities after emancipation. Haney's vivid images of city streets teeming with enslaved Africans and African Americans raise important questions about gender: did enslaved women move as freely as men in the city? Visions of black families and communities gathering behind locked doors in Chappell's and Vlach's essays warrant further inquiry into the religious, social, and burial societies formed beyond watchful

white eyes. Hafertepe's and Tolbert's views of life on the edges of the frontier should encourage others to look to the relationships between urban and rural contexts. How did enslaved people on plantations interact with those in cities? Finally, what did urban slavery mean for the lives of African Americans after emancipation? How did its specific conditions impact black migration, social organization, and political action during Reconstruction?

*Slavery in the City* proves that answers to these questions will be found through multidisciplinary inquiry, close attention to context, and analysis of the built environment. The logic, clarity, and readability of its essays make it hard to believe that this is the very first collection of essays on urban slavery. Their openness, creativity, and empathy leave room for much more to come.

AUTHOR BIOGRAPHY

**Lydia Mattice Brandt** is an associate professor at the University of South Carolina. Her book, *First in the Homes of His Countrymen: George Washington's Mount Vernon in the American Imagination* (2016) chronicles the image of America's most famous plantation house in preservation and popular architecture.

---

**Melanie Kiechle**
*Smell Detectives: An Olfactory History of Nineteenth-Century Urban America*
Seattle, University of Washington Press, 2017.
xviii + 331 pages, 35 illustrations.
ISBN: 978-0-2957-4193-2, $34.95 HB

Review by Nicolas Kenny

---

Melanie Kiechle's thoroughly researched and highly evocative journey through the olfactory landscape of American cities in the nineteenth century is a welcome contribution to a rapidly growing body of scholarship interrogating the past through the perspective of

the senses.[1] Long classified with taste and touch as one of the lower senses—intuitive and animalistic, unlike the supposedly more rational and objective senses of sight, and to some extent, sound—smell has captured growing attention as scholars have sought to problematize this sensory ranking inherited from the Enlightenment.[2] As Kiechle notes in her introduction, "nineteenth-century Americans took smell seriously," thus requiring historians to pay equally serious attention to it (7), and to enrich their narratives by searching for the meeting point between lay and scientific conceptions of environmental realities (10). Indeed, smell was a perpetual concern throughout the period, says Kiechle, exploring what life was like in a time and in places characterized by powerful, frequent, and ever intensifying stench. Marshaling an impressive body of evidence, *Smell Detectives* reveals not just the fears and anxieties about odors that permeated representations of cities in all quarters, but more broadly, the way understandings of smell itself shifted as city dwellers sought to navigate and make sense of their changing environment during this period of unprecedented, and very stinky, urbanization.

Borrowing the term from Charles Frederick Chandler, president of the New York City Board of Health from 1873 to 1883, Kiechle defines smell detectives as "anyone who followed her nose" in trying to locate the origins of and attribute meaning to the smells enveloping cities. While smells might have paled in comparison to other urgent political issues of the day, Kiechle's unearthing of complaints, debates, legal proceedings, journalistic investigations, and scientific research shows how "they were a continuous concern that shaped the lives of Americans and the physical, governmental, and social development of American cities" (16). As such, virtually anyone could be, and was, a smell detective, so pervasive were repugnant odors in crowded industrial cities where sanitary measures were initially nonexistent, then slow to be adopted. Indeed, the range of voices the author draws on is vast, and throughout the work we hear from physicians, sanitarians, scientists, politicians, domestic advice writers, and a wide array of what we might call ordinary citizens, women and men of various class, ethnic, and racial backgrounds.

At stake in these conversations and throughout the century, Kiechle convincingly argues, were competing understandings of the legitimacy of these detectives' differing olfactory observations in identifying the cause and assessing the dangers of the smells that so haunted American cities. When Chandler coined his term, he was in fact denying the capacity of ordinary citizens to arrive at accurate understandings of these phenomena through their noses. In doing so, he sought to reinforce the social and cultural authority of a growing class of scientists and physicians attempting to leverage their expertise into political authority. This process, suggests Kiechle, ultimately resulted in a decreasing reliance on the sense of smell in gauging the salubriousness of the environment and in making decisions about how cities should be organized.

It is in these nineteenth-century developments that the author situates the relative absence of smell from public discourse in contemporary American society, though not without pointing to occasional flare-ups where mysterious smells continue to elicit serious concerns. This shift occurred slowly, accompanying but not always directly correlating to scientific developments, the most transformative of which was the advancement of germ theory. In advocating for politics and the law to account for scientific evidence in purifying the city, experts initially shared in, but later found themselves running up against, what Kiechle playfully calls "common sense," the lived experience of urbanites whose noses told them their environs were unpleasant and by extension unsafe, and whose interpretations of the cause of these smells, and what should be done about them, often differed from those of people in power. In adopting a broad temporal sweep, the au-

thor successfully shows how science came to trump common sense in the popular olfactory imagination.

The book is in many ways anchored around the fourth of eight chapters in which Kiechle identifies the Civil War as a crucial turning point in urban Americans' attitudes toward smell. Prior to the conflict, the conventional wisdom of miasma theory held that it was smells themselves that caused disease. In the first three chapters we thus follow medical doctors condemning the inaction of governments in fighting stench and pushing for health reform, urban dwellers holding up nosegays and fleeing the city in search of fresh air, and domestic advice writers advising women of the best ways to keep their homes free of unpleasant odors, and by extension disease. In these early decades of the century, most Americans lived outside of cities, but the dense and smelly "instant cities" that were Civil War camps brought urban conditions to rural environments, exposing large portions of the population to the stench of death and decay, as well as to the powerful odors of the chemical disinfectants used in hospitals. The intensity of these smells and the fear of disease associated with them, argues Kiechle, made Americans more willing to invest medical authorities with political and legislative power, ushering in the recourse to expertise covered in the second half of the book. While germ theory would debunk the notion that smells cause disease, popular acceptance of the new science was slow to take root as urban dwellers continued to rely on their common sense to advocate for reform of the industrial practices that made unpleasant odors a ubiquitous feature of urban life. Ironically, in delegitimizing the sensory experiences of residents, the newly empowered experts became less responsive to the claims of those whose health they were meant to protect. By the progressive era, conversations about smell had "splintered in various directions" such that smell lost its potency as a call to action for more healthful cities for all, and instead became a premise for "the social

condemnation of congested immigrant and minority neighborhoods" (258).

The arguments in *Smell Detectives* are compelling, and Kiechle's evocative use of the redolent language pervading her sources give the text an odorous vividness that occasionally makes the reader think, "yuck!" At the same time, the book raises various questions, the most lingering of which is how common this common sense really was. Kiechle devotes considerable attention to how women shaped ideas about smell and is careful to show how various groups, including workers and ethnic or racialized communities, experienced smell differently while also being constrained by dominant society's thinking on odors. But we are not presented with evidence to suggest that marginalized groups did in fact share in attitudes defined by middle-class intellectuals, writers, scientists, and politicians. One wonders, for instance, how much time the shantytowns dwellers recently examined by Lisa Goff might have had for the sanitary prescriptions and amenities portrayed as essential in the domestic manuals and plumbing advertisements read by well-to-do homeowners settling in leafy suburbs.[3]

In focusing on multiple urban settings, Kiechle shows how larger societal trends were also inflected by local circumstances, and her thought-provoking portrayal of the Civil War as a turning point in smell culture shows how the story was shaped by the specific national context that frames her study. Yet Kiechle also gives the impression of a hermetically American story by largely ignoring how changing understandings of smell in the United States, and the science propelling these shifts, were bound up to conversations taking place on an increasingly global level during the period. Indeed, while an extensive bibliography contains several key references, the author does not engage directly with the recent, and growing, historiography on the senses that would have allowed her to situate her work in this larger context. A more thorough dialogue with her fellow researchers might also

have avoided certain eyebrow-raising assertions, such as that historians of the senses
have ignored the spatial context of their narratives or failed to acknowledge the paradox
that urban dwellers sought to mitigate smells
even as they actively pursued the industrial
growth that caused them. On balance, however, Kiechle does live up to her promise of
taking smell seriously and of showing how
urban dwellers experienced and imagined
their environments through their noses.
Readers interested in urban, environmental,
and sensory history should certainly pick up
this book, hold their noses, and dive in.

## AUTHOR BIOGRAPHY

**Nicolas Kenny** is a member of the history
department at Simon Fraser University. His
research examines sensorial and emotional
experiences of the urban environment in the
nineteenth and twentieth centuries. He is the
author of *The Feel of the City: Experiences of
Urban Transformation* (2014).

## NOTES

1. For a running tally of recent work in the
field, see the "books of note" section on www
.sensorystudies.org.

2. See for example Constance Classen, David
Howes, and Anthony Synnott, *Aroma: The Cultural
History of Smell* (London: Routledge, 1994); Alain
Corbin, *The Foul and the Fragrant: Odor and the
French Social Imagination* (Cambridge, Mass.:
Harvard University Press, 1986); Mark M. Smith,
*Sensing the Past: Seeing, Hearing, Smelling, Tast-
ing, and Touching in History* (Berkeley: University
of California Press, 2007); and Jonathan Reinarz,
*Past Scents: Historical Perspectives on Smell* (Ur-
bana: University of Illinois Press, 2014).

3. Lisa Goff, *Shantytown USA: Forgotten Landscapes of the Working Poor* (Cambridge, Mass.: Harvard University Press, 2016).

---

**Benjamin D. Lisle**
*Modern Coliseum: Stadiums and American
Culture*

Philadelphia: University of Pennsylvania Press, 2017.

328 pages, 76 black-and-white illustrations.

ISBN: 978-0-8122-4922-4, $34.95 HB

ISBN: 978-0-8122-9407-1, $34.95 EB

Review by J. Philip Gruen

---

It is hardly novel to study architectural modernism in the United States. Even those problematic developments that rose (or fell) amid
urban and suburban schemes in the post–
World War II years, from publicly funded
inner-city high-rises to developer-driven tract
homes on the suburban edge, have received
their scholarly due. Yet the written landscape
of the American built environment is still
missing the huge stadiums of the postwar
years: the reinforced concrete, largely circular, and occasionally domed facilities planned
and built across the country from the 1950s
through the 1970s to accommodate major
league baseball, professional football . . .
and automobiles. Once politically, economically, imaginatively, and often geographically
central to cities such as Atlanta, Cincinnati,
Houston, Los Angeles, New York City, Philadelphia, Pittsburgh, San Francisco, Seattle,
St. Louis, and Washington, D.C., these stadiums have today all but vanished from the
land, their one-time presence considered an
aberration in the history of the twentieth-
century American city, if they are considered
at all. For the most part, sports facilities of
all periods have been neglected by historians
despite their central locations in the metropo-
lis; their impacts on race, class, and gender;
their effects on neighborhood character; and
their role in preservation and memory.[1] Only
economists, bent upon targeting stadiums
as exemplary of fiscal mismanagement and
waste, and journalists, who wax nostalgic
about the days of yore when smaller ballparks

apparently made more intimate connections
to their neighborhoods, serve as general exceptions to this historiography.

Benjamin Lisle's *Modern Coliseum: Stadiums and American Culture* offers a far more
historically grounded, and thus refreshing,
view and scope. Lisle's effort is ambitious:
though his focus is on the postwar stadiums
and he excludes the glorified wooden grand-
stands erected for professional baseball and
football in the late nineteenth century, he
traces the rise of American stadiums over
the past hundred years while situating them
within their political, economic, geographical, cultural, and social climate. Although the
book is loosely chronological, Lisle employs
a case study approach to tease out major
themes of stadium development. He directs
his attention principally to the kaleidoscope
of issues surrounding the construction of
Shea Stadium in New York City (1961–64), the
Astrodome in Houston (1962–65), and Busch
Memorial Stadium in St. Louis (1964–66) and
cites them—and their contemporary ilk—for
setting in motion a commercialism, exclusivity, and artificiality that has reached extreme
proportions in the wave of "retro" ballparks
built in the late twentieth and early twenty-
first centuries. Well written, thoroughly researched, and appropriately illustrated, *Modern Coliseum* is long overdue.

Following an introductory section highlighting the shifting demographics that allegedly necessitated the construction of
different stadiums in Washington, D.C., in
the initial chapters Lisle introduces readers
to the roiling ethnic, political, and economic
considerations that surrounded the gradual
abandonment of stadiums in the New York
City boroughs of Brooklyn (Ebbets Field) and
Manhattan (Polo Grounds), built or rebuilt
in the 1910s, and the construction of those
in Los Angeles (Dodger Stadium) and San
Francisco (Candlestick Park), begun in the
late 1950s. He marshals a variety of primary
sources to contend that the rowdy, mixed-race
crowds at the older ballparks, together with
augmented African American neighborhood

populations and difficult parking, inspired New York Giants' owner Horace Stoneham, Brooklyn Dodgers' owner Walter O'Malley, and New York City Parks Commissioner Robert Moses to seek architecturally distinctive and spacious accommodations (with ample parking) for an increasingly affluent—and white—suburban middle-class and upper-middle-class clientele.

This new collection of potential fans, and potential capital, comprise the human contingent from which the middle three chapters, the core of Lisle's book, draw their material. Lisle introduces Shea Stadium, the Astrodome, and Busch Memorial Stadium with respect to their local and national postwar conditions, from the ethnic makeup of neighborhoods and the formation of redevelopment agencies to urban renewal, white flight, suburbanization, engineering innovation, the space race, and a rising culture of consumption. Historians are familiar with these cultural conditions, of course, but less familiar with the role that stadiums played in illustrating, if not symbolizing, them. Lisle's narrative suggests that these years, and the stadiums erected within them, marked the beginning of a progressive decline of professional sports into sheer spectacle, as owners scrambled to build technologically advanced stadiums to entertain fans who might otherwise stay home and watch the games on television—a theme he develops more comprehensively in his final chapter. The "retro" stadiums, including Baltimore's Oriole Park at Camden Yards (1989–92) and Pittsburgh's PNC Park (1999–2001), also find a place in the final chapter, albeit hardly a lofty one. Lisle argues that their urbanistic and architectural nods toward an earlier time cloud a gentrification and class-based separation that has completely transformed professional sports into a manufactured experience for the well-to-do; these stadiums have removed the public almost entirely from the game, even though that public is still mostly responsible for footing the construction bill.

The enduring legacy of *Modern Coliseum*, however, may be its revisionist perspective that situates, or re-situates, the stadium within twentieth-century urban and architectural history. This alone is a vital contribution, but Lisle goes well beyond simply laying out the historical context. He demonstrates, for example, that team owners' claims to build new stadiums appealing to a broad public were couched in an "official" discourse that favored certain publics and employed the rhetoric of contagion to justify the destruction or abandonment of poor, ethnic, or African American neighborhoods in the inner city. The postwar stadiums were typically separated from these neighborhoods, either by distance or by design. The new home for baseball's New York Mets, Shea Stadium, built on the northern edge of Flushing Meadows Park in New York City's borough of Queens, for example, made no attempt at social progress. It was built far from the inner city, with broad, cantilevered decks that eliminated obstructed view seating and, stadium promoters boasted, removed bleacher seats as well. Yet bleachers, Lisle reminds us, were usually the most inexpensive seats in any stadium, home to the working class and the youth. They were readily available at New York's old Polo Grounds in the predominantly African American neighborhood of Harlem, where the Mets played their first two seasons prior to moving to suburban Queens.

Lisle highlights several instances of such inequity in *Modern Coliseum*, architectural and otherwise, underscoring the dwindling public sphere that characterized the postwar stadiums and providing support for a reading of these facilities as exclusive and hierarchical. Who or what constituted the "public," an issue Lisle raises in the introduction, was based largely upon who produced the "dominant or official meanings" surrounding stadium development (7–8). Drawing upon the work of Stuart Hall, Lisle contends that those who controlled the discourse were politicians, owners, journalists, and public relations officers in addition to engineers and architects who helped bring the plans into reality. Any allegedly inclusive rhetoric about the "public," regardless of who funded stadium construction, meant a rather specific public: a typically well-off one which served to benefit most from the new stadiums, and could most easily access, and afford, the events held there. The postwar stadiums, Lisle informs us in the book's final pages, were part of a "fundamental project" to reshape the stadium public and experience (259). This project removed stadiums from the diversity of their urban milieu and, through creature comforts and on-site entertainment catering to a mostly white, suburban population, removed fans from encountering the otherwise unpredictable nature of the game—or experiencing the game at all. That it takes until the last chapter for Lisle to make this point explicitly is perhaps a reflection of the progressive corporatization of professional sports, which took several decades to develop. It may also reflect Lisle's desire to provide a balanced view, which necessitates a series of concessions to the populist appeal of the postwar stadiums, which—on the surface, anyway—did enjoy some popular support.

Indeed, many of the details Lisle provides regarding the construction and promotion of the postwar stadiums mark some of the most enlightening, if not entertaining, aspects of *Modern Coliseum*. The marketing frenzy and features surrounding Houston's Astrodome are Exhibit A: though Lisle acknowledges that its dome, out-of-downtown location, and glass-enclosed box seats had earlier precedents, he essentially locates an entire culture of profligacy, distraction, and decadence in its countless sideshows. It was in the Astrodome's early years that stadium attendants dressed up in spacesuits, custodians vacuumed the cushioned seats, well-heeled fans enjoyed meals in themed restaurants, outfielders dove for fly balls on plastic grass, and home runs crushed by Astros' hitters set off an exploding scoreboard—all in air-conditioned comfort under a dome in the "eighth wonder of the world." Whether the Astros actually won their games (and in the 1960s, usually they did not) was of entirely little consequence. Several priceless images, which Lisle uses to illustrate these and other long-forgotten or rarely brought-to-light circumstances (including renderings and models of stadium proposals), are appropriately sprinkled throughout the narrative.

Perhaps more seriously, Lisle's work exposes the racial landscape that contributed to the proliferation of postwar stadiums, and he discusses the often discriminatory practices or claims of owners and local politicians as they sought new stadiums in suburban locations or in "revitalized" city centers that catered to moneyed suburbanites. This was the case with Walter O'Malley, who claimed that his decision to move the Dodgers in 1957 from dense, ethnically-diverse but increasingly African American Brooklyn to a site in Los Angeles north and west of downtown (itself housing a long-standing Mexican American community) had only to do with his desire for greater profit—not race (38). In St. Louis, Lisle discusses a city whose municipal population shifted from 13 percent to 41 percent African American in the three decades between 1940 and 1970, and one whose African American population in the vicinity of Sportsman's Park—the previous home of the St. Louis Cardinals baseball club—had grown at an even faster rate. "Any spatial project" in the Gateway City, Lisle contends, "was *also* a racial project" (195).

The postwar stadiums were gendered constructions, too, and *Modern Coliseum* does more than any book-length study on American stadiums to show how women were objectified through stadium design and development. Lisle offers a perceptive analysis of owner, designer, and even journalistic attempts to "domesticate" the postwar stadium in order to lure more women, although he exposes rather depressing (if predictable) motives that cast women either as uneducated about sports or deemed them as little more than aesthetic fodder for male fans. In this vein, it is perhaps unsurprising that journalists likened Shea Stadium, for example, to

a large, suburban split-level home, featuring modern appliances, cheerful colors, and a huge "television" (actually, a rear projection screen atop the scoreboard), all available at an enormous scale in a new outdoor "living room" (133–39). Lisle also shows that stadium officials often employed women as ushers, hoping their presence and charm would bring "class" to an otherwise unruly, typically male-dominated space. At the Houston Astrodome, which pushed a space-age theme to dimensions that today may seem rather anachronistic, women who worked as ushers—the "Spacettes"—were required to attend etiquette school before donning orange pillbox hats and gold lamé suits and leading fans to their seats. Apparently, not any woman would do—whether as a "Spacette" or a fan. "The domed stadium," Astros' owner Roy Hofheinz declared, "was designed for beautiful women" (180).

Postwar stadiums themselves also were highly designed objects. Lisle dedicates several pages to the architectural gestures and engineering prowess of these "machines for sport," setting their efficiency, symmetry, and order within a larger rationalist discourse of architectural modernism. In this fashion, Lisle incorporates into this discourse the stadiums' expressive circulation ramps, Edward Durell Stone's decorative arches atop Busch Memorial Stadium (which mirrored the shape of Eero Saarinen's nearby Gateway Arch), and even the "wind baffle" encircling the upper lip of San Francisco's Candlestick Park, regardless of its inability to lessen the effect of howling winds that regularly swirled into the facility. Lisle's discussion of futuristic stadium proposals by Norman Bel Geddes and Buckminster Fuller for the Brooklyn Dodgers demonstrate that the sleek lines and technological experiments of postwar stadiums, including cantilevered decks, escalators, and retractable roofs, had an earlier, albeit visionary, provenance. Discussions of these and other well-known designers may satisfy traditionalists wishing to situate the stadiums within a modernist architectural canon. Yet

this is hardly Lisle's purpose. *Modern Coliseum* remains focused upon illuminating the complexity of circumstances that enveloped the emergence of the postwar stadiums, revealing locally distinctive issues of politics and race within a rising culture of technology, consumption, and affluence.

Lisle's writing is not thoroughly immune from bouts of nostalgia, however, and there are instances where it could benefit from some clarification. Ebbets Field, Lisle contends, is "the iconic urban ballpark" and the touchstone for when the "story of the modern stadium begins" (9). Yet he neither discusses the notion of iconicity nor that of the modern enough to permit readers a clear understanding of what constituted a modern stadium (or whether, or when, the "modern" constituted a generalized modern American culture or a more specific *modernist* architecture, the latter arguably better exemplified by the postwar stadiums than those built in the early twentieth century, such as Ebbets Field). Moreover, Lisle also claims there was "genuine" diversity inside and outside the early twentieth-century urban ballparks, yet never fully unpacks what makes diversity "genuine" as opposed to, say, artificial (4). If a racially diverse crowd is not economically diverse (or vice versa), is it still diverse? Is it genuine?

It is also unfortunate that Lisle occasionally reverts to the all-too-common aesthetic refrain of the postwar stadium as a "concrete mushroom" (9) or its various ilk, such as a "multipurpose monster" (11), "engineered behemoth" (123), "anonymous cylinder" (232), or "placeless machine" (234). His overall narrative, by contrast, offers a far more nuanced investigation of these stadiums that emphasizes their local peculiarities and links them to a new sense of "place" in the postwar years—a notion of place seemingly desired by many people, regardless of the various problems and inequities that ensued. Even Lisle admits that the "incredible Astrodome" (65), which he otherwise castigates as the epitome of postwar artificiality and hedonism, was nonetheless "certainly a marvel" (157); and that Dodger Stadium featured several exciting design moves, though he critiques its private financing, Hollywood glamour, and disengaged audiences. "But what a stadium," Lisle writes, "it was" (96).

Given Lisle's overall achievement with *Modern Coliseum*, which elevates postwar stadiums to a critical place in the history of the twentieth-century city, these quibbles are minor. His wide-ranging methodology ultimately illuminates these stadiums less as stunning architectural designs than as cultural products through which one can read inequality, hierarchy, and power—*in addition* to innovation and spectacle.

AUTHOR BIOGRAPHY

**J. Philip Gruen** is associate professor of architecture in the School of Design and Construction at Washington State University. He is the author of *Manifest Destinations: Cities and Tourists in the Nineteenth-Century American West* (2014).

NOTE

1. Notable exceptions include Aaron Cowan's chapter on Pittsburgh's Three Rivers Stadium in *A Nice Place to Visit: Tourism and Urban Revitalization in the Postwar Rustbelt* (Philadelphia: Temple University Press, 2016), 101–26; Bruce Kuklick, *To Every Thing a Season: Shibe Park and Urban Philadelphia, 1909–1976* (Princeton, N.J.: Princeton University Press, 1991); Jerald Podair, *City of Dreams: Dodger Stadium and the Birth of Modern Los Angeles* (Princeton, N.J.: Princeton University Press, 2017); Daniel Rosensweig, *Retro Ball Parks: Instant History, Baseball, and the New American City* (Knoxville: University of Tennessee Press, 2005); and Robert C. Trumpbour and Kenneth Womack, *The Eighth Wonder of the World: The Life of Houston's Iconic Astrodome* (Lincoln: University of Nebraska Press, 2016).

**Stefan Al**

*The Strip: Las Vegas and the Architecture of the American Dream*

Cambridge, Mass: MIT Press, 2017.

254 pages, 82 color and black-and-white illustrations.

ISBN: 978-0-2620-3574-3, $34.95 HB

Review by Chester H. Liebs

When asked to review *The Strip* for *Buildings & Landscapes* I initially demurred. I assumed it was a sequel in the mold of Robert Venturi, Denise Scott Brown, and Steven Izenour's *Learning from Las Vegas* (1972). While indisputably important and groundbreaking, perhaps this earlier work's most enduring takeaway, the alluring deduction that the Las Vegas Strip is composed of "Ducks" and "Decorated Sheds," continues to pose the danger of being applied without one fully grasping its authors' sophisticated thought that led up to it. This was eerily demonstrated by several international architecture students, a few years ago, when I was teaching in Tokyo. As we walked down a street lined with *machinami* (traditional merchant buildings), each time we passed a structure bearing a business sign, to my great surprise, someone would call out in English, "Decorated Shed!" After reading Stefan Al's *The Strip*, such too-quick reduction and application would be far more difficult. Here the reader is deluged with a barrage of fascinating facts and stories, in a series of chapters-cum-typologies, linking social and economic history, owner and designer biographies, and many other factors with the design evolution of Las Vegas's casino resorts and the audiences they are pitched to attract.

The first chapter, "Wild West (1941–1946)," chronicles the early casinos that began springing up in the Mojave Desert, just beyond the official town border of Las Vegas, to form what is today's Las Vegas Strip. Casino number one, the El Rancho, was built by Thomas Hull, a California hotelier, and opened up in 1941. Planned as a motel, with a casino added "as an afterthought" (15), the El Rancho sported an interior featuring a nostalgic décor of cowhide curtains and wagon-wheel chandeliers. The Western-themed Frontier followed shortly in 1942. Designers of these early resorts took their thematic cues from the adjacent former mining town of Las Vegas, which was busy promoting itself at the time as a tourist destination that was "Still a Frontier Town" (11).

Next the late forties morphed into "Sunbelt Modern (1946–1958)," where characters such as gangster Benjamin "Bugsy" Siegel built hotels like the Flamingo with its scalloped-edge, Olympic-size pool. Siegel, along with other entrepreneurs, often with Mafia financing according to Al (30), lined the emerging Las Vegas Strip with "clean modern forms" (29). Cowboy town was out. The Frontier's stonework was covered over with pink paint (33). "By the late 1950s, the Strip had become a catalog of modern suburban homes on steroids" (30). Wagon wheels and buffalo heads gave way to "Cadillac-like grilles and tail-fin shapes" (30).

Then came "Pop City (1958–1969)," initiated by former bootlegger Toney Cornero and his brainchild, the Stardust casino. Now dazzling giant neon signs—the Dunes' sign was twenty stories high (59), the Thunderbird's electric-sign-covered façade as long as two football fields—along with lots of cheap rooms lured middle-class patrons increasingly arriving by jet plane and interstate highway. At Teamsters Union–funded Caesars Palace, which offered visitors experiences including the Circus Maximus theater and "cocktails inside a moving Cleopatra's barge" (95), in the words of Caesars' owner, Jay Sarno, "Everybody is a Caesar" (95).

Moving on, the author points out that ironically, at the same time observers like Venturi et al. "celebrated the Strip's Electrographic Architecture and Decorated Sheds" (107), the Pop City era was already beginning to decline. Mafia influence, while not disappearing, waned, and corporate ownership increased. Things were headed in a new direction—"Corporate Modern (1969–1985)." The result was the evolution of a new, sanitized, less flamboyant Las Vegas Strip. This change accelerated as a consequence of the huge quantity of electricity needed to power Pop City Strip's dazzling array of neon and energy-guzzling incandescent lights. Energy shortages caused by the 1973 Arab oil embargo were a wakeup call for the casino industry. Complying with a national call for voluntary conservation, Las Vegas even "went dark and stayed that way for five whole months" (122).

By the late 1970s the Strip was transformed into a series of "large, efficient hotel buildings that looked little different from corporate hotel chains or office buildings elsewhere in the world" (109). As for signage, "architecture had struck back with a vengeance, putting the sign back in its place as an inferior reference to a building" (109). Neon and incandescent bulbs gave way to cheaper backlit "white acrylic reader boards illuminated from within" (122).

Then by the mid-1980s developers, in the hope of attracting more families, turned to emulating Disney theme parks as a formula for success. However, the author points out that exact copies of Disney imagery had to be ruled out because of copyright concerns. Consequently, in "Disneyland era (1985–1995)," the Strip became adorned with a collage of Disney-inspired attractions. Now one could encounter "a bronze pyramid, an erupting volcano, and a sinking eighteenth-century ship, smack on the Strip" (134). Following Disneyfication came the "Sim City (1995–2001)," where design along the Strip "evolved from mimicking Disney fairy tales to simulating authentic architectural heritage" (169). Visitors were offered a "condensed version of a Grand Tour, now endowed with American commercialism and convenience" (169). They could experience Venice complete with a Campanile, canals, and a Rialto Bridge ascended by escalators instead of stairs; an Eiffel Tower

and Styrofoam Paris opera house; and New York City landmarks including the Statue of Liberty and Empire State Building "congealed into a single mass like a souvenir slow [*sic*] globe" (176).

However, just as the 1973 Arab oil embargo helped kill the energy-intensive Pop City, another catastrophic event helped put an end to the Sim City Strip. After 9/11, as things Middle Eastern became associated with terrorism, customers started avoiding the recently completed Aladdin casino, with its copies of buildings from Cairo and Marrakesh. Before long the Strip entered the final phase covered in the book, the age of "Starchitecture (2001–present)," where casino moguls commissioned renowned architects, from Daniel Libeskind to César Pelli, to design stylish high-rise casinos enlivened with pop-art adornments such as Claes Oldenburg and Coosje van Bruggen's giant "Typewriter Eraser" sculpture. Inside, Starchitecture casino resorts sported art galleries, shopping malls, and celebrity-chef restaurants. This formula, that the author calls "Casinopolitanism" (211), spread to a number of cities around the world.

While the author marks the Starchitecture Strip as continuing to the present, the text relates how its construction was significantly slowed by the 2007–2008 financial crisis when "images of unfinished construction projects, cranes suspended in midair, and empty casino floors made for eerie sights" (217). However, Al then describes how the Strip has rebounded with post-foreclosure fixer-uppers, concert arenas, and urban parks. As for the future, since the book was published before the tragic October 1, 2017, mass shooting during an open-air concert, one wonders how a need for increased security will influence the design of the Strip as have earlier cataclysmic events.

Among the work's many strong points, each chapter of *The Strip* is crammed with fascinating details and anecdotes. For example, in 1956, to attract more gamers to his

Hacienda casino, owner Warren "Doc" Bayley began buying up planes to provide package deals to his resort that included low-cost airfare. His operation swelled to thirty aircraft by 1962, causing the Civil Aeronautics Board to shut it down as an unlicensed airline (54). The seven-foot-tall centurions at the base of the 1966 Caesars Palace sign were modeled from twenty-five-cent toy centurion figures found at a variety store (92). In Sheldon Adelson's Sim City Venetian casino, gondoliers steer guests along a Grand Canal "dyed monthly to keep its azure color" (188).

Al also writes with an engaging wit and sense of irony. He muses how Paris, Las Vegas, a sanitized American stereotype, has offered a cure for the much publicized "Paris syndrome," where Japanese visitors to the real Paris are shocked "that the French do not all dress like fashion models and smell of Chanel No. 5" (193). He also observes, in a somewhat mischievous reference to *Learning from Las Vegas,* that "the Strip was never guided by architectural theory, but by profit: it was Scrooge Mc Duck, not the Long Island Duck, who ruled the Strip" (102). *The Strip* is also profusely illustrated with a spatial timeline on the inside of the front and back covers along with dozens of fascinating historical photos, period advertisements, and original plans, many of them in color. Their captions are excellent and greatly support and illuminate the text.

Inevitably in a book of this scope, there are also shortcomings and factual errors. For example, many of the excellent illustrations just mentioned are unfortunately undated, and their sources are relegated to a small, hard-to-read abbreviated list in the front matter. There is a conflation of terms such as ranch house and bungalow, and the assertion that the second tower of the Venetian "ended up overtaking the Pentagon as the United States' tallest building" (204) is surely in need of correction. Also, there does not seem to be any mention of possible similarities and cross-influences in the evolution of the nation's roadside commercial strips and Las Vegas's famed linear landscape.

In his concluding remarks Al suggests that "the Strip is both a promoter of hyper capitalism and a paragon of modernity in which 'all that is solid melts into air'" (222). Whether that thought gives joy or gloom to the reader, the book will likely become the classic study of the Las Vegas Strip for some time to come.

AUTHOR BIOGRAPHY

**Chester H. Liebs** is professor emeritus of history at the University of Vermont and author of *Main Street to Miracle Mile: American Roadside Architecture*, first published in 1985.

---

**Ioanna Theocharopoulou**

*Builders, Housewives and the Construction of Modern Athens*

London: Artifice Books on Architecture, 2017.

192 pages, 154 illustrations (maps, color plates, print media, photographs).

ISBN: 978-1-9089-6787-9, $39.95 PB

Review by Eliana Abu-Hamdi

---

Ioanna Theocharopoulou's *Builders, Housewives and the Construction of Modern Athens* is a historical study of development in Athens, one that traces the theoretical roots of construction, design, nationalism, class, and gender. In so doing, her analysis offers a comprehensive view of the city's political history, well supported by a tableau of empirical and archival evidence. Each chapter is grounded in archival documents, offering a springboard to primary analysis, from which Theocharopoulou expands the critique, often with her own insight as a local resident of Athens. Theocharopoulou argues that Athens is historically overshadowed by its monumental past, so much so that its modern self, its modern architecture in particular, is not seen as emblematic of the city's development. Instead Athens is seen as an embodiment of a historicized Aegean rural architecture—its vernacular roots. Theocharopoulou's significant contribution is in her examination of the term vernacular, turning its traditional use on its head, arguing that not only can modern development be vernacular, in turn the fabric of a modern city can be understood as vernacular as well. In so doing, Theocharopoulou does well in expanding the definition and conventional interpretation of the vernacular.

The methodology to advance this argument is presented through a new set of tools, ones that recognize urbanism as a mode of life and that the intricacies of planning are nuanced practices along a spectrum of politically and socially motivated development decisions, ones that transcend the general paradigm of formal versus vernacular, planned versus chaotic, and modern versus classic. As an example, Theocharopoulou uses the construction of *polykatoikia*, multifamily dwellings, as a unit of analysis capable of presenting a historical and theoretical account of planning and construction in Athens. The *polykatoikia* is the embodiment of family structure, class structure, development, and, most importantly, the role of the builder and the professionalization of architecture in Athens.

The book traces the historical development of a major point of contention in Athens' identity: its European or neoclassical roots. Neoclassical style imported from elsewhere in Europe in the nineteenth century had a long-enduring impact on local culture and memory in Athens. While the nineteenth-century middle class welcomed the adoption of the neoclassical style, viewing it as a symbol of pride and prestige, Greek scholars considered the style a destructive departure from old "Athenian" houses and a source of alienation from Greek culture and origins. Ultimately, to them, neoclassical architecture was self-orientalizing, a colonization from within.

Though to the middle class the adoption of neoclassical style was heralded as a "national rebirth," informal development, namely the domination of the home builder, persisted as a stylistic opposition to European influence. The tumultuous political history of Greece throughout the nineteenth and twentieth centuries disrupted the rules for builders and architects in the race to accommodate the numerous refugees who relocated to the city, causing a major housing shortage in Athens. For this reason, home builders dominated the development arena, constructing residential units without restriction by development policy or building code. Construction was largely craft based, and embraced the multifamily style of the *polykatoikia*, systematically sacrificing single-family neoclassical houses for this more dense and efficient residential unit.

Construction by experienced craftsman persisted in Athens up to the mid-twentieth century, but it faced opposition upon the return of internationally educated professional architects, schooled in the science of design and construction. The professionalization of architecture introduced a formal process of design, but also caused confusion, as the role of the architect had to be reconciled with the dominant role of local craftsmen and builders. The city, lacking any formal policy or building restrictions, decreed that builders could continue to construct homes without the council of engineers, the scientifically educated architects of Athens. During this time, a hierarchy of builders developed, from master builders, responsible for procuring materials, projects, and building contracts, to those who executed the actual construction. Implicit within this new craft hierarchy was class, and while the technical architect remained at the top of the hierarchy, the stratification among builders became more nuanced.

Throughout the interwar period housing continued to be increasingly important for the city, but it also became highly symbolic of "modern" Athens, particularly as its neoclassical recent past was gradually demolished to make room for the *polykatoikia*. These housing units appear to be modern, influenced by the international style, with flat planes, large windows, white unadorned façades, some even with pilotis at the ground level for cars. The author argues, however, that this modern appearance was deceiving, as the similarities in the architecture of these dwellings ended at basic aesthetics, as they were constructed informally and in an unplanned manner, a complete departure from the rigors and restraint of the international style.

Theocharopoulou introduces a series of characters, among them Constantinos Apostolos Doxiadis, an officer in the Greek military who later became chief town planning officer for the Greater Athens Area. Doxiadis, like many other Greeks, felt that Athens was losing its identity, the simplistic *polykatoikia* dominating the aesthetic of the city. Unable to curb the booming housing market, as housing was a highly sought after and necessary commodity, Doxiadis operated through informal channels to develop postwar recovery schemes. For Doxiadis the solution was simple: to strengthen Greek identity, development had to establish a continuity with ancient Greece. In his opinion, as well as that of like-minded scholars, development had to take on the form of rural settlements, not urban multifamily dwellings that increased density and congestion. It is at this point in the historical narrative that Theocharopoulou's strengths shine—her tremendous use of archival sources, skillfully referenced to narrate the history of Athens and the tensions among residents and scholars. Specifically, Theocharopoulou presents primary evidence from scholars who traveled rural areas documenting both the damages incurred from the war for reconstruction, and also the housing and settlement typology of the countryside— the Greek vernacular.

Theocharopoulou convincingly argues that Doxiadis was intent on his scheme to usher settlements to the countryside as pods, or nuclei of houses, because he believed that rural architecture more closely represented Greek identity. In turn Theocharopoulou demonstrates how government officials embraced conventional understandings of vernacular, applying value to the style, sensationalizing the architecture of the countryside as authentic. Theocharopoulou focuses on this point, challenging the standard understanding of vernacular and informal practice to build her overall argument that Athens' vernacular is not that which is classic or traditional, but can be the alternate—that which is classified as modern. In this way, the critique shifts to the construction practice of the *polykatoikia*, claiming that if indeed the vernacular is that which is constructed through informal, nontechnical, and unregulated practices, then the *polykatoikia*, constructed as such, qualify as Greek vernacular, able to inform Greek identity.

While Theocharopoulou's title highlights housewives, the issue of gender and the role of the housewife is unfortunately only presented in the final chapter, and more expansion of this discussion would be welcome. Theocharopoulou's study of gender and gender-based roles is interesting particularly because the author's voice is most present in this chapter's narrative. As a local Athenian, she has much insight to offer, as well as personal anecdotes from her own family, which were entertaining and engaging for the reader. The strengths of the book lie in her compelling argumentation, well supported with a breadth of evidence and visual materials. The book provides an abundance of color images, historical black-and-white photographs, and floor plans. Theocharopoulou's engaging writing style and the images make the book highly readable and appealing to a broad audience.

In *Builders, Housewives and the Construction of Athens* Theocharopoulou sets out to challenge the long-established traditional narrative of the vernacular and makes great strides toward shifting away from the conventional categories and toward a more interrogative and timely analysis of architectural practices, particularly ones that do not rely upon the overwhelming dichotomies of formal versus informal and modern versus traditional.

AUTHOR BIOGRAPHY

**Eliana Abu-Hamdi** is the Global Architectural History Teaching Collaborative Project Manager at MIT and adjunct assistant professor of political science at Hunter College. She is an urbanist, designer, and Middle Eastern/Global South scholar with published articles in academic journals and chapters in academic press collections.

---

**Francesco Vallerani and Francesco Visentin, eds.**

*Waterways and the Cultural Landscape*
London and New York: Routledge, 2017.
266 pages, 34 black-and-white illustrations.
978-1-138-22604-3, $140 HB
978-1-315-39846-4, $54.95 EB

Review by Giulio Verdini

---

*Waterways and the Cultural Landscape* is the outcome of an international conference held in Venice in 2015 on the heritage dimensions of waterscapes and historic canals. Vallerani and Visentin framed this collection in the spirit of collecting some of the most meaningful contributions on this emerging topic. This is never an easy task, given the usual heterogeneity of contributions received, but this variety is by no means a demerit for this edited book.

The book is divided into two parts. The first part, "Cultural Visions," covers a wide range of waterways and waterfronts with high cultural value and unique environmental heritage. Stephen Daniels's interpretation of the River Trent in the English Midlands as a literary river echoes the narrations of Italian writer Gianni Celati used by Giada Peterle and Francesco Visentin to observe and interpret the geography of the Po Delta. Peter Coates's account of the renaissance of the River Tyne, where artists have recently interpreted the rebirth of the river through the reappearance of salmon, draws a historic parallel with artists' attempts to restore a symbiotic union between the Dolomites and the Venice Lagoon in the nineteenth century, as described in the erudite contribution of William Bainbridge. Past water histories, such as those described by Annika Aires related to the wood-processing industry on the waterfront of Lathi in Finland and Queensborough in Canada, and by Chandra Mukerji on women's labor and laundries along the Canal du Midi in France, are occasions to reveal forgotten social and productive practices. Similarly, the rediscovery of the ideological discourse behind the sharing of the Saimaa Canal between Finland and the former Soviet Union described by Elena Kochetkova and the lead mining sough disputes in Derbyshire discussed by Georgina Endfield and Carry Van Lieshout reveals underlying historical social and political tensions around water in such regions.

The second part, "Touristic Perspectives," provides an overview of different strategies employed to develop sustainable tourism along waterways and their surrounding regions. Bruce Prideaux reassures readers about the positive impact that canal tourism might have, assuming the canal lifecycle concept is an opportunity to reconnect the past and the present. In the same vein, Francesco Vallerani examines the potentiality of river tourism in northwest Croatia, as do Lucyna Nyka for the Vistula River Delta in Poland, Andrew McKean and John Lennon for Scottish canals, Aurelio Nieto Codina for the Manzanares River in Madrid, Federica Cavallo and Domique Crozat for the Canal du Midi in France, and Eriberto Eulisse and Francesco

Visentin for Venice's historic waterways. These two parts are preceded by an evocative introductory chapter from Francesco Vallerani, "flowing consciousness and the becoming of waterscapes," and a conclusion from Francesco Visentin on the fascinating topic of humanistic hydrology.

While the contributions of the two editors provide an overarching and original reflection on the cultural importance of hydrography and everyday life in waterscapes, and therefore of the social relevance of historic waterways, the two main parts in which the book is articulated reaffirm the centrality of two broad topics traditionally well established in cultural landscape studies. I refer to the nexus between culture and nature, hence the ecological relevance of historic waterways in part one, and the relationship between cultural tourism and sustainable development, hence their potential economic relevance, in part two.

The resurgence of interest in cultural landscapes within the broader field of heritage studies in recent years has found international legitimacy with the UNESCO recognition of "cultural landscape" as a category of protection in 1992. Since then, an important amount of literature has been produced to reconcile *in primis* the concept of culture and nature overcoming the "pre 1990s . . . division, and hence tension, between cultural and natural heritage conservation."[1] More recently an important effort has been made to understand the conditions by which cultural landscapes can survive. As the expression of social and economic practices, their long-term survival is bound to the capacity to protect and reproduce both their material forms and their socioeconomic dynamics. It goes without saying that cultural tourism has often been seen as a panacea, and great effort has been placed on studying ways to improve its complex management, particularly when applied to cultural routes.[2]

Nevertheless, warnings have been also sounded regarding the fact that cultural

landscapes are "faced with the dilemma of tourism being an erosive factor . . . and [at the same time] a tool for economic development and sustainability of the communities."[3] The dilemma around the conflictual relationship between community and (touristic) development has been an object of intense debate for some time, but this debate seems to have consolidated in "a noticeable shift from largely negative ethnographic critiques of the cultural impacts of tourism to a more balanced discussion of travel and tourism as a social and cultural phenomenon."[4] Along these lines, contemporary theorists have overcome the seemingly sterile discussion on authenticity to embrace a more optimistic evaluation of cultural commodification by looking at the proactive and more empowered role of communities in this process.

Vallerani places the rediscovery of water, or the emerging "new aquatic scholarly sensibility" (19), in his personal experience of rediscovery of Veneto hydrography back in 1992 together with Daniel Cosgrove, as they visited the region to study the Palladian landscape. It was along those rivers that the two could appreciate "unexpected insights into traditional rural landscapes, so far untouched" (3) in an area that had experienced devastating urban sprawl in the phase of the Italian economic boom and well beyond. Thus, in the intellectual experience of a geographer, this exploration represents a *j'accuse* against a certain economic modernity and a stimulus to advocate for "more attentive interventions of local administrators to prevent the dispersion (of) the uniqueness of tangible waterscapes" (10). More than that, it is a way to rediscover seductive landscapes, being composed of precious everyday life expressions and memories of river communities. He would then require "the development of a sort of hydraulic humanism, which should underpin not only the support and reorganization of hydrography governance but also a participating consciousness that is able to rediscover the large repository of hidden memories, particularly involving minor rivers and historic canals" (10).

Visentin, in contrast, traces some "liquid conclusions," drawing on the variety of contributions presented on sustainable and supposedly "sincere" forms of cultural tourism (188). He reiterates the ecological relevance of waterscapes, outlining the importance of the watery turn in heritage and landscape studies alongside the rediscovery of its ordinary dimension. More interestingly, he relates the historical material and everyday qualities of water landscape and heritage with the notion of nostalgia, memory, and the life cycle of objects. He then concludes with a suggestion to use the concept of nostalgia as a process, far from the hidden "irrational belief of the superiority of the past over the present time" and for a resilient use of memory, which is meant to be aware of "a risk of a reproduction of a particular hegemonic cultural memory" and works instead "somewhere between the public and the private, between the official histories and those small histories of individuals and families" (251). In the postindustrial era, the life-cycle model requires transformation and regeneration: this can be narrowly interpreted as a recycle of images or memories, or as a more promising adaptation of places and communities to new conditions.

However, while both Vallerani and Visentin set an ambitious agenda to develop a new humanistic hydrology, some of the concerns that they manifest remain largely unexplored in the collection of essays. In these, cultural tourism is *a priori* understood as beneficial or as an opportunity for sustainable development. Communities are generally seen as potential beneficiaries of such development. Risks are associated, in the best scenario, to lack of funding, accessibility, or services for stimulating tourism. The dilemma of whether tourism can be also an erosive factor is not questioned. The fact that the elegant "cultural visions" provided are primarily instrumental in the development of tourism might be controversial. These local narratives are cultural resources deemed to be essential for local communities. They are expressions of their livelihood and they forge their own identity. On the other hand, they might not be enough to fight decline or landscape alteration, especially when communities are affected by external forces such as tourism and residential redevelopment processes.[5] It is a consequence of what Airas describes as "the making of arbitrary distinctiveness," which paradoxically encourages "ignorance of cultural history and heritage . . . limiting diverse development options for such areas in the future" (38).

The boundary between mass tourism and cultural tourism, given the prediction of tourism growth in the years to come, is increasingly unclear, and consequently the risk of decline of waterscapes' everyday life and the question of the real benefits for local communities should be more and more considered. While the discussion on the commodification of culture has been biased by a slippery notion of authenticity, and therefore I would agree with the proactive role here attributed to nostalgia, I would also warn about some economic distortions implicit in tourism development and heritagization, particularly in fragile sociocultural environments. These might be related to the politics of cultural tourism with associated issues such as the deterioration of labor conditions in the tourism sector, the power relationship between culturally or economically hegemonic and marginalized stakeholders, or the overall negative environmental externalities of seasonality, just to mention a few.[6] In light of this, the very essence of a new humanistic hydrology could be undermined and, in the absence of a specific critical inquiry into such contradictions, the old dilemma on tourism would unfortunately remain valid.

This book surely stands as a fundamental cornerstone for further developing a humanistic hydrology in cultural heritage studies. It is a promising path to reintroduce an ethos of cultural landscape protection along waterways, and also to avoid some of its associated risks, when protection is purely functional to cultural commodification. *Waterways and the Cultural Landscape* has the merit of bringing together diverse and multidisciplinary insights into a fascinating topic that will deserve increasing attention in the future.

AUTHOR BIOGRAPHY

**Giulio Verdini**, an urban planner and urban economist, is senior lecturer in Planning at the University of Westminster in the U.K. He is one of the lead contributors to the UNESCO Global Report *Culture for Sustainable Urban Development* (2016) and the editor of the newly established Routledge book series Planning, Heritage, and Sustainability.

NOTES

1. Ken Taylor and Jane Lennon, "Cultural Landscapes: A Bridge Between Culture and Nature?" *International Journal of Heritage Studies* 17, no. 6 (2011): 538.

2. United Nations World Tourism Organization (UNWTO), *Global Report on Cultural Routes and Itineraries* (Madrid: UNWTO, 2015).

3. P. J. Fowler, *World Heritage Cultural Landscapes 1992–2002* (Paris: UNESCO World Heritage Center, 2003), World Heritage Papers no. 6, 89.

4. Melanie Smith and Greg Richards, *The Routledge Handbook of Cultural Tourism* (New York: Routledge, 2013), 191.

5. Giulio Verdini, "Culture as a Tool for Harmonious Territorial Development," in UNESCO, *Culture: Urban Future. Global Report on Culture for Sustainable Urban Development* (Paris: UNESCO, 2016).

6. See part 3, "Authenticity and Commodification," in Melanie Smith and Mike Robinson, eds., *Cultural Tourism in a Changing World: Politics, Participation, and (Re)presentation* (Buffalo, N.Y.: Channel View Publications, 2006).

**Caitlin DeSilvey**

*Curated Decay: Heritage Beyond Saving*

Minneapolis: University of Minnesota Press, 2017.

233 pages, 8 black-and-white illustrations (color in Kindle edition).

ISBN: 978-0-8166-9436-5, $105.00 HB

ISBN: 978-0-8166-9438-9, $27.00 PB

Kindle $25.63


**Daniela Sandler**

*Counterpreservation: Architectural Decay in Berlin Since 1989*

Ithaca, N.Y.: Cornell University Press, 2016.

255 pages, 14 black-and-white illustrations.

ISBN: 978-1-5017-0316-4, $89.95 HB

ISBN: 978-0-5017-0317-1, $29.95 PB

ISBN: 978-1-5017-0680-6, $29.95 EB

Review by Michael R. Allen

---

Historic preservation in the United States is a paradoxical field, where its methods are constantly the subject of anxiety among practitioners and its limits are nonetheless inscribed fairly rigidly by most of its constituency. Preservation conferences are rife with discussions of the inadequacy of historic preservation *as it is now* to address global climate change, to incorporate the urgency of Black Lives Matter, to understand how to survey and preserve resources in shrinking cities. This discourse often attends to perceived limits of knowledge, invoking needs to engage planners, artists, activists, and others who are supposedly outside of the field. Both of these discursive patterns form a fickle horizon, in which historic preservation is always an emergent, self-deprecating, and only tenuously interdisciplinary field. Narratives often end at the national borders.

Preservation may be guilty of incorporating too many conflicting projects—the project of professionalization of practice; the project of cultural advocacy for the built environment; (sometimes) the project of political resistance to place erasure and cultural hegemony; the project of legal Gnosticism around the National Historic Preservation Act and its subsidiary parts; and the project of physical building repair, rehabilitation, and restoration. This field is a multitude of fields, not a singularity. Yet it often chases its own tail trying to assert a normative method—usually a law or vocational principle—while remaining a field of stunning opacity and contradiction. Further, there is very little preservation theory to ground critical reflection, and little international consciousness.

The two volumes under review offer a set of theoretical posts within the field, although neither dares to offer any conclusive principles. They interpolate the problem of the restoration ethic, an often unstated and unquestioned motive to historic preservation. The tendency to take buildings and sites back closer to or exactly at a supposed origin drives preservation practice, law, and narratives. Restoration fundamentally even infects "rehabilitation" with a quest for some removal of later layers, and privileges historicizing buildings and landscapes as designed objects instead of questioning whether use and maintenance are not equally significant components of the physical authenticity of place.

The operative definition of "preservation" seems to have been forgotten in American practice, which assiduously presents "authenticity" as a historicized material being located in the past, rather than the material being of the present. The foundational error is the National Register of Historic Places' linking integrity to a "period of significance," an ontological principle that castigates decay and change as always deleterious, and discards even the field's own early definitions of "preservation" as a mode of stewardship. For instance, the conceptual model for level of intervention developed by James Marston Fitch begins with "preservation" as maintenance of an artifact in the condition at first encounter.[1] DeSilvey and Sandler seem to be reviving this fundamental starting point.

Caitlin DeSilvey's *Curated Decay* studies cases where heritage artifacts are inherently temporary, gusseted by climate changes and material decay. In *Counterpreservation*, Daniela Sandler presents rugged methods of stewardship and alteration of Berlin buildings that constitute a "reflective nostalgia" instead of "restorative nostalgia," revealing preservation as a productive practice with its own embedded political and cultural editorial power.

Remarkably, DeSilvey and Sandler expiate the trepidation within the historic preservation field by close theoretical examination of physical heritage sites. Both authors unpack their own work with European cultural heritage (there are only a few American sites invoked in each book) to critically examine (at least centrally) American preservation's perceived norms of identification, evaluation, and intervention. The work in each volume should find its way into the hands of American preservationists, because the authors offer essays in methods that lack large constituencies here—and fall outside of emergent critical heritage practices such as Jorge Otero-Pailos' "experimental preservation" and activist calls for removing memorials to Confederates and white nationalists. The pair of books in fact illustrate how every day, sometimes unnoticed choices about conservation open moments for critical reflection on the act of intervention.

DeSilvey questions not only whether heterodox conservation methods are more appropriate for certain sites, but also whether the planned loss or erasure of heritage itself should be a managerial option. The emblematic chapter in *Curated Decay*, "When the Story Meets the Storm: Unsafe Harbor," lays out the physical conservation and political complication of the Mullion Cove breakwater in Cornwall. In 2005, Britain's National Trust published *Shifting Shores: Living with a Changing Coastline*, where it evaluated the probity of continuing to protect and conserve heritage resources constantly being damaged by changes to coastal conditions. The report acknowledged that climate change may be culpable, and stated that coastal resources like historic stone breakwaters may now be "conserved and enhanced as far as practicable, whilst not necessarily seeking to protect them indefinitely" (48).

The 1890s stone breakwater was acquired by the National Trust in 1945 and listed by English Heritage in 1984. Since acquisition, however, the Trust dealt with frequent damage due to storms and wave surges. The author narrates her own attempt to grapple with the paradox of abandoning future conservation of the protected resource. DeSilvey poses "anticipatory history" that removes the heritage conservationist privileging of built heritage, instead positioning the physical artifact as a chapter in a narrative in which the ecological past and unknowable future were as worthy of consideration as "authentic" manifestations of the site.

This telling, which challenges narratives of historic preservation's tendency to historicize sites, is just a beginning. DeSilvey encounters Bob Felce, a local historian, whose website contests the National Trust by narrating successive storm events as far back as 1867 that were as devastating as those since 2005. Not only does the sanctity of the breakwater dissolve in the telling, but so does the authority of heritage conservation organizations and trained preservationists. DeSilvey presents a rare and riveting account of local preservation, in which community contestation of both the National Trust and DeSilvey's own points is in full display. In the end, the veracity of climate change becomes an open question. DeSilvey hints that preservation may have a problem in terminal narratives—sites are either worth painstaking restoration each time they are damaged, or they are assumed to be victims of climate change and left to fall. Felce and others suggest alternative regimes of maintenance that are contingent upon shared authority and balancing contemporary ecological knowledge with historic accounts.

The book further collapses nature and ar-chitecture as diachronic forces through tours of Duisburg, Orford Ness, the Cornish Mining World Heritage Site, Kilmahew/St. Peter's, and a lighthouse left to certain loss. Throughout these case studies, DeSilvey makes requisite points to consider ideas of ruin offered by Georg Simmel, Timothy Edensor, and Gordon Matta-Clark. The invocation of Edensor's appreciative gaze toward "emergent aesthetics" of ruin benefits from connecting the neo-romantic impulses with updated analysis of ecological science. That is, DeSilvey urges historic preservation toward acceptance of decay not simply for its optic allure, or for an admission of the futility of restoration, but because of empirical evidence of the benefits of biodiversity (even the possible benefits of flora growing in the mortar joints of historic buildings, whose removal could cause severe damage). Yet DeSilvey asks few questions about the economic and political structures that may produce ruin, or those that allow for certain places to become protected heritage sites (often those associated with state, feudal, or economic power) while others meet demolition (most often vernacular architecture of working class communities and sites related to marginalized groups).

Still DeSilvey speeds along an inquiry that would assist with broader preservation of heritage sites whose conditions defy historicized, temporally-fixed determinations of integrity. The author proposes shifting practices away from preservation of original "fabric and function" and toward "letting be," where decay and disintegration may be accepted outcomes of heritage conservation work. This ethic would also allow for selection within conservation, where some elements may be restored while others would be removed, left unmaintained, or repaired enough to avoid loss (such as what is happening at the Orford Ness Ministry of Defense site, used during the Cold War).

DeSilvey conjures the old essay by Aloïs Riegl, "The Modern Cult of Monuments," which has been long neglected in historic preservation.[2] Riegl's category of monuments significant for "age value" justifies conservation programs that distinguish them from commemorative or historical value, which would compel physical conservation and long-term restoration. The preference for "age value," which compares to Walter Benjamin's "aura," allows preservationists to steward the living evolution of the physical nature of heritage sites, and permit consilience of architecture and nature.

Sandler attenuates DeSilvey's interest in the physical decay of heritage by exploring the reciprocal relationship between publics and heritage sites—a fundamentally political relationship. The idea of "counterpreservation" becomes a deliberate choice to circumvent aesthetic programs attributed to capitalist gentrification, historical record cleansing, and social forgetting. Berlin offers a locus where the contests of heritage cannot be concealed beneath the sheens of preservation orthodoxy—if trepidation over Confederate monuments' future is the American standard today, almost no Germans came to the defense of preserving Nazi history sites, and many were obliterated without challenge. Others remain open to question, as do sites related to the less historically clear legacy of Soviet occupation in East Berlin.

The re-gentrification of Berlin in the 1980s and 1990s becomes central to the narrative of *Counterpreservation,* which considers the conservation of historic buildings to open Lefebvre's "social space" where meaning may invite conflict (45). Sandler starts with a presentation of the *Hausprojekte*—the collective houses that are often squats—as a conflictual occupation that required symbolic rejection of repair to enunciate a political opposition to gentrification. Sandler presents the stories of KA86 and Tuntenhaus by evaluating the choices of allowing or only slightly repairing physical decay as part of the political optics of communities of anarchists, artists, or queer people who felt increasingly marginalized by the rising property values in Berlin. As

Prenzlauer Berg, Kreuzberg, Friedrichshain, and other districts gentrified, buildings left to decay or sporting wounds from World War II and the Cold War were glamorized by restoration programs consonant with normative historic preservation. The *Hausprojekte* was not simply electing against repair due to poverty or illegality, but to champion a presence of historical memory that needed the signifier of the unrepaired building.

Sandler takes the questioning of historic preservation to a level of political critique, connecting the decay of Berlin buildings with intentional management rooted in liberatory politics. It is difficult to dismiss these claims by resorting to orthodoxy; instead, the presentation of these projects as preservation projects lays bare the relationship of contemporary historic preservation and exclusionary capitalism. Sandler's examination of art centers like Haus Schwarzenberg and Tascheles only underscores an urgency to counterpreservation. This is a method of asserting a right to inhabit a globalized, capitalized, and historically sanitized Berlin. As the author states, the preservation work she profiles marks an engagement with history as much as with history's artifacts (20).

*Counterpreservation* concludes with a particularly illustrative case study with Daniel Libeskind's never-built competition entry for the SS barracks at the Sachsenhausen Concentration Camp Memorial in Oranienburg outside Berlin. Libeskind originally proposed flooding the barracks where the torturers and murderers dwelled, so that the buildings would gradually deteriorate underwater but still be visible to visitors. This was a punitive preservation, but one that would have provoked the sorts of questions that DeSilvey raises about British heritage sites interacting with coastal flooding. Namely, is preservation an act of saving or rescuing, or is it an act of letting be? And can preservation also be an act of intentionally letting go, of instigating or allowing the process of destruction while narrating that destruction to prevent the loss of

historical engagement? Libeskind's proposal, anathema to American preservation practice today, would have inhabited the problematic while not avoiding a moral choice about the fate of Nazi relics. Instead of the architect's daring proposal, though, today the barracks are in use as Brandenburg Police Department's training facility. Should preservationists rejoice? The buildings remain in a use close to their original use, and new buildings have been built to match. In use and appearance the place now very much resembles its origins as an SS barracks.

To Sandler, a new practice of preservation demands an "active and critical participation from the inhabitants, users, and designers of buildings" (243). It is not a static engagement with material, nor is it an open admission of ecological factors of decay. Preservation is the generation of the public who make political demands on heritage artifacts, with the demands productive of new social arrangements that improve historic injustices. The book's concluding narrative of the dismantling of the Soviet Palace of the Republic, wrought through public art by Raumlabor and others, shows that the process need not always be militant or dour. The work of preservation can be joyous even in confrontation of a building's loss or its willful destruction. Sandler invokes Freud's theory of transience to support the claim that the built artifact is always a transitory, physically unstable one. Counterpreservation is the commitment to witness and guide the transitions, rather than a prescriptive theory that would urge categorical practices based on historic association or physical condition.

Counterpreservation reads into post-preservation as a more fully-developed version—one is a genus and the other a species. Both also share a historic echo with E. R. Robson's essay "Restoration in France," where the author writes that "I could multiply the instances in which the French are *restoring* when they ought to be preserving."[3] In fact, there is a recurrent narrative within heritage

conservation that has postulated the vitality of the other side of a dichotomy between restoration and something called preservation, ruin or, per Stewart Brand, "how buildings learn." This school of thought has been immolated in the United States under the weight of preservation orthodoxy, but has flourished occasionally throughout Europe and other parts of the world.

Heretical ideas about place split off into cultural studies and geography, finding patronage from writers from J. B. Jackson to Camilo Jose Vergara, who generally avoid any real discussion of historic preservation praxis. DeSilvey and Sandler find a closer referent in Stephan Tschudi-Madsen, who poses, "The falsification of history is one side of the matter; the other is the ethical and religiously inclined attitude where responsibility to the past becomes evident in relation to the coming generations."[4] Tschudi-Madsen reported that the field of what Americans call historic preservation had been divided even earlier, when in 1877 William Morris publicly objected to Sir Gilbert Scott's proposed restoration of the fifteenth-century appearance of Tewkesbury Abbey (or Tewkesbury Minster per Morris' original text). Morris emphatically rejected the possibility that lost appearances could ever rematerialize, and lauded the age value of the old church. DeSilvey offers a gentler interrogation in *Curated Decay*, asking: "Is all that we can hope for honesty about our ambivalence, and the contradictions that riddle any attempt to collaborate with ecological and chemical process?" (125). The author hopes that the answer is that honesty will be followed with revised conventions of practice and heritage laws around the world. In *Counterpreservation*, Sandler, on the other hand, suggests that many people are not waiting for authority to change the historic preservation rules, but have already made new ones in full effect. Hopefully these two volumes' well-supported inquiries return the productive discourse of critical heritage theory to the American field of historic preservation, at a time when it seems to be reaching an intellectual impasse. These volumes may spur the field to reconsider that very basic mode of always interrogating, sometimes appreciating, and often conserving heritage artifacts as we find them—which has long been called simply *preservation*.

AUTHOR BIOGRAPHY

**Michael R. Allen** is a senior lecturer in architecture, landscape architecture, and urban design, Washington University in St. Louis, and director of the Preservation Research Office, a heritage consultancy.

NOTES

1. James Marston Fitch, *Historic Preservation: Curatorial Management of the Built World* (New York: McGraw-Hill, 1982), 46.

2. Aloïs Riegl, *Der Moderne Denkmalkultus: sein Wesen und seine Entstehung* (Wien: K. K. Zentral-Kommission für Kunst-und Historische Denkmale, W. Branmüller, 1903). Translation first published as Aloïs Riegl, "The Modern Cult of Monuments: Its Character and Its Origins," trans. Kurt W. Forster and Diane Ghirardo, in *Oppositions* 25 (Fall 1982): 21–51.

3. E. R. Robson, "Restoration in France," *The Ecclesiologist* XXI (1861): 215.

4. Stephan Tschudi-Madsen, *Restoration and Anti-Restoration: A Study in English Restoration Philosophy* (Oslo: Universitetsforl, 1976), 48.

# List of Editors: *Buildings & Landscapes*

*Perspectives in Vernacular Architecture* 1 (1982), 2 (1986)
EDITOR: Camille Wells

*Perspectives in Vernacular Architecture* 3 (1989), 4 (1991)
EDITORS: Thomas Carter and Bernard L. Herman

*Gender, Class, and Shelter: Perspectives in Vernacular Architecture* 5 (1995)
*Shaping Communities: Perspectives in Vernacular Architecture* 6 (1997)
EDITORS: Elizabeth Collins Cromley and Carter L. Hudgins

*Exploring Everyday Landscapes: Perspectives in Vernacular Architecture* 7 (1997)
*People, Power, Places: Perspectives in Vernacular Architecture* 8 (2000)
EDITORS: Annmarie Adams and Sally McMurry

*Constructing Image, Identity, and Place: Perspectives in Vernacular Architecture* 9 (2003)
*Building Environments: Perspectives in Vernacular Architecture* 10 (2005)
EDITORS: Alison K. Hoagland and Kenneth A. Breisch

*Perspectives in Vernacular Architecture: The Journal of the Vernacular Architecture Forum* 11 (2004), 12 (2005), 13.1 (2006)
EDITORS: Jan Jennings and Pamela Simpson

*Perspectives in Vernacular Architecture: The Journal of the Vernacular Architecture Forum* 13.2 (2006/2007), Special 25th Anniversary Issue
EDITORS: Warren Hofstra and Camille Wells

*Buildings & Landscapes: Journal of the Vernacular Architecture Forum* 14 (Fall 2007), 15 (Fall 2008), 16.1 (Spring 2009), 16.2 (Fall 2009)
EDITORS: Howard Davis and Louis P. Nelson
BOOK REVIEW EDITOR: Marilyn Castro

*Buildings & Landscapes: Journal of the Vernacular Architecture Forum* 17.1 (Spring 2010), 17.2 (Fall 2010), 18.1 (Spring 2011), 18.2 (Fall 2011), 19.1 (Spring 2012), 19.2 (Fall 2012)
EDITORS: Marta Gutman and Louis P. Nelson
REVIEW EDITOR: Andrew K. Sandoval-Strausz

*Buildings & Landscapes: Journal of the Vernacular Architecture Forum* 20.1 (Spring 2013), 20.2 (Fall 2013), 21.1 (Spring 2014), 21.2 (Fall 2014), 22.1 (Spring 2015), 22.2 (Fall 2015)
EDITORS: Cynthia G. Falk and Marta Gutman
REVIEW EDITOR: Andrew K. Sandoval-Strausz

*Buildings & Landscapes: Journal of the Vernacular Architecture Forum* 23.1 (Spring 2016), 23.2 (Fall 2016), 24.1 (Spring 2017), 24.2 (Fall 2017)
EDITORS: Anna Vemer Andrzejewski and Cynthia G. Falk
REVIEW EDITOR: Matthew Lasner

*Buildings & Landscapes: Journal of the Vernacular Architecture Forum* 25.1 (Spring 2018)
EDITORS: Anna Vemer Andrzejewski and Carl Lounsbury
REVIEW EDITOR: Matthew Lasner

*Buildings & Landscapes: Journal of the Vernacular Architecture Forum* 25.2 (Fall 2018)
EDITORS: Anna Vemer Andrzejewski and Carl Lounsbury
REVIEW EDITOR: Andrew Johnston and Jessica Sewell

# UNIVERSITY OF MINNESOTA PRESS

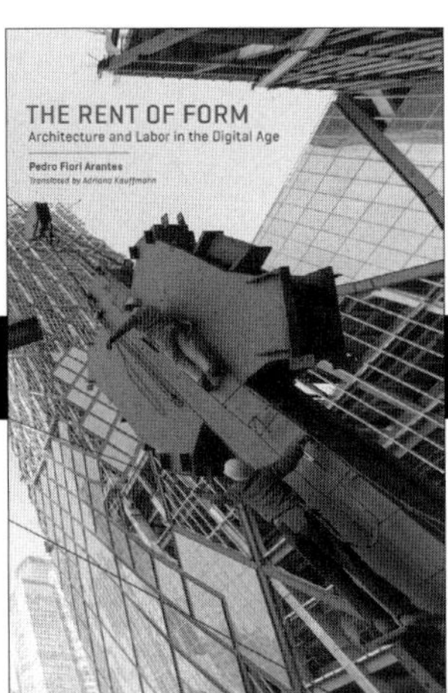


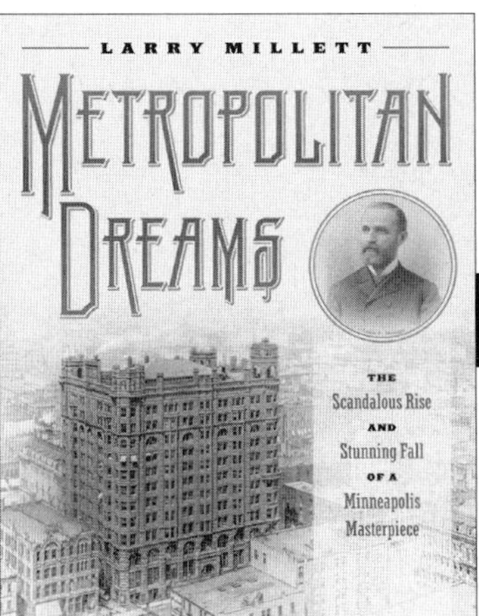


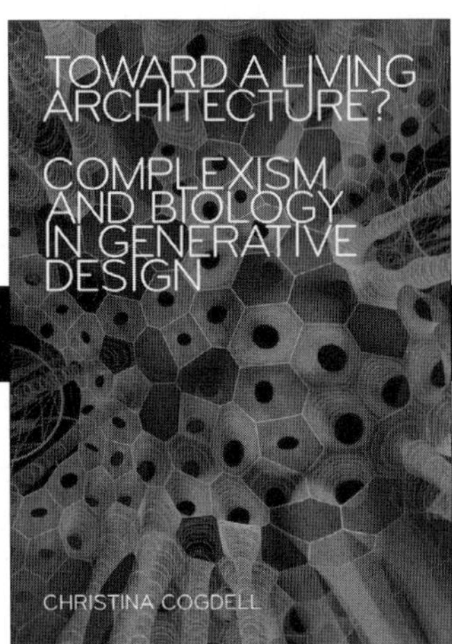


## Graphic Assembly
### Montage, Media, and Experimental Architecture in the 1960s
Craig Buckley

An innovative look at the contribution of montage to twentieth-century architecture

$34.95 hardcover | 400 pages | 228 images
Available January 2019

## The Rent of Form
### Architecture and Labor in the Digital Age
Pedro Fiori Arantes
Translated by Adriana Kauffmann
Foreword by Reinhold Martin

A critique of prominent architects' approach to digitally driven design and labor practices over the past two decades

$30.00 paperback | $120.00 cloth | 312 pages | 55 images
Buell Center Books in the History and Theory of American Architecture Series

## Metropolitan Dreams
### The Scandalous Rise and Stunning Fall of a Minneapolis Masterpiece
Larry Millett

The story of one of Minnesota's most famous and most mourned buildings, set against the history of downtown Minneapolis

$29.95 hardcover | 256 pages | 140 images

## Toward a Living Architecture?
### Complexism and Biology in Generative Design
Christina Cogdell

A bold and unprecedented look at a cutting-edge movement in architecture

$35.00 paperback | $140.00 cloth | 296 pages | 71 images
Available January 2019